I COULD NOSH

ALSO BY JAKE COHEN

Jew-ish: Reinvented Recipes from a Modern Mensch

I COULD NOSH

Classic Jew-ish Recipes
Revamped for Every Day

JAKE COHEN

HARVEST

An Imprint of WILLIAM MORROW

FOR JAMIE, MY SISTER, BEST FRIEND, AND TOUGHEST CRITIC

"This is literally the worst thing I've ever tasted!"

—Jamie Cohen, *a hater of rose water and cardamom, upon trying my Havdalah Snickerdoodles (page 258)*

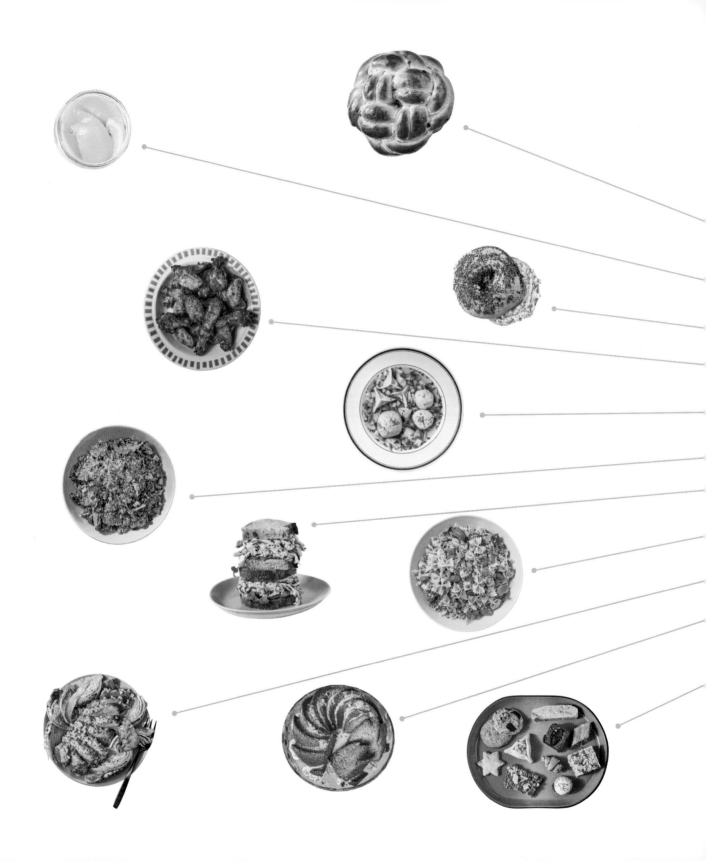

Contents

Preface

Nice to see you again! Or maybe we're meeting for the first time. Before we chat all things noshes, I wanted to write a little preface to catch up and let you know why I chose to write this book, which I love so deeply.

It's been a wild couple of years. When I released *Jew-ish* in March 2021, I had grandiose fantasies of how it was all going to play out. And with a lot of work and a lot more luck, everything went better than I could have ever dreamed. But as I made my way through the tour of interviews and press, two questions kept popping up that I couldn't stop thinking about.

Question One: What's next?

Well, obviously this book is the answer. But this question bothered me a bit. We have a tendency when reaching any milestone to turn our attention to the next one, diminishing prior accomplishments by focusing on what's next, what's bigger and better.

You lose fifteen pounds, but you won't celebrate until you lose *another* five. You get a promotion and a raise, but you'll *really* feel you've made it when you get the next one. You cook a gorgeous feast, but you're dwelling on that *one* dish that didn't come out like you planned.

In my case, I wrote a bestselling cookbook, and for a while, I needed to figure out how to do it again as quickly as possible to prove my worth.

But honestly, fuck that.

When we focus too much on what's next, we lose our sense of gratitude and ignore one of my favorite Hebrew words of all time: *dayenu*. Most Jews, even secular ones, know it from the Passover song, and can even belt out a few lines of the jingle. Often though, when I ask people if they know what it means, they're clueless.

It translates to "it would have been enough." The song goes through every single miracle of the Exodus, exclaiming that if only one such miracle had happened, *it would have been enough*. The irony of the song is, perhaps, that without all these miracles happening together, it actually would *not* have been enough to free us from the shackles of slavery in Egypt. Yet still, we focus on constant and wholehearted gratitude for every blessing we receive. It's a powerful way to think and I try to bring that perspective to most aspects of my life, career, and relationships.

To truly feel gratitude for accomplishing the feats I'd always dreamed of, I had to learn to stop immediately moving the goalpost forward. I began shifting my focus elsewhere, to studying Torah, reading about Stoicism, volunteering at my neighborhood food pantry, and cooking for friends and family with no motive beyond that of spreading love through food. (FYI, these are all things I'd highly recommend putting some time toward!)

In these moments when I need to feel grounded, I turn to the kitchen to recharge, feeding my soul while I try to tap into joy and inspiration. I dove into my family's old recipe box, and adapted recipes that survived the Holocaust and their journey from Europe to Cuba and finally to New York City. My mother-in-law, Robina, whom you may remember as the queen of tahdig from both my last book and my TikTok, would sit down with me when we'd visit, and recount newly unlocked memories of dishes from her upbringing in Iran and Israel. Alex, my husband and forever muse, would constantly throw ideas or concepts my way, listing ingredients and flavor profiles he thought I should experiment with. He'd then serve as my favorite taste tester, of course. In these spaces of playful discovery, so many of the recipes in this book were born. I hope all of them bring the same amount of love into your kitchen as they have for me.

Question Two: When are you going to branch out from just Jewish food?

I began telling interviewers who asked me this question to imagine how it would sound posing it toward a cookbook author representing any other minority group. (I hope in your head, you're cringing as much as I am.) Society has this blind spot for Jewish food—and really, Jews in general, but that's for another rant—in which it's acceptable to devalue our rich and diverse cuisine, which has traveled throughout the Diaspora to America against all odds. Since Jewish assimilation was so successful, naturally my goal should be to move on from kugel and kasha and start cooking mainstream American food, whatever that means.

But the thing is, when I started writing about Jewish food and culture, I felt more like myself than ever before. Every memory I have surrounding food from my childhood is linked to a Jewish holiday or culinary tradition, building my relationship to cooking on a foundation of shared moments and opportunities to use a meal as a vessel for deeper connection and community. As I've explored my connection to Judaism and Jewish food, I've been able to see how much of my life and the decisions I make are influenced by the Jewish values I was raised on. So, anything I touch will be a little Jewish—*Jew-ish*, if you will—because my Jewishness has shaped my entire perspective on food and hospitality and their power to nurture every relationship in my life. I could spend my entire career focusing just on Jewish food and its evolution, like so many of my culinary idols have, and still just scratch the surface of our recipes and traditions and the ways in which they've nourished our vastly diverse communities. I'm not saying I plan to do that, but that's my decision to make.

Too often, food content focuses so much on pandering to the opinions of others—to be loved, to sell books, to get likes—to the point that authors and creators find themselves silencing their unique perspective in favor of what they think will be most marketable. And I get it! Capitalism! We all must play the game to some

degree! But here's the thing: I've always found when people strive to be loved by everyone, their work tends to inspire no one. So, my hope with this book is that some of you adore it and passionately cook every recipe (tagging me in all the stories and TikToks of your creations, of course), while some of you flip through it at your local bookstore and decide it's not for you. Hopefully not in an "I hate Jews" kind of way, but in an "I hate Jake" kind of way. I truly don't mind! Everything I create is saturated with my authentic self, offering a window into the imperfect, gay, tradition-honoring, tradition-breaking, wildly insecure, family-oriented, 420-loving, dirty joke–obsessed, community-centered, Larry David–esque, and proudly Jewish Jake. I get that I'm not for everyone, and that's ok!

I always described my first book as my and my husband's love story, as we blended families and ventured to uncover our own narrative as a young Jewish couple. This book is a story of self-love. It traces my journey toward a deeper understanding of and passion for my Jewish identity, an identity I hope will infuse my everyday actions and life. It's too easy to think about your Jewish culture and heritage only on special occasions: its presence is felt during the High Holidays or when you go to temple or when you visit your bubbe. This was all too true on my last book tour. If you saw me on TV or read about my book in a magazine, it was probably in the context of Passover, Rosh Hashanah/Yom Kippur, or Hanukkah—the only three times of year you will ever see Jewish food featured in mainstream media.

If being Jewish is such a huge part of who I am, why shouldn't I create space for it on any night of the week, at any time of year?

The power to uplift other cultures through the recognition and reverence of their food traditions is immense. Look at your personal cookbook collection and notice how it spans far beyond the cuisine of your individual heritage. Think about the conversations you have debating what you're going to cook or order for dinner. How often is the answer to that question "Italian," or "Japanese," or "Mexican." And how frequently, or infrequently, does Jewish food fit into that picture?

Although Jewish guilt is very powerful (just ask my mother), with everything I do in my life and work, I strive to focus on Jewish joy. This book is meant to capture the joy I've felt these past two years, cooking for those who mean the most to me. My only hope is that by bringing Jewish food into some part of your daily routine, I can share that joy with you—whether you're Jewish, Jew-ish, or not Jewish at all.

Shall we get noshing?

Nosh It

NOSH
/näSH/

noun: food; a snack or small item of food.

plural: noshes

"If you want a nosh, I have some rugelach on the counter.
You know what, I'll pack you up the rest to take home, too."

verb: to eat food enthusiastically or greedily; to eat between meals.

third-person singular: noshes; past tense: noshed; past participle: noshed;

gerund or present participle: noshing

"Here, bubuleh, I made you a tuna sandwich to nosh on
while I get closer to death without any grandchildren."

"Are you hungry?" is always one of the first questions any Jewish mother or grandmother will ask you, posed in a tone both equally loving, worrisome, and aggressive. No matter if you are ravenous, disgustingly full, or anywhere in between, the only acceptable response for any Ashkenazi Jew is, of course, "I could nosh."

While this Yiddish gem of a word may literally translate to simply "a snack or nibble," the concept of noshing has come to mean much more than that. Not to get too philosophical, but I feel passionately that noshing is more about the person providing the noshes than the one who gets to nosh on them. It's about setting an intention to make sure those you love are nourished. To say you're full isn't just turning down food, it's turning away an act of love.

Noshing is a lifestyle, one where you are taking the step to elevate your kitchen into the epicenter of hospitality in your life, filling it with ready-to-eat food or ingredients stocked to whip something up. For me, this mentality has always been the core of what turns a house into a home, creating a space to build lasting memories and connections. My blueprint for this was my grandmother's house. Every time we visited Grandma Annie, she would prepare a feast as if it was a holiday, while also having at least two freezers and a pantry full of noshes to cover any craving we had, from liverwurst sandwiches to fresh crepes dusted with sugar. I look back on those moments with such adoration for the way we were cared for. Those memories are a blessing that still bubble up feelings of intense gratitude, feelings that have shaped my desire to cook for others into my own love language, paying it forward to my family and friends.

How do we embrace our inner bubbe? Well, in my very best Kim Kardashian voice, "Get your fucking ass up and cook. It seems like nobody wants to cook these days." I get that we all have work and responsibilities and all these excuses for why we can't carve out space in our schedules for cooking. But if you have the time to scroll through the Instagram stories of people you don't even like for forty-five minutes every day, you can shift some of that energy toward something that will bring joy to your life and those around you. Treat it like meditation or working out, where it's more about the discipline than your skill level. Everyone is going to start somewhere, and I just want to help you carve out time for cooking so you can unleash that fierce confidence in the kitchen, even if that doesn't happen overnight.

Just scrap any expectations for yourself. You don't need a big table or fancy pans or even a fully stocked pantry. You just have to do you. Put some headspace toward what that means. How do you like to eat? Do you prefer fast and simple recipes to knock out at a moment's notice? Do you prefer taking time for project recipes that yield leftovers to stretch the week? Is your ideal setup a hearty meal or an array of snacks? What's the ideal number of people you can cook for while keeping your cool? What are the flavors and ingredients that bring you the most comfort? These are mainly rhetorical questions because nobody is a monolith. Your mood, schedule, and cravings probably all shift daily in tangent with your answers. But the more you ask them to yourself, the more you see the patterns in cooking and entertaining that bring you joy. And that's the missing ingredient.

When you're able to tap into that joy, that's when those around you will begin to "taste the love" in whatever you make. And that's what I'm here for. Recipes that work are the bare minimum for my job. I want to help you have fun in the kitchen. I want to help you become the host you want to be. I want to help you find peace and contentment in the kitchen even when juggling a full menu of dishes. I want to help you feel confident in taking my recipes and making them your own. I want to help you find the same excitement I have found by infusing Jew-ish food into my life every day. And we can do it, trust me.

10 Commandments of Kitchen Life

But before we even decide on what we're in the mood for, I've broken down my ten kitchen commandments that keep me sane.

1. Be equipped.

You don't need a million-piece set of pots and pans or every random kitchen gadget to be a better cook. If anything, I find having too much clutter in your kitchen brings more stress than help. I frequent the same items every time since it all boils down to what cooking technique I'm trying to accomplish. A lid for every pot, ya know? I always try to have my entire menu accomplished between four burners and the oven, so less is more when it comes to pots and pans. You don't have to have everything here, but here's how I stock my kitchen, for reference.

The pots and pans I'm reaching for the most:

- **7-ish-quart dutch oven:** My most-used pan! I use it for almost anything, such as sautés, braises, soups, stews, anything fried, etc.

- **10- to 12-inch nonstick pan:** Frying eggs, cooking fish, flipping pancakes, or making food that tends to stick happens in this pan. I just try to use only wood or silicone utensils to prevent any chance of scratching.

- **10- to 12-inch cast-iron pan:** Cast iron is always my move for any high-heat cooking, from searing steak and chicken to shallow-frying foods like latkes. Doubles as a great vessel for skillet cookies and cobblers!

- **8-quart stock pot:** You need one for making chicken soup, of course, and for any pasta party or vegetable-blanching session.

- **2-quart saucepan:** This is for all the accoutrements, like sauces, toasting/candying nuts, cooking grains, and browning butter.

- **Two rimmed half sheet pans (13 × 18 inches):** You know what to do on a sheet pan, lol.

- **Two rimmed quarter sheet pans (9 × 13 inches):** If you don't need a full half pan, use a quarter sheet pan to save space. When I preroast veggies, etc., I'll consolidate them on quarter sheet pans for reheating.

- **Glass 9 × 13-inch baking dish:** You need one for baking everything from cakes to lasagna. Glass is my go-to because you can see the bottom when making tahchin, but I have metal (my favorite for cakes) and ceramic (my favorite for any dish getting served on the table) 9 x 13s as well.

- **Metal 9-inch square baking pan:** Snacking cakes and brownies make up so much of my diet that I bring my pan wherever I travel for baking!

I pull these out once in a while, but I'm so glad I have them:

- **12-inch high-sided skillet:** A big-boy pan for bigger projects. Typically I'm using it for pastas (both one-pan and for finishing cooked pasta with sauce) or large-batch shallow-frying jobs like schnitzel.

- **4-quart nonstick pot:** This is my tahdig pot! Yes, I mainly use it for this one function, but it also works so well as a secondary pasta pot or for making and holding mashed potatoes.

- **Various cake pans:** I have a set of two 9-inch and three 8-inch round cake pans. They don't get the same love as my 9 × 13-inch and 9-inch square pans, but I love to have them for when the mood strikes for a layer cake (though there are none in this book!). I love a good Bundt. (Whenever I serve one, I always scream, *"There's a hole in this cake!"*) So I have a couple of Bundt pans with different designs, all nonstick.

- **5-ish-quart dutch oven:** A backup when you're making smaller quantities of any of the dishes you would make in a larger dutch oven.

Make some room for these countertop appliances:

- **High-speed blender:** Invest in a good blender. Trust me, it makes a noticeable difference in how well your soups and sauces are blended. I use a Vitamix, and while the cost is high, it's a great investment piece (and you can wait for it to go on sale at Costco and snag one)!

- **Food processor:** I have both an 8-cup and a 2-cup food processor, which I choose depending on the project, but truthfully, they're both recent additions to my kitchen. They are the appliances I use the least, but when you need to grate 5 pounds of potatoes or finely chop nuts or make any of my schmears, it just makes your life so much easier.

- **Stand mixer:** The shocking truth is I use a KitchenAid mini stand mixer (3½ quarts) for everything I do. It's all I need to make anything from challah and cookie dough to meringues and cake batters. And it's small enough to always keep out on the counter without taking up too much space.

- **Immersion blender:** A magic stick! While I mainly use it for making homemade mayo and other emulsions, it's perfect for blending soups when you don't want to clean the blender or want to retain some texture.

Shove these in your tool belt:

- **Kitchen scale:** If you don't own a kitchen scale by now, what are you doing?! It's one of the most important tools in my kitchen. I am telling you right now. Please, please, please use a scale to weigh flour whenever you are baking! A cup of flour should weigh 135g (that's my standard, but for many others they do a 120g cup, which I think is a bit of a stretch). The only way for accuracy and consistency when baking is to use your scale. They're cheap and compact and the easiest way to become a better baker overnight.

- **Instant-read thermometer:** Same deal. If you don't own an instant-read thermometer by now, what are you doing?! You need to temp everything. We're not psychic! Chicken, steak, challah, and cakes all have internal temperatures we're looking for to yield the best result, every time without fail. Don't leave anything up to chance!

- **Bench scraper:** Use it to scrape your bench! I have a silicone and a metal bench scraper to portion any dough I make, but I mainly use them to transfer prep from my cutting board to elsewhere. Stop using your knife to do that since it dulls the blade!

- **Microplane:** Finely grate whatever your heart desires, from citrus zest and hard cheeses to ginger and garlic. I use mine every day, and you will, too!

- **Offset metal spatula:** For spreading and swooshing!

- **Silicone spatula:** For stirring when mixing!

- **Silicone brush:** For brushing!

- **Wooden spoon:** For stirring when cooking!

- **Slotted spoon:** For picking up things without liquid!

- **Slotted fish spatula:** For flipping things both fishy and not!

- **Metal tongs:** For picking things up!

- **Knives:** For cutting things! You need sharp knives, but I'm not going to tell you what brand or style—that depends on what is most comfortable for you. I use German knives since they're a little heftier for my *Seinfeld man hands* but find what feels right for you. You need at least a 9-inch chef's knife, a paring knife, and a serrated knife, though I also love my 5-inch petty knife (the in-between knife when you need something smaller than a chef's but bigger than a paring).

2. Get to know your appliances.

Let's talk about your oven. All (functioning) ovens are beautiful, but they're not the same. Hot spots, ovens that run hot or cold, and the location of the heating element all affect cooking times and temperatures. GET TO KNOW YOUR OVEN!

It's a relationship you must be present in and that I couldn't possibly predict. The more you use it, the more you'll get to know its quirks.

- The first thing I always recommend is getting an oven thermometer to hang on one of the racks, so you always know the exact temp. When it's time to cook, the standard rule is you should preheat your oven 30 minutes before you start baking or roasting, no matter when it dings that it's preheated.

- Rack city, bitch! The placement of your oven rack is crucial because it determines the food's proximity to the heating elements. For example, when baking challah, I always place the rack one notch below the middle so the challah can be perfectly centered in the oven—if it's too high or low you'll risk burning the top/bottom. However, when I'm roasting chicken or potatoes, I put the rack on the upper third just for that reason, since I'm looking to get more color. Location is going to depend on what you're cooking. Use that noggin to think about it before you even turn the oven on, and if I don't specify a specific rack position in the recipe that means keep it in the middle!

- Limit how often you open the oven door. Every time you do so, you're releasing the heat and dropping the temperature. If you're impatient and keep opening and closing the oven to check on your food, it will take much longer than any recipe suggests. I find the same happens if you're trying to cook multiple dishes in the oven at once. I'm not saying that's impossible, but remember that every recipe's times are based on it cooking solo.

Similar rules apply with your refrigerator! If you're trying to chill something and are continuing to open and close it, you're releasing the cold air and lengthening the time it will take to chill!

3. Curate your oil collection.

Extra-virgin olive oil is typically what I'm reaching for, but it all comes down to what temperature I'm cooking at. EVOO is great for a standard sauté and even baking (its acidity reacts with the leaveners for a fluffier result), but if I'm searing steak or cooking at a super high temp for a prolonged amount of time, I want a more refined oil with a higher smoking point (can take more heat without smoking and making everything taste bitter/burnt). I love avocado, sunflower, and grapeseed equally. It's not that deep. If you want to play around and swap fats, just go for it. Hello, flex that schmaltz if you have some! As for frying, you can stick to vegetable or canola, but grapeseed, peanut, and soybean are also great options.

4. Everyone is salty in their own way.

My mother refuses to cook with salt, while my husband adds a heavy pinch to just about everything he eats. Everyone has their own definition of salty and you're the best judge of what that should look like. That's why most recipes I develop ask you to season with salt to taste, allowing you to curate to your guests/ self. With baked goods or instances where you season before cooking, I give amounts of kosher salt that I find are centered on the spectrum of seasoning, but feel free to scale back if you know you're sensitive to salt. Just remember that my measurements are for kosher salt, with Diamond Crystal being my brand of choice. If you use another type of salt, the recipe may be more or less salty depending on the size of the salt crystals. For example, fine sea salt is finer (duh) than Diamond Crystal, and therefore a teaspoon of it weighs more, making it "saltier." If you're swapping with fine sea salt, reduce the amount by half to ensure the only thing salty are your haters.

5. Be a dairy or nondairy queen.

Like many with Jewish stomachs, I've been trying to reduce the amount of dairy in my diet. The result was a beautiful challenge that aligned with my desire to make this book as kosher friendly as possible. (I think there's only one recipe that's really *treif* beyond adaptability.) That means you'll get to explore the beauty of pareve desserts and what's possible in the world of dairy-free baking. And there are such incredible dairy-free alternatives now, that wherever you see butter, yogurt, or sour cream, you can make swaps as you see fit. But that also means there will be moments where you're embracing dairy in all its glory, no matter what the digestive repercussions are! In those cases, if you're kosher, treat yourself to all the cheese and cream cheese frosting you deserve! I'm a big believer in cutting back on meat and having a plant- or fish-based menu if it means you can have more pie and cake.

6. Embrace the pivot.

So many of my recipes have been shaped by moments where I didn't have an ingredient, or something went wrong and I had to pivot. You forgot to buy rosemary, but have thyme in your fridge? Use it! You don't like cardamom, but love cinnamon? Swap it! Your Bundt cake sticks and falls apart? Cut it up and layer with whipped cream and fruit and call it a trifle! Allergic to pine nuts? Swap with sunflower seeds! Get creative and don't be afraid to experiment. I receive so many beautiful messages of how people take my recipes and pivot based on what they have or like. It's those moments that build confidence and start to shape your intuition in the kitchen. Sometimes the pivot doesn't work out like you hoped. In those cases, order a pizza and remember that the thought and effort you put into the moment is not lost—think of this as a beautiful lesson on your culinary journey!

7. Put some pep in your prep.

While it may seem like I can just seamlessly throw something together at a moment's notice, the headspace I put toward prep is what keeps my blood pressure in check. That means I have my fridge, pantry, and freezer stocked with the ingredients I frequent the most, as well as a bottle of white wine always chilled. That means in my spare time I whip up some cookie dough or pie dough to keep in the freezer, or my favorite sauces and condiments to keep in the fridge. That means if I know someone is coming over or even if I'm making the decision to cook for just myself and my husband in the coming days, I think about how far I can prep in advance without sacrificing quality. That means I wash and dry all my herbs, toast my nuts, soak my beans, prep any other aspect of the recipe that I can and should get out of the way. When you break up cooking into these little vignettes, it becomes so much more approachable and makes entertaining that much more enjoyable. I give shout-outs in every headnote about how to prep every recipe and how far in advance you can start.

8. The most important ingredient is patience.

We want it all and we want it now! In a world that focuses on instant gratification, cooking, like so many disciplines, requires patience. That means when I ask you to let something cool completely or rest overnight, please listen. Slicing into hot cake releases steam that otherwise gets reabsorbed into the crumb, resulting in leftovers that are significantly drier. Not waiting for your challah dough to double in size will result in a denser loaf, where the strands pull apart. Not letting your cookie dough properly chill will cause the cookies to spread more and come out less than ideal. And I'll repeat my earlier sentiment: constantly opening and closing the oven door to check on something releases the heat, messing with both how it cooks and how long it takes. There are so many more examples of why this matters, but you won't have to deal with any of them since you're going to put intention toward being patient.

9. Leftovers are a blessing.

As important as prep is for throwing something together quickly, the same goes with being stocked on leftovers to heat up a plate any time of day. So much of Jewish food tastes better the next day (and even best on day two or three). Lean into that. Having soups, stews, braises, and salads ready in the fridge or freezer to pull out for lunch, dinner, or last-minute company is a pro move. Having cakes and cookies on your counter to nosh on with coffee or tea is just self-care. It's why I personally hate recipes that yield only a tiny amount of food. I want abundance! You deserve abundance! Cook when it's convenient for you and reap the benefits for days.

10. As with everything, nothing really matters. Don't take anything too seriously.

Some of my fondest memories of dishes my mom would make are all rooted in Betty Crocker cake mixes or Wish-Bone Italian dressing packets. While I'm not telling you to go full Sandra Lee (unless we're measuring vodka, of course), I am trying to remind you that it's just food. You get to choose your path of how much you want to lean into cooking and baking, so be sure the path you choose fits into your life and fuels your happiness. My mother worked full time (and still does), so my focus will never be on the corners she cut when baking a cake, but the intention she put toward creating sweet memories. For me, the true gauge of being a good cook is how you make those around you feel, not turning into Julia Child overnight. So do as much or as little as you like, and I'll be right there cheering you on. This is not a *Moonstruck*-SNAP-OUT-OF-IT revelation, but a mantra you must continue to remind yourself. This book is about tapping into joy through food, so there will be no tears or kvetching allowed!

The *I Could Nosh* Ingredient Collection

I always explain that cookbooks are often like fashion collections, reflecting the author's obsessions and styles during the snapshot of recipe development. Because of that, you'll find some culinary motifs throughout this book that I wanted to highlight. This isn't my all-time pantry, but the ingredients to be stocked up on for cooking through this book.

Baharat

While it literally translates to "spice" in Arabic, *baharat* is also a catchall name for a blend of black pepper, cumin, cinnamon, paprika, and plenty of other earthy and warm spices to season everything from rice to meat. The blend will vary from family to family, and the same goes for store-bought varieties. I've included a recipe in the book from my husband's family (page 46), but it's become increasingly easy to find jars of baharat at supermarkets, spice shops, and online. I love the blends from La Boîte and New York Shuk (theirs runs spicy).

Preserved Lemons

These are simply lemons pickled in salt and their own juices. Just give them a couple of weeks and the whole lemon (even the rind) turns into a jammy, complex citrus masterpiece. If you're patient, I have a recipe to make them from scratch (page 49). If you're not, you can find jars of these lemons online, in specialty spice stores, and even in many supermarkets, by the jarred olives.

Dried Persian Limes

These are tiny limes that are left in the sun until they've totally dried and turned black, adding a complex acidity to everything they touch. I always have two types in my cupboard: the whole limes for long stews, and a ground version for quick seasoning, like in the Ghormeh Sabzi Paneer (page 194). They're going to be at most specialty spice stores or easily available online. Just note when shopping: you'll sometimes find them sold as black limes or Omani limes, too. For the ground limes, I love Burlap & Barrel or Sadaf, both of which you can order online.

Kasha
While *kasha* can often be used to describe any whole cereal, we're talking about buckwheat groats here. You'll see them as pasta's trusty Eastern European sidekick in kasha varnishkes (pages 178–184), but don't stop there. Treat them like any other grain and add the most magical toothsome chew to any dish. You can sometimes find them in the grain section with all the Bob's Red Mill products, but I typically order mine on Amazon.

Osem Consomme
My mother-in-law, Robina, swears by a spoon of Osem in whatever she cooks, to add extra flavor and depth. And she's absolutely correct. It's very much the same vibe as my mom throwing a couple of bouillon cubes in any and every simmering pot on her stove. I'm obsessed and demand you order some on Amazon immediately!

Ground Sumac
This crimson spice is made up of dried and ground berries that will give tang to any dish. Most commonly you'll see it sprinkled over yogurt dips, grilled meats, or salads, but don't sleep on dessert! Something magical happens when you mix it with dark chocolate or berries. You can find it at any spice shop, but I particularly love the cured sumac from Burlap & Barrel.

Date Syrup/Silan
Easily one of the best sweeteners in the world! Made from cooked-down dates, silan is like the consistency of molasses with a balance of floral sweetness and rich caramel notes. I love it in baking as much as I do when roasting veggies or marinating meat. It might be the item on this list that makes the most cameos in this book! You'll find it in more and more supermarkets, by the maple syrup, or easily online (I love the brand Just Date).

Honey
Don't just grab any plastic bear! I'm a big believer in using honey that's local to where you are cooking or baking for a layer of poetic terroir. Past that, honey takes on such vastly different flavor profiles depending on what flowers the bees are pollinating and what time of year. Go to your local farmers market and taste what's available!

Almonds in Every Form
You're going to find whole almonds, slivered almonds, almond flour, almond extract, and marzipan (a sweetened almond confection) throughout the recipes in this book. It's one of the ingredients that touches so many corners of the Diaspora, so stock up!

Sour Cream
Always have a container of it on hand because it's one of the few kitchen staples that adds both richness and acidity, making it perfect for everything from dips and sauces to cakes and cookies.

Dill
It's my favorite herb! You better always have a bunch on hand!

1

CHALLAH BACK

Get that bread.

Challah saved me.

I know that sounds dramatic but leave it to a gay Jew to know a thing or two about drama.

This story begins at the start of the pandemic with me on the verge of a breakdown. I went from hosting huge Shabbat dinners to not even being able to see my closest family and friends. I felt stripped of my community and routine, moping around my apartment in a wardrobe consisting exclusively of onesie pajamas. But while everyone in the world started baking sourdough, I turned to challah. What was once a special-occasion baking project became a weekly Shabbat ritual that I fell in love with. For extra motivation, since flour was so hard to come by at that time, I ordered fifty pounds online. Because I am what? Unwell!

After a few months, my challah started to get lighter and shinier, and even picked up more love on Instagram and TikTok (not that I should be basing my worth on social media, but I'm working on that!). I grew to understand what a proper hydration and gluten structure felt like. I gained confidence in the realm of proofing and knowing how to pivot depending on the weather. I literally scrapped the original recipe from my first book before it went to press, and redid the whole thing at the eleventh hour to reflect my learnings. The version in this book now uses bread flour for an even better gluten structure to get the best possible texture.

But most importantly, baking challah brought me a sense of peace and fulfillment that was lacking during this time.

I've downloaded many meditation apps, but nothing was quite like this. Every Friday morning, I would block out the world, put on some music or a podcast, and get my hands into the dough. It helped me feel grounded in a ritual of repetition that yielded the most glorious result. It's the anchor of presence with your loved ones, creating a vessel to literally nourish all at the table. While I wasn't gathering the usual big crowds, I was blessed to have a *Marvelous Mrs. Maisel* setup and live in the same building as my mother and sister, allowing for the magic of Friday night dinner to take a familial focus for a hot second. And you better believe we ate an entire loaf of challah every week. You would, too.

And even once the world opened back up again, I never stopped. For me, baking fresh challah every Shabbat is still non-negotiable. I get as much joy out of making it as my family and friends do eating it. As I look back at this journey, I have so much pride for having learned how to work with this yeasted dough rooted in Jewish history. If you have followed a similar path, I hope you feel the same way and find continued passion exploring some of the variations in this section. And if you're new to challah, I'm going to tell you every tip and trick that has helped me along the way!

Before we get into baking, the two most important things to remember . . .

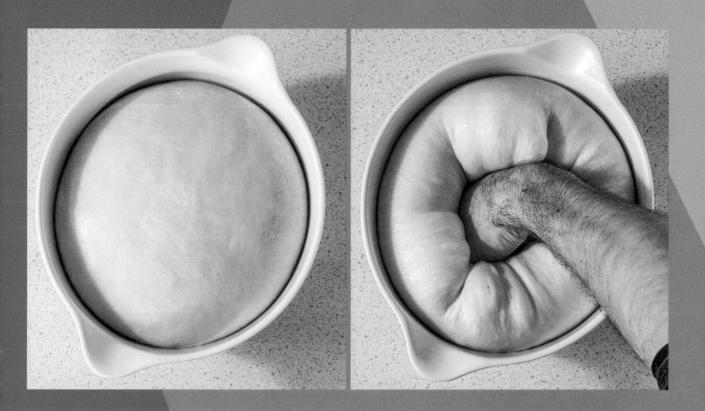

KNEAD UNTIL A SMOOTH, TACKY-BUT-NOT-STICKY DOUGH FORMS

WAIT FOR IT TO DOUBLE IN SIZE

JAKE'S CHALLAH

Makes 2 loaves
Prep Time: 40 minutes,
plus 3 to 4 hours of
proofing time and at least
1 hour cooling time
Cook Time: 30 minutes

For the Dough
1 cup water, heated to
   115°F
½ cup (100g)
   granulated sugar
1 (¼-ounce) packet
   active dry yeast
   (2¼ teaspoons)
¼ cup vegetable, olive,
   sunflower, or avocado
   oil, plus more for
   greasing
¼ cup honey
3 large eggs
5½ to 6 cups (745g to
   810g) bread flour
2 teaspoons kosher salt

1. Make the dough: In the bowl of a stand mixer fitted with the whisk attachment, mix the warm water and 2 tablespoons of the sugar to dissolve, then sprinkle the yeast over the top. Let stand until foamy, 5 to 10 minutes. Add the remaining 6 tablespoons of sugar, the oil, honey, and eggs, then whisk on medium speed until incorporated.

2. Switch to the dough hook. Add 5½ cups (745g) of the flour and the salt to the mixture in the bowl and, beginning on low speed and gradually increasing to medium, knead until a smooth, elastic dough forms, 3 to 4 minutes. (Your dough will be tacky but shouldn't be sticky. If it's sticky, mix in flour, a few tablespoons at a time, until tacky.) Transfer to a lightly floured work surface, and with floured hands, continue to knead by hand, dusting with flour as needed, until a very smooth ball forms, another 3 to 5 minutes. (Alternatively, if you make this dough entirely by hand, it will require about 10 minutes of kneading on a clean work surface after incorporating the flour.)

3. Grease a medium bowl and your hands with oil and add the dough ball, turning gently to coat. Cover with plastic wrap or a kitchen towel and set aside in a warm place until doubled in size, 1½ to 2½ hours.

4. Transfer the dough to a clean work surface and divide in half (the full dough should weigh about 1400g, so about 700g each). Working with one half at a time, and keeping the other half covered, divide the dough into 4, 6, or 8 equal pieces. Fold each piece of dough onto itself to release any air bubbles and form a smooth surface with 1 single crease, then roll each into a long rope, about 16 inches in length. The ropes should be slightly thicker at the center and tapered at both ends. Lay out all the ropes vertically with their creases facing down, then link the tops of the ropes and pinch them together to seal.

For After Braiding
1 large egg, lightly beaten
Assorted seeds, such
   as white and black
   sesame, fennel, poppy,
   nigella, cumin, and/
   or everything bagel
   seasoning, for garnish
   (optional)
Flaky sea salt, for garnish
   (optional)

5. For any even number of strands, you repeat the same four steps in repetition. Take the second rope from the right and cross it all the way to the far left. Take the farthest rope on the right and cross it over to be in the middle (there should be 1 more number of ropes on the left of it than on the right). Then, take the second rope from the left and cross it all the way to the far right. Now, take the farthest rope to the left and move it to the middle (there should be 1 more number of ropes on the right of it than on the left). Repeat this process until you've braided the lengths of the ropes, then pinch the ends of both sides and tuck them under each end of the challah.

6. Repeat this entire process with the other half of dough to form another challah. Using your hands, carefully transfer the challot (plural of challah) to a parchment-lined sheet pan, placing them on a diagonal, 4 inches apart. (Alternatively, see other uses for your second half of challah dough on pages 33–37.)

7. After braiding: Brush about half of the beaten egg liberally on the challot. Let them rise again, uncovered, until doubled in volume and puffy in appearance, 1 to 1½ hours.

8. Preheat the oven to 350°F with a rack one level below the center. Brush the challah loaves again with the remaining beaten egg, then sprinkle with seeds and a heavy pinch of flaky salt, if using.

9. Bake, rotating the pan halfway through the cooking time, for about 30 minutes, until the challah is golden brown and has reached an internal temperature of 190°F. Remove from the oven and let cool completely before slicing. Serve the challah the same day you bake it.

1 Divide your dough in half; each half should be about 700g. (Please use a scale!)

2 Divide 1 (700g) piece of dough into 4 equal pieces, each about 175g. (Please use a scale!)

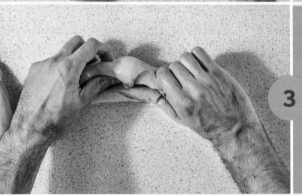

3 Using both thumbs, fold a piece of dough onto itself to release any air bubbles and form a smooth surface with 1 single crease when pinched closed. Repeat with the remaining 3 pieces of dough.

4 Use both palms to roll each piece of dough into a long rope, about 16 inches in length. The ropes should be slightly thicker at the center and tapered at both ends.

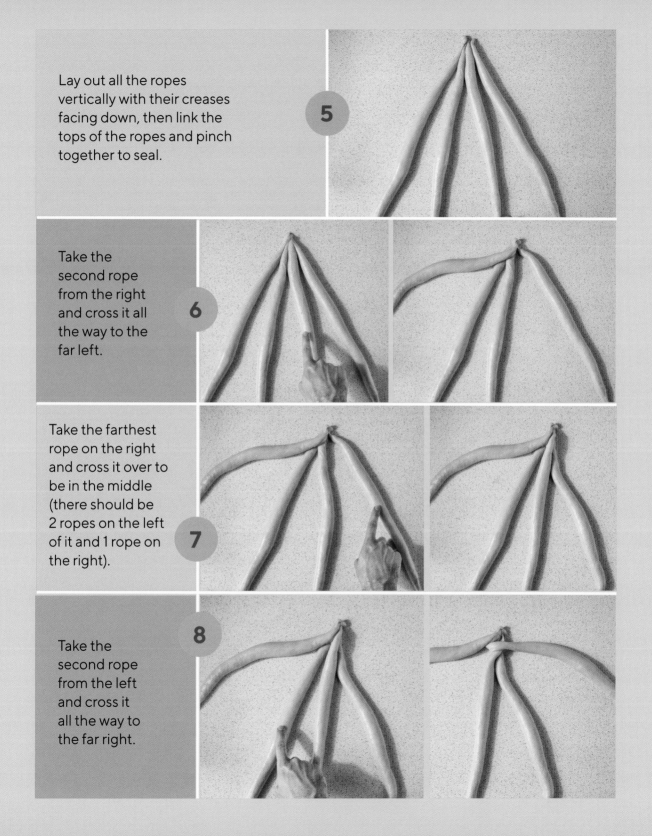

5 Lay out all the ropes vertically with their creases facing down, then link the tops of the ropes and pinch together to seal.

6 Take the second rope from the right and cross it all the way to the far left.

7 Take the farthest rope on the right and cross it over to be in the middle (there should be 2 ropes on the left of it and 1 rope on the right).

8 Take the second rope from the left and cross it all the way to the far right.

9 Take the farthest rope to the left and move it to the middle (there should be 1 rope on the left of it and 2 ropes on the right).

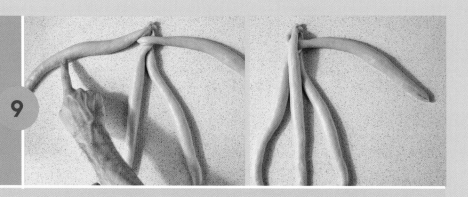

10 Return to step 6 and repeat steps 6 through 9 until there is no more rope to braid.

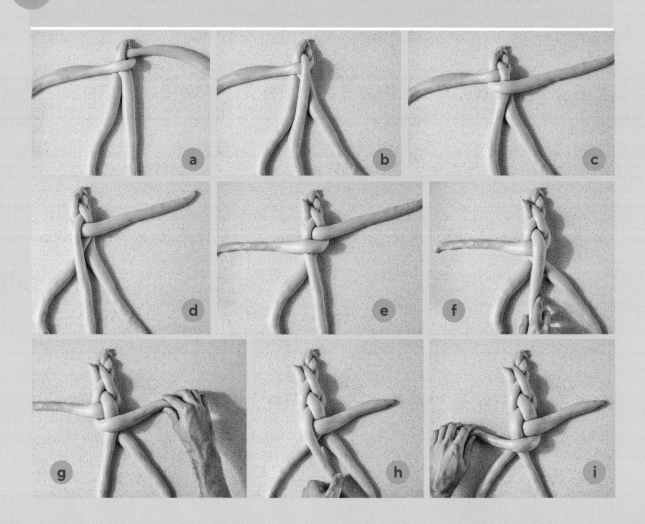

10. Continued

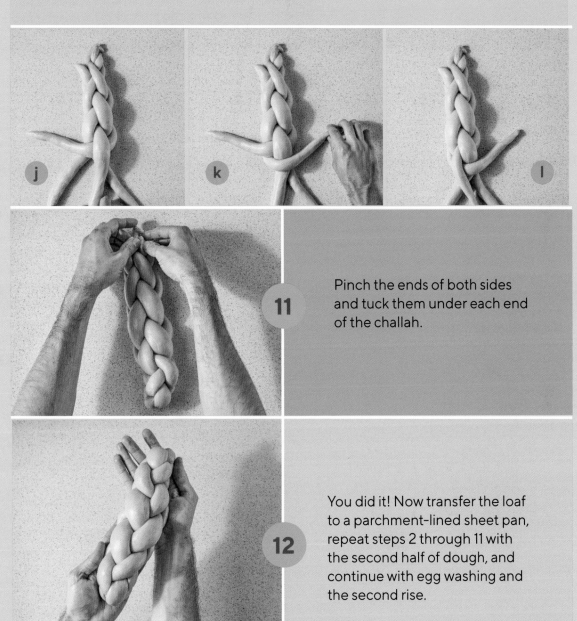

j

k

l

11 Pinch the ends of both sides and tuck them under each end of the challah.

12 You did it! Now transfer the loaf to a parchment-lined sheet pan, repeat steps 2 through 11 with the second half of dough, and continue with egg washing and the second rise.

1 Divide your dough in half; each half should be about 700g. (Please use a scale!)

2 Divide one of the halves (700g) into 4 equal pieces, each about 175g. (Please use a scale!)

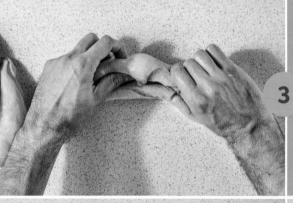

3 Using both thumbs, fold a piece of dough onto itself to release any air bubbles and form a smooth surface with 1 single crease when pinched closed. Repeat with the remaining 3 pieces of dough.

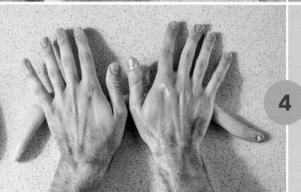

4 Use both palms to roll each piece of dough into a long rope, about 16 inches in length. The ropes should be slightly thicker at the center and tapered at both ends.

Arrange 2 ropes horizontally, spaced 2 inches apart. Lay the remaining 2 ropes, vertically and perpendicular, on top of the first two, and space them 2 inches apart. Alternate which vertical rope goes over and under the horizontal ropes, to form a lattice.

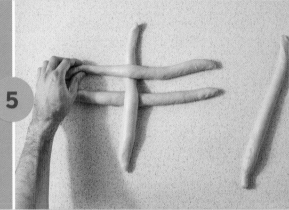

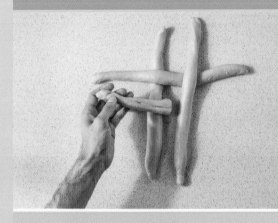

You'll always be working with 2 parallel ropes at a time, crossing them over each other. To start, you'll be working with the groupings at 12, 3, 6, and 9 o'clock.

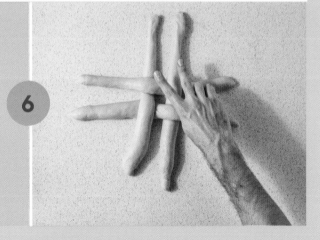

To continue the lattice, alternate which rope goes over and under. The left rope went under in the crosshatch so it goes over when you cross. The right rope went over in the crosshatch so it goes under when you cross.

7

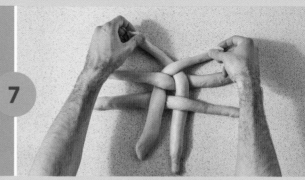

Once you've crossed all the ropes once, you'll continue with new groupings approximately at 2, 4, 8, and 10 o'clock.

8

For the final groupings, it will return to 12, 3, 6, and 9 o'clock.

9

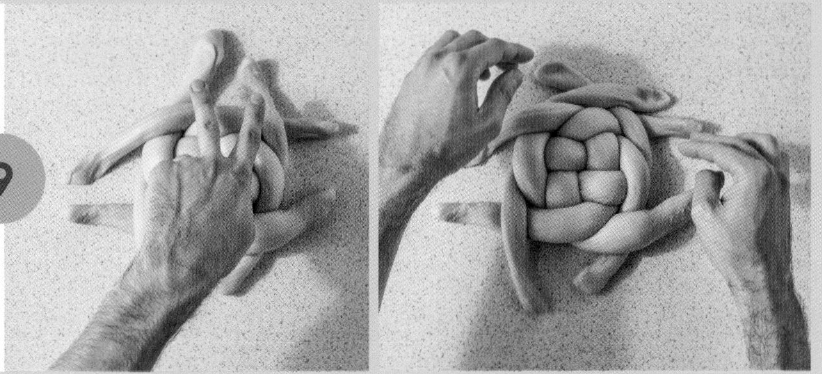

Once fully braided, tuck all the ends of the ropes tightly underneath the challah.

10

You did it! Now transfer the loaf to a parchment-lined sheet pan, repeat steps 2 through 10 with the second half of dough, and continue with egg washing and the second rise.

11

Making Your Dough Ahead

If your Friday is going to be hectic, you can make the dough Thursday night and do the first proof (rise) in the refrigerator overnight. The next morning, divide and braid and continue with the recipe. Since your dough will be cold, it will take longer to double in size, so cushion in a relatively longer second proof.

Freezing Your Dough

You can freeze the finished challah, or freeze the dough after the first proof. Simply punch down the dough and put it in a greased, sealable plastic bag before freezing. The night before you want to bake it, transfer to the refrigerator to defrost overnight, then, the next morning, let it sit at room temperature for 1 hour before braiding and continuing with the recipe. The dough will be colder so your second proof will be longer. (I tried freezing a braided challah pre–second proof, but condensation formed on the outside as it defrosted, causing bubbles and cracking when it baked.)

For a Round Challah

Between Rosh Hashanah and Yom Kippur, it's traditional to bake a round challah as a nod to the cyclical nature of a new year. Divide the dough in half, then divide each half into 4 or 8 strands (an 8-strand round is done the same way as a 4-strand round, just with groupings of 2 strands) and roll them out just as you would in a traditional braided challah. See photos (pages 26–29) for braiding instructions. These take 35 to 40 minutes to bake since they're wider than a traditional challah, and feel free to tent with aluminum foil if it's golden but still has not reached 190°F internally.

For a Vegan Challah

Swap the honey with an equal amount of date syrup (silan) and replace the 3 eggs in the dough with $\frac{1}{2}$ cup aquafaba (the liquid from a can of chickpeas). This dough will need a bit more flour than the classic, so you should use the higher end of the flour range and may need even an extra $\frac{1}{4}$ cup on top of that. Same rules apply: tacky, not sticky! For the post-braiding and second-proof glaze, I use a combo of 2 tablespoons aquafaba mixed with 2 tablespoons date syrup, which helps give a beautiful golden color and shine.

For a Gluten-Free Challah

I'm still working on that, but the second I crack the code I'll share it with you all!

For Flour Swaps

I get lots of requests on how to incorporate alternative flours (mainly whole wheat). I play around with whole wheat and rye flour often! The secret is easy: Swap out $1\frac{1}{2}$ to 2 cups of the bread flour with whatever you want. I find any more than that will result in a dry, tough challah since every flour is different and has a different hydration/protein content. Think of this as a journey of experimentation where this swap ratio is a jumping-off point to explore. A fully whole wheat–based or alternate gluten flour–based challah is possible; it just requires a different ratio of fat, eggs, and water than my recipe, which is why you can't just go rogue.

For Mix-ins

I'm partial to the glorious magic of a warm, sweet classic loaf of challah, but on occasion I like to lace the challah with all sorts of flavorings. You can have classic mix-ins such as chocolate chips or raisins, which you incorporate by adding during the last minute of mixing in the mixer. However,

you can also play with the oil and water for other flavors. The warm water in which you bloom ("activate to get foamy") the yeast can be infused with everything from saffron and turmeric (one of my combos below) to Earl Grey tea or instant espresso (a great addition when adding chocolate). The oil you use can be infused with garlic and herbs (another combo below) or any aromatics such as chiles, ginger, and/or spices that you like, with the option to either strain out for just flavor or keep in the solids for visual appeal and texture. Simply combine the oil and aromatics and bring to a simmer, then remove from the heat and let cool completely before adding to the dough.

Some ideas for you . . .

Cacio e Pepe. Infuse the oil with 1 tablespoon coarsely cracked black pepper and add 1 cup grated Pecorino cheese during the last minute of kneading in the mixer.

Saffron & Turmeric. Infuse the water with 1 teaspoon ground turmeric and ¼ teaspoon saffron threads, finely ground. I like to top these challot with nigella seeds.

Garlic & Herb. Infuse the oil with 3 tablespoons minced herbs, such as rosemary, sage, and thyme, and 8 minced garlic cloves. I do not strain the solids out, as I like the chunks of herbs and garlic laden throughout. In the spring, I'd recommend playing with adding wild ramps instead of garlic!

Chocolate & Citrus. Infuse the water with 1 bag of Earl Grey tea or ½ teaspoon instant espresso. Infuse the oil with 1 tablespoon finely grated orange zest. Add in 1 cup dark chocolate chips (or 6 ounces finely chopped dark chocolate bars) and ¼ cup finely chopped candied orange peel (optional) during the last minute of kneading in the mixer.

Spiced Raisin. In a small saucepan, combine ½ cup spiced rum and ½ teaspoon ground cinnamon and bring to a simmer. Pour the mixture over 1 cup raisins in a heatproof bowl and let cool completely to soak. Strain the raisins and add them in during the last minute of kneading in the mixer. Reserve the strained rum and brush it on the challot immediately after baking.

I've made many a stuffed challah over the past few years and have come to a potentially controversial opinion: The only acceptable stuffing for challah is schmear. It holds its shape without spilling out onto the tray and it adds a hint of moisture to the dough. If you're looking for a pizza challah, check out my challah calzones (*Chall-zones*) instead (page 34). If you're looking for a cinnamon roll challah, you're actually just looking for a babka (page 36) or you should check out my challah Monkey Bread (page 35).

But for a schmear-stuffed challah, simply roll out half of my challah dough recipe (about 700g) into a 10 × 15-inch rectangle, ¼ inch thick and aligned horizontally. Spread 1 cup of any of my schmear recipes (pages 55–59) in an even layer, leaving a 1-inch border clean. Starting with the edge closest to you, tightly roll up the dough into a log, then take one end of the log and coil it into a spiral. Place the coiled dough seam side down on a parchment-lined sheet pan. A stuffed challah takes about 40 minutes to bake.

Master Challah Dough and the Variations Are Endless!

The main reason I wanted to have an entire challah section in this book is because mastering a yeasted dough is something to celebrate. There is a giddiness I have when I bake a challah and it comes out both gorgeous and delicious, and that never goes away, no matter how many loaves have come out of my oven. And while some might see this as a stepping stone to more complex baking, I think it's a perfect opportunity to dive deeper into challah and learn all the alchemic creations you can derive from this one dough. Many of these variations are rooted in more history than you think. Long before buttery, gooey babkas were being torn into across the country, the original version was made by Jews in Eastern Europe, who rolled up extra challah dough with cinnamon sugar or jam as a treat for Shabbat. My goal for this section is that when you make my challah recipe and divide your dough in half, you use one portion for challah and the other for a new nosh to bring to the table. Let's explore!

Reminder: full batch of dough = 1400g, half batch of dough = 700g

Another reminder: I'm talking about dough that has already gone through its first rise, and I specify the recipes that should have that first rise happen in the refrigerator overnight.

Final reminder: The refrigerator is your friend. Use it to slow down your second rise if needed to work with your schedule.

MOSES IN A BLANKET

If there is one nosh you make from this book, it should be challah-wrapped hot dogs.

A full batch of the challah dough will work for 20 hot dogs. If doing the full batch, roll out the dough into a 10 × 20-inch-wide rectangle, about ¼ inch thick and aligned horizontally. Slice vertically into 20 (1-inch) strips. Wrap each hot dog in a strip of dough like you're wrapping it in a bandage, overlapping the edges of the dough slightly, then arrange on two parchment-lined sheet pans, tucking the ends under the bottoms and spacing them 2 inches apart. If using a half batch of dough, roll into a 10-inch square, then cut it into 10 (1-inch) strips to wrap 10 hot dogs. Alternatively, you'll be using 70g of dough for each hot dog, so if you're just looking to make a few, you can weigh out the dough and roll it out with your hands into a long rope to wrap around each hot dog. Let the challah-wrapped hot dogs rise until puffed, 30 to 45 minutes, then bake at 400°F, rotating the pans halfway through the cooking time, for 15 to 20 minutes, until golden.

BURGER BUNS

Brioche buns, but make them Jewish!

A full batch of the challah dough will make about 14 buns. Divide the dough into 100g-sized pieces and, using one hand, roll the dough against your work surface in a circular motion to form a smooth, tight ball. Arrange on parchment-lined sheet pans, spacing them 3 inches apart, and brush with beaten egg. Let rise until puffed, about 45 minutes. Brush again with beaten egg and garnish with sesame seeds, if desired. Bake at 375°F, rotating the pans halfway through the cooking time, for 15 minutes, until golden.

GARLIC KNOTS

Soft and chewy and covered in roasted garlic butter, these knots are a crowd-pleaser for all ages.

A full batch of the challah dough will make about 20 knots. Divide the dough into 70g-sized pieces and roll each into a 12-inch-long rope. Tie each rope into a single knot, tucking the ends of the rope into the center of the knot. Arrange on parchment-lined sheet pans, spacing them 2 inches apart, and brush with melted Roasted Garlic Butter (page 48). Let rise until puffed, about 30 minutes. Bake at 400°F, rotating the pan halfway through the cooking time, for 12 to 14 minutes, until golden. Remove from the oven and immediately brush with more Roasted Garlic Butter, then serve alongside a warm bowl of my Spicy Vodka Sauce (page 47).

CHALL-ZONES

Challah makes for such a perfect pocket of pizza.

Roll out half of the challah dough into a 9 × 16-inch oval, aligned horizontally. In a bowl, stir together 1 (6-ounce) can tomato paste with 1 teaspoon garlic powder, 1 teaspoon dried oregano, and ¼ teaspoon crushed red pepper, then season with salt and black pepper. Spread on the lower half of the dough, leaving a 1-inch border clean along the bottom. Spoon over 3 tablespoons of prepared pesto, then top with 1 cup (4 ounces) shredded low-moisture mozzarella. Fold the top half of the dough over the filling, then use a fork and crimp the edges to seal. Transfer to a parchment-lined sheet pan, oriented in a crescent shape to fit. Brush with beaten egg, then let rise for 30 minutes. Brush again with beaten egg, then cut three 1-inch slits on the top to allow any steam to vent. Garnish with sesame seeds, if desired. Bake at 350°F, rotating the pan halfway through the cooking time, for 25 to 30 minutes, until golden. Let cool slightly, then slice and serve.

PLETZEL

While traditionally made with a higher-hydration dough, this old-school focaccia-meets-bialy-esque flatbread is just as delicious with a challah base.

Grease a sheet pan with 2 tablespoons olive oil. Place half of the challah dough on the pan and, using your fingers, stretch the dough to cover the bottom. Drizzle with another 2 tablespoons olive oil and let rise for 1 hour. Meanwhile, in a large skillet, heat 3 tablespoons olive oil over medium heat. Add 2 finely chopped sweet onions and 2 heavy pinches of salt and cook, stirring occasionally, until softened and lightly caramelized, 10 to 12 minutes. Remove from the heat and set aside until the challah is finished rising. Scatter the onions over the top of the dough, then sprinkle with 2 teaspoons poppy seeds and a heavy pinch of flaky salt. Bake at 400°F, rotating the pan halfway through the cooking time, for 15 to 20 minutes, until golden and has reached an internal temperature of 190°F.

MONKEY BREAD

Hands down the dessert I've gotten the most compliments on and by far my favorite variation using challah dough.

Using a bench scraper, cut half of the challah dough into 1-inch pieces, then transfer to a large bowl. Toss with 6 tablespoons melted butter. In a separate bowl, stir together ½ cup granulated sugar, 2 teaspoons ground cinnamon, ½ teaspoon ground nutmeg, and ½ teaspoon kosher salt to combine. Sprinkle over the dough and toss to coat, then transfer to a Bundt pan in an even layer. Cover and set aside in a warm area until puffed to fill the pan, 45 minutes to 1 hour. (Alternatively, if you're braiding and baking your challah long in advance of serving the monkey bread, once assembled in the Bundt pan, cover and refrigerate. Let come to room temperature 1 hour before baking.) Bake at 400°F for 15 to 20 minutes, until golden. Remove from the oven and let sit for 5 minutes. Place a platter over the pan and carefully but quickly invert them together, then remove the pan to reveal the monkey bread. In a bowl, whisk together 1 cup confectioners' sugar, 1½ tablespoons water, 1 teaspoon vanilla bean paste or extract, and a pinch of salt until smooth. Drizzle over the monkey bread and serve warm.

BABKA

You can't beat it.

Roll out half of the challah dough (works best when the first rise is done in the refrigerator overnight so the dough is cold) into a 12 × 16-inch rectangle, aligned horizontally. Spread ½ cup Nutella chocolate-hazelnut spread evenly over the surface of the dough, leaving a 1-inch border clean. Sprinkle ½ cup mini chocolate chips over the Nutella. Starting with the edge closest to you, roll up the dough tightly into a log. Using a serrated knife, carefully cut the roll lengthwise in half. Twist the strands together and pinch the ends to seal. Carefully place the babka in a greased loaf pan. Cover loosely with plastic wrap or a clean kitchen towel and set aside in a warm area until the dough expands to fill the pan, about 45 minutes. Brush with beaten egg. Bake at 350°F, rotating the pan halfway through the cooking time, for 35 to 40 minutes, until the babka is golden and has reached an internal temperature of 185°F. Remove from the oven and immediately brush with simple syrup (optional). Let cool slightly in the pan, then transfer the loaf to a wire rack and let cool a bit more before slicing and serving. (Served warm is always the best!)

SCHNECKEN

From an old family recipe card for these German "snails," schnecken are pretty much yeasted cinnamon rolls with dried fruit and nuts. My schneck, my snack!

In a bowl, stir together 6 ounces (1½ sticks) melted butter, 1½ cups packed light brown sugar, 2 tablespoons honey, 2 teaspoons ground cinnamon, and 1 teaspoon kosher salt to combine. Spread half of the mixture in a 9 × 13-inch baking dish to coat the bottom. Roll out half of the challah dough (works best when the first rise is done in the refrigerator overnight, so the dough is cold) into a 10 × 18-inch rectangle, aligned horizontally. Spread the remaining half of the brown sugar mixture in an even layer over the dough, leaving a 1-inch border at the top. Scatter ½ cup chopped walnuts and ½ cup raisins on top. Starting with the edge closest to you, roll up the dough tightly, then slice it crosswise into 12 disks. Place them cut side down in the prepared baking dish. Cover with plastic wrap or a clean kitchen towel and set aside in a warm place, until they've doubled in size, 45 minutes to an hour. Brush with 2 tablespoons melted butter and bake at 375°F for 20 to 25 minutes, until golden brown and have reached an internal temperature of 185°F. Place a platter over the baking dish and invert them together, then remove the dish to reveal the schnecken. Serve warm.

SUFGANIYOT

Hanukkah came early, because you can split the dough and turn half into challah and half into sufganiyot. Go nuts for doughnuts.

Roll out any amount of the challah dough to ½ inch thick. Cut the dough into 2-inch squares, like beignets, and place on a parchment-lined sheet pan. Cover with plastic wrap or a clean kitchen towel and set aside in a warm place until puffed, about 30 minutes. (Alternatively, if you're braiding and baking your challah long in advance of frying and serving the sufganiyot, once cut, cover and refrigerate. Let come to room temperature 15 minutes before frying.) In a large dutch oven, heat 2 inches of oil to 375°F. Line a sheet pan with paper towels. Working in batches, fry the doughnuts, flipping once, until golden brown and puffed, 1 to 2 minutes per side. Transfer to the paper towel–lined sheet pan to drain. Repeat until all the doughnuts are fried. Dust with confectioners' sugar, then serve while warm alongside a bowl of warm jam or Nutella for dipping.

2

PANTRY
Powerhouses

Harissa Honey

Tahini Ranch

Spicy Green Sauce

Dill-Pickled Jalapeños

**Sweet & Salty
Onion Crunch**

Sumac-Pickled Onions

Master Meat Rub

Susi's Dressing

Sandwich Schmear

Baharat

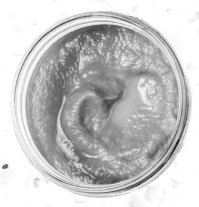

Spicy Vodka Sauce

Za'atar Bread Crumbs

Roasted Garlic Butter

Dukkah

Preserved Lemons

HARISSA HONEY

Makes about 1¼ cups
Prep Time: 5 minutes, plus
cooling time
Cook Time: 5 minutes

1 cup honey
¼ cup harissa paste
Pinch of kosher salt

We love a sweet and spicy moment! While there are many ways to make hot honey, I'm partial to spiced magic that happens when you simmer harissa, a powerhouse North African hot chile paste, with floral honey. Spoon it over some cream cheese schmeared on challah; drizzle it over pizza right after it comes out of the oven; brush it on grilled chicken or roasted wings. Just use it wherever you need a little sweet heat!

In a small saucepan, stir together the honey, harissa, and salt over medium heat. Bring to a simmer, then remove from the heat and let cool completely in the pan. Store in an airtight container in the refrigerator for up to 2 weeks.

TAHINI RANCH

Makes about 1½ cups
Prep Time: 10 minutes

¾ cup tahini
2 teaspoons dried or fresh
    minced dill
2 teaspoons dried or fresh
    minced parsley
2 teaspoons dried or fresh
    minced chives
1 teaspoon onion powder
1 teaspoon garlic powder
1 garlic clove, finely grated
Kosher salt and freshly
    ground black pepper
¼ cup freshly squeezed
    lemon juice
½ cup cold water

So really this sauce is like making a typical tehina sauce but with all the ranch mix-ins, and I mean, what can be bad about that?! The tahini adds richness, while the lemon provides tang, and both fresh grated garlic and garlic powder give a sharp punch. Amped up with either fresh or dried herbs, this sauce has become my go-to topping for any roasted vegetables I serve when entertaining. Something as simple as a tray of charred broccoli or cauliflower will be transformed into a next-level side that may just outshine the entrée!

In a medium bowl, whisk together the tahini, dill, parsley, chives, onion powder, garlic powder, grated garlic, and 2 heavy pinches each of salt and pepper to combine. Slowly whisk in the lemon juice, followed by the water, until a smooth sauce forms. Taste and adjust the seasoning with salt and pepper. Use immediately or store in an airtight container in the refrigerator for up to 3 days. Once chilled, the sauce will firm up. Before using, whisk in water as needed to thin out, and season again with salt and pepper.

SPICY GREEN SAUCE

Makes about 3 cups
Prep Time: 15 minutes

2 cups plain full-fat Greek
    yogurt
1½ cups fresh dill fronds
    and tender stems
½ cup fresh parsley leaves
    and tender stems
½ cup fresh basil leaves
2 tablespoons olive oil
2 tablespoons freshly
    squeezed lemon juice
1½ tablespoons honey
2 garlic cloves, smashed
    and peeled
1 jalapeño, stemmed
Kosher salt and freshly
    ground black pepper

This sauce really is as vers as they come. I've been making it for years, mashing up vibes of Yemeni schug with Indian chutney and my Ashkenazi obsession with dill into a verdant, tangy, and spicy third-culture concoction. It's great served alongside any roasted or grilled protein (feel free to swap in coconut yogurt to make it pareve!) or veg, but that's just the tip of the iceberg. It's great used as a salad dressing, especially for grain bowls, as well as maybe my favorite dipping sauce for fries or any preparation of the almighty potato. Happy saucing!

In a food processor, combine the yogurt, dill, parsley, basil, olive oil, lemon juice, honey, garlic, jalapeño, and a heavy pinch of salt and pepper. Process until a smooth, thick sauce forms. Taste and adjust the seasoning with salt and pepper. Store in an airtight container in the refrigerator for up to 5 days.

DILL-PICKLED JALAPEÑOS

Makes about 1 cup
Prep Time: 10 minutes,
plus cooling time
Cook Time: 5 minutes

4 jalapeños, stemmed and
    thinly sliced
2 garlic cloves, smashed
    and peeled
3 sprigs dill
½ cup distilled white
    vinegar
½ cup water
¼ cup granulated sugar
1 tablespoon kosher salt

When in doubt, pickle it. I always find myself with an excess of jalapeños in my fridge, so before they get too wrinkled and sad, I love to give them the dill pickle treatment. It's a superfast and easy pickle that yields beautifully spicy rings for topping pizzas, tacos, and nachos, while the brine is lovely splashed in salad dressings or even in pickle-back shots (if you're brave enough).

In a heatproof 2-cup glass jar, combine the jalapeños, garlic, and dill. In a small saucepan, combine the vinegar, water, sugar, and salt and bring to a simmer over medium-high heat. Cook, stirring, until the sugar and salt have dissolved, 1 to 2 minutes. Pour over the jalapeños and let cool completely before sealing the jar. Store in the refrigerator for up to 2 weeks.

SWEET & SALTY ONION CRUNCH

Makes about 3 cups
Prep Time: 10 minutes,
plus cooling time
Cook Time: 25 minutes

2 cups vegetable oil
2 medium yellow onions,
    thinly sliced
½ cup slivered almonds
½ cup chopped pitted
    dates
Kosher salt

While my intention for this recipe is to serve as the ultimate topping for any bowl of rice (which of course it is), I've found that often I'm just standing in my pantry eating handfuls of it like it's trail mix. Combining the deep sweet umami punch of fried onions with crunchy golden almonds and chewy, sugary dates, this combo brings every texture and flavor you'd want to sneak into a dish. Just be aware that every onion has a different water and sugar content, so frying times will vary. The almonds and dates take only 2 minutes, so really you're sneaking them in right when the onions are all golden but not too dark. Be sure to sprinkle this over my Date-Roasted Vegetable Tahchin (page 217)! The best part is the strained oil you fry everything in, which is perfumed with caramelized onions and perfect for roasting veggies or salad dressing or turning into mayo!

In a large skillet, combine the vegetable oil and onions over medium heat. Cook, stirring occasionally, until the onions are completely golden, but not too dark, 18 to 22 minutes. Stir in the almonds and dates and cook until the almonds are golden, another 2 minutes. Transfer the fried onion crunch to a paper towel–lined sheet pan to drain, then immediately season with a heavy pinch of salt. Let cool completely, then store in an airtight container for up to 1 week.

SUMAC-PICKLED ONIONS

Makes about 2 cups
Prep Time: 10 minutes,
plus overnight pickling

2 medium red onions,
    thinly sliced
¼ cup red wine vinegar
1 tablespoon granulated
    sugar
2 teaspoons kosher salt
1 teaspoon ground sumac

All pickles are beautiful, but these rosy quickles (quick pickles) truly just make everything a little tastier and prettier. Shaken up with a little vinegar, salt, and sugar, red onions melt into soft pink curls, speckled with crimson flakes of tangy sumac. They add just a bit of brightness to anything they touch, from bagels with lox to salads to grilled meats. It's like a shake weight that yields the most delicious reward for your little arm workout.

In a 24-ounce jar, combine the red onions with the vinegar, sugar, salt, and sumac. Seal and shake the jar well to combine. Refrigerate overnight and, if possible, give it another shake or two throughout the process. Store in the refrigerator for up to 2 weeks.

MASTER MEAT RUB

Makes about ¼ cup
Prep Time: 5 minutes

1 tablespoon black
　peppercorns
1 tablespoon coriander
　seeds
1 tablespoon ground sumac
1 tablespoon garlic powder
1 tablespoon packed light
　brown sugar
1 tablespoon kosher salt

This rub is my quintessential seasoning for any protein (it works with vegetables, too), combining equal parts salt, sugar, and all of my favorite spices to bring out the most flavor in whatever you're cooking. The key is freshly grinding the black peppercorns and coriander seeds, resulting in a textured rub that gets gorgeously crispy. I love to just empty my pepper mill and throw them both in to coarsely grind, though you can also use a spice grinder or mortar and pestle. While I love making this blend often so it stays fresh, you can double it to have more on hand!

Using a mortar and pestle, spice grinder, or empty pepper mill, coarsely grind the black peppercorns and coriander seeds. Transfer to a medium bowl and stir in the sumac, garlic powder, brown sugar, and kosher salt to combine. Transfer to an airtight container and store at room temperature for as long as you want (though try to use it within 2 months for peak freshness).

SUSI'S DRESSING

Makes about 2½ cups
Prep Time: 15 minutes

¾ cup olive oil
½ cup balsamic vinegar
2 tablespoons honey
2 tablespoons dijon
　mustard
1 teaspoon dried thyme
1 teaspoon dried oregano
1 orange, zested and juiced
1 lemon, zested and juiced
1 small shallot, minced
1 garlic clove, finely grated
Kosher salt and freshly
　ground black pepper

Whenever my aunt Susi comes for holidays, she can always be expected to bring two items: a magnum of Yellow Tail white wine and her iconic salad. This recipe is a version of her balsamic dressing, which she always stores in a recycled Grey Poupon or Bonne Maman jar. Over the years, I've fallen in love with the combo of using both vinegar and fresh citrus juice for simultaneous layers of brightness and tang, while dijon, minced shallot, and grated garlic add a bit of zip that will make any salad irresistible. But don't stop at salad; if you make my Iceberg Slice Salad (page 142) you'll discover this dressing makes the best marinade for any protein!

In a 16- or 24-ounce mason jar, add the olive oil, vinegar, honey, dijon, thyme, oregano, orange zest and juice, lemon zest and juice, shallot, garlic, and 2 heavy pinches each of salt and pepper. Close the lid tightly and shake until emulsified. Store in the refrigerator for up to 1 week.

SANDWICH SCHMEAR

Makes about 1¼ cups
Prep Time: 5 minutes

1 cup mayonnaise
3 tablespoons minced
    fresh dill
1 tablespoon dijon mustard
2 teaspoons honey
1 teaspoon hot sauce
1 garlic clove, finely grated
Kosher salt and freshly
    ground black pepper

Summer of 2020, Alex and I got really into sandwiches. Like REALLY into them. Every weekday for lunch I'd make us a turkey pastrami sandwich layered with butter lettuce, heirloom tomatoes, and pepperoncini on sourdough, slathered with this sandwich schmear. And we ate it five days a week for about three months without any complaints. Mayo is already the superior condiment, only improved by a bit of sweetness from honey, heat from hot sauce, tang from dijon, bite from garlic, and freshness from dill. It's a simple swap to step up your sandwich game!

In a medium bowl, stir together the mayonnaise, dill, dijon, honey, hot sauce, and garlic to combine. Taste and adjust the seasoning with salt and pepper. Store in an airtight container in the refrigerator for up to 1 week.

BAHARAT (ARABIC SPICE MIX)

Makes about ⅔ cup
Prep Time: 10 minutes

2 tablespoons freshly
    ground black pepper
2 tablespoons ground sumac
2 tablespoons ground
    coriander
2 tablespoons ground cumin
1 tablespoon sweet paprika
1 tablespoon ground
    cinnamon
2 teaspoons ground allspice
2 teaspoons ground
    cardamom
¼ teaspoon cayenne pepper

You're going to see this ingredient pop up a bit in this book, so have a batch in your pantry ready to pull from. *Baharat* literally translates to "spice" in Arabic and it's meant to be the master blend you use to season just about anything. It's a fragrant mash-up of earthy, pungent flavors, with warm spices you'll find in rice and grain dishes as well as grilled meats and hearty stews. And if you omit the cumin and cayenne, the blend also works beautifully in desserts, like a Middle Eastern pumpkin spice. While I love my recipe, it's quite easy to purchase baharat from specialty spice shops, but just like the homemade jars of baharat in the cupboards of all my husband's aunties, the blends will vary from shop to shop. Experiment and find one you love!

In a small bowl, stir together the black pepper, sumac, coriander, cumin, paprika, cinnamon, allspice, cardamom, and cayenne pepper to combine. Store in an airtight container for up to 6 months.

SPICY VODKA SAUCE

Makes about 2 quarts
Prep Time: 10 minutes
Cook Time: 40 minutes

3 tablespoons olive oil

6 garlic cloves, thinly sliced

2 medium yellow onions, finely chopped

½ to 1 teaspoon crushed red pepper

Kosher salt and freshly ground black pepper

½ cup vodka

2 (28-ounce) cans crushed tomatoes

¼ cup fresh basil leaves

1 cup heavy cream

This is my go-to recipe for a velvety vodka sauce, perfect to have in the fridge for any weeknight pasta party as well as pizza bagels (page 112), eggplant parm (page 224), or anything you just want a little saucy. I'm a big fan of pureeing my sauce for a creamy, glossy consistency, but if you're a fan of chunky sauce, by all means you do you!

1. In a medium pot or dutch oven, heat the olive oil over medium-high heat. Add the garlic, onions, crushed red pepper, and 2 heavy pinches each of salt and black pepper, and cook, stirring often, until softened and lightly caramelized, 5 to 7 minutes. Pour in the vodka, then stir continuously with a wooden spoon for 1 minute to scrape up any browned bits on the bottom of the pot. Add the crushed tomatoes, basil, and another 2 heavy pinches of salt and black pepper, then bring to a simmer.

2. Cover and cook, reducing the heat to maintain a simmer, for 30 minutes. Remove from the heat and let cool slightly.

3. Using an immersion blender or working in batches in a high-speed blender, puree the sauce until smooth. Stir in the heavy cream. Taste and adjust the seasoning with salt and black pepper. Use immediately or store in an airtight container in the refrigerator for up to 5 days or in the freezer for up to 6 months.

ZA'ATAR BREAD CRUMBS

Makes about 1 quart
Prep Time: 10 minutes, plus cooling time
Cook Time: 20 minutes

12 ounces sourdough bread, finely torn by hand or with a food processor

¼ cup olive oil

2 tablespoons za'atar

Kosher salt

A knockoff version of one of my favorite Sweetgreen salad toppings! Finely torn sourdough is baked with grassy za'atar for a crunchy topping that I adore sprinkled on anything needing a little crunch. Of course you can tweak and adjust this recipe however you want. It's not that deep, it's just bread crumbs!

1. Preheat the oven to 350°F.

2. On a sheet pan, toss the sourdough with the olive oil, za'atar, and 2 heavy pinches of salt. Bake, tossing halfway through, for 20 to 25 minutes, until golden and crisp. Let cool completely on the pan.

3. Store in an airtight container for up to 1 week or in the freezer for up to 6 months.

ROASTED GARLIC BUTTER

Makes about ¾ cup
Prep Time: 15 minutes, plus cooling time
Cook Time: 1 hour

3 heads garlic, tops trimmed to reveal the cloves
1 tablespoon olive oil
Kosher salt
4 ounces (1 stick) unsalted butter, at room temperature
½ cup finely grated parmesan cheese
2 tablespoons minced fresh basil
¼ teaspoon crushed red pepper

I went a little viral on the internet with my roasted garlic bread, made using this compound butter in which whole roasted heads of garlic are squeezed out in the most disturbing and oddly satisfying manner. More than forty-five million views later, I still love this butter schmeared on bread, spooned into pastas, or brushed onto Garlic Knots (page 34) for a bit more caramelized sweetness. If you're looking to follow the garlic bread route, I spread a nice layer of this butter on a halved baguette and bake at 400°F for 12 to 15 minutes, until golden and crisp. Bring on the garlic breath!

1. Preheat the oven to 400°F.

2. Place the garlic on a double layer of aluminum foil. Drizzle with the olive oil and season with a heavy pinch of salt, then wrap in the foil to seal. Roast for 1 hour to 1 hour and 15 minutes, until the cloves are softened and golden. Let cool completely, then squeeze the cloves into a medium bowl, discarding the skins.

3. Using a fork, mash the roasted garlic into a paste. Add the butter, parmesan, basil, and crushed red pepper and stir until well incorporated. Taste and adjust the seasoning with salt. Store in an airtight container in the refrigerator for up to 2 weeks or the freezer for up to 6 months.

DUKKAH

Makes about 2 cups
Prep Time: 15 minutes
Cook Time: 5 minutes

½ cup peeled hazelnuts
½ cup shelled pistachios
½ cup shelled sunflower seeds
¼ cup sesame seeds

I'm obsessed with dukkah and hopefully you will be, too. Traditionally this Egyptian condiment of ground nuts and spices would be served with bread and vegetables; you'd dip the bread into olive oil and then into the dukkah to stick. And while I adore doing just that with a fresh loaf of challah on Shabbat, I find that one of my favorite uses for it is as a garnish for roasted vegetables or as a crust on fish. Just sprinkle it on top of any white fish, such as black cod or halibut, and drizzle with olive oil before baking. It's an easy entrée that leaves no fishy odor in your kitchen and tastes like it took much more work than it did!

1/4 cup coriander seeds

2 tablespoons cumin seeds

2 tablespoons black peppercorns, coarsely ground

1 tablespoon fennel seeds

1½ teaspoons kosher salt

½ teaspoon granulated sugar

1. In a medium skillet, heat the hazelnuts, pistachios, and sunflower seeds over medium heat. Cook, shaking the pan often, until toasted and fragrant, 3 to 6 minutes. Transfer the nuts to a food processor.

2. To the skillet, add the sesame seeds, coriander seeds, cumin seeds, black peppercorns, and fennel seeds. Cook, shaking the pan often, until toasted and fragrant, 2 to 3 minutes. Transfer the seeds and spices to the food processor along with the salt and sugar.

3. Pulse until a coarse mixture forms. Transfer to an airtight container and store in the refrigerator for up to 2 weeks or the freezer for up to 6 months.

PRESERVED LEMONS

Makes about 1 quart
Prep Time: 15 minutes, plus 1 month pickling

6 small lemons, scrubbed clean, plus another 3 to 4 lemons for juicing

½ cup kosher salt

While I'm not a serial pickler, I do find that there is something truly wonderful about preserving your own lemons. Requiring only two ingredients (three, if you include patience), this recipe pickles whole lemons in salt and their own juice until they transform into soft, jammy pockets of sunshine. I'm not going to lie; I was mainly buying them jarred from the store, but the second I took the plunge to make them at home, I never looked back. It's so easy and, in true Ina fashion, homemade is better! The best part is that you can then use the entire lemon, rind and all. I finely chop a bit to add into sauces, pastas, salad dressings, or anything that needs a little brightness. You can add whatever flavors to the preserved lemons you want, with some whole peppercorns, a pinch of saffron threads, or any other spice you love. I just tend to keep it classic, since I'll want to save some for my Preserved Lemon and Olive Oil Loaf Cake (page 236)!

Trim the very ends of the lemons, then cut an X down through the length of each of them to almost quarter while leaving the quarters attached at the base of one side. Pack a few teaspoons of the salt into each cut lemon and then pack into a clean quart jar, sprinkling with the remaining salt on top and pressing the lemons down to fit. (As you pack in the lemons you should begin to squeeze out some of their juice.) Once the jar is full, pour enough freshly squeezed lemon juice to cover the lemons, then seal the jar. Let sit at room temperature for 1 month, occasionally shaking the jar to make sure the salt is dissolved. Once preserved, store in the refrigerator for up to 6 months.

3

THE BREAKFAST AND THE FURIOUS

Nothing to schmear but schmear itself.

Hot Honey

Za'atar & Tahini

Schmears

Brown Butter

Veggie Supreme

Herbalicious

Sugar & Spice

Preserved
Lemon &
Harissa

Pickled
Everything

Frizzled
Scallion &
Garlic

Lox & Seeds

Schmear Campaign

There is no breakfast move like serving a spread of bagels and lox. Whether for just your family or Shabbos brunch or any occasion that requires carbs and smoked fish, I'm a believer in sourcing the best bagels and fish you can find, while putting a little effort into making some homemade schmears to go with all the fixings. This mentality really began when I was passed down my grandmother's lox tray a few years ago: an ornate, giant wooden board shaped like a salmon, of course, adorned with a silver head and tail. It's the most extravagant serving platter I own, making me immediately want to be as extra as it is. These schmears span a range of flavors that take the nostalgic classics to the next level and create unique combos that will make you question everything you thought you knew about your bagel order. And they're all ridiculously easy, so you can be stocked with your favorite ones to schmear on bagels for breakfast or challah on Shabbat without having to think twice!

PICKLED EVERYTHING SCHMEAR

Makes about 1 cup
Prep Time: 10 minutes

1 (8-ounce) package full-fat cream cheese, at room temperature
¼ cup coarsely chopped dill pickles
¼ cup fresh dill fronds
2 tablespoons drained pepperoncini
1 tablespoon drained capers
Kosher salt and freshly ground black pepper

In a mini food processor, combine the cream cheese, pickles, dill, pepperoncini, and capers. Pulse until well incorporated. Taste and adjust the seasoning with salt and pepper. Store in an airtight container in the refrigerator for up to 5 days.

PRESERVED LEMON & HARISSA SCHMEAR

Makes about 1 cup
Prep Time: 10 minutes

1 (8-ounce) package full-fat cream cheese, at room temperature
2 tablespoons harissa
1 small preserved lemon (page 49), quartered
Kosher salt and freshly ground black peppe

In a mini food processor, combine the cream cheese, harissa, and preserved lemon. Pulse until well incorporated. Taste and adjust the seasoning with salt and pepper. Store in an airtight container in the refrigerator for up to 5 days.

LOX & SEEDS SCHMEAR

Makes about 1¼ cups
Prep Time: 10 minutes

1 (8-ounce) package full-fat cream cheese, at room temperature
4 ounces nova lox
2 tablespoons everything bagel seasoning
Kosher salt and freshly ground black pepper

In a mini food processor, combine the cream cheese, lox, and everything bagel seasoning. Pulse until well incorporated. Taste and adjust the seasoning with salt and pepper. Store in an airtight container in the refrigerator for up to 5 days.

SUGAR & SPICE SCHMEAR

Makes about 1 cup
Prep Time: 10 minutes

1 (8-ounce) package full-fat cream cheese, at room temperature
2 tablespoons packed light brown sugar
2 tablespoons honey
½ teaspoon ground cinnamon
½ teaspoon ground nutmeg
½ teaspoon ground ginger
½ teaspoon freshly ground black pepper
Pinch of kosher salt

In a mini food processor, combine the cream cheese, brown sugar, honey, cinnamon, nutmeg, ginger, pepper, and salt. Pulse until well incorporated. Store in an airtight container in the refrigerator for up to
5 days.

VEGGIE SUPREME SCHMEAR

Makes about 1½ cups
Prep Time: 15 minutes, plus cooling time
Cook Time: 15 minutes

1 medium carrot, chopped (¾ cup)
1 small red bell pepper, stemmed, seeded, and chopped (1 cup)
½ small red onion, chopped (¾ cup)
1 tablespoon olive oil
Kosher salt and freshly ground black pepper
1 (8-ounce) package full-fat cream cheese, at room temperature
2 teaspoons fresh thyme leaves

1. Preheat the oven to 450°F.

2. On a sheet pan, toss the carrot, red bell pepper, and onion with the olive oil and a heavy pinch each of salt and black pepper. Roast for 15 minutes, until softened and lightly golden, then let cool completely on the pan.

3. Transfer the cooled vegetables to a mini food processor along with the cream cheese and thyme. Pulse until well incorporated. Taste and adjust the seasoning with salt and black pepper. Store in an airtight container in the refrigerator for up to 5 days.

HOT HONEY SCHMEAR

Makes about 1 cup
Prep Time: 10 minutes, plus cooling time
Cook Time: 5 minutes

¼ cup honey
¼ to ½ teaspoon crushed red pepper
1 (8-ounce) package full-fat cream cheese, at room temperature
Kosher salt

1. In a small saucepan, combine the honey and crushed pepper over medium heat and bring to a simmer. Remove from the heat and let cool completely in the pan.

2. Transfer the cooled honey to a mini food processor along with the cream cheese and a heavy pinch of salt. Pulse until well incorporated. Taste and adjust the seasoning with salt. Store in an airtight container in the refrigerator for up to 5 days.

HERBALICIOUS SCHMEAR

Makes about 1¼ cups
Prep Time: 10 minutes

1 (8-ounce) package full-fat cream cheese, at room temperature
¼ cup minced fresh chives
¼ cup minced fresh dill
¼ cup minced fresh parsley leaves and tender stems
¼ cup minced fresh basil
1 teaspoon finely grated lemon zest
Kosher salt and freshly ground black pepper

In a mini food processor, combine the cream cheese, chives, dill, parsley, basil, and lemon zest. Pulse until well incorporated. Taste and adjust the seasoning with salt and pepper. Store in an airtight container in the refrigerator for up to 5 days.

ZA'ATAR & TAHINI SCHMEAR

Makes about 1¼ cups
Prep Time: 10 minutes

1 (8-ounce) package full-fat cream cheese, at room temperature
¼ cup tahini
2 tablespoons za'atar
1 garlic clove, smashed and peeled
Kosher salt and freshly ground black pepper

In a mini food processor, combine the cream cheese, tahini, za'atar, and garlic. Pulse until well incorporated. Taste and adjust the seasoning with salt and pepper. Store in an airtight container in the refrigerator for up to 5 days.

FRIZZLED SCALLION & GARLIC SCHMEAR

Makes about 1¼ cups
Prep Time: 10 minutes, plus cooling time
Cook Time: 5 minutes

½ cup olive oil
6 scallions, thinly sliced
4 garlic cloves, thinly sliced
1 (8-ounce) package full-fat cream cheese, at room temperature
Kosher salt and freshly ground black pepper

1.   In a small saucepan, combine the olive oil, scallions, and garlic over medium-high heat. Cook, stirring often, until golden, 5 to 7 minutes. Strain and let cool slightly, reserving the oil for another use.

2.   Transfer the scallions and garlic to a mini food processor along with the cream cheese. Pulse until well incorporated. Taste and adjust the seasoning with salt and pepper. Store in an airtight container in the refrigerator for up to 5 days.

BROWN BUTTER SCHMEAR

Makes about 1 cup
Prep Time: 10 minutes, plus cooling time
Cook Time: 5 minutes

4 tablespoons (2 ounces) unsalted butter
1 (8-ounce) package full-fat cream cheese, at room temperature
Kosher salt and freshly ground black pepper

1.   In a small saucepan, melt the butter over medium-high heat. Cook, stirring constantly, until browned and nutty in aroma, 4 to 6 minutes. Transfer to a heatproof bowl and let cool completely.

2.   In a mini food processor, combine the cooled brown butter and cream cheese. Pulse until well incorporated. Taste and adjust the seasoning with salt and pepper. Store in an airtight container in the refrigerator for up to 5 days.

BEC CHALLAH STRATA

Serves 6 to 8
Prep Time: 15 minutes
Cook Time: 40 minutes

8 ounces (5 thick-cut slices)
    bacon
6 large eggs
2 cups whole milk
2 tablespoons maple syrup
1½ teaspoons kosher salt
1 teaspoon freshly ground
    black pepper
1 pound day-old challah,
    cut into 1½-inch cubes
8 ounces aged cheddar
    cheese, coarsely grated
3 scallions, thinly sliced

Meet your new favorite hangover cure! Or if you don't drink, like me, meet the cozy casserole of your dreams! This recipe takes the bodega trifecta—a bacon, egg, and cheese—and marries it into a strata (like a savory bread pudding) made with leftover challah for a sweet and smoky and cheesy and insanely delicious breakfast. It was born out of my predilection for lazy cooking, finding a shortcut for all the Shabbat mornings I would spend slicing challah and making individual BEC sandwiches for my family. It's one of those casseroles that's truly just as great fresh as it is reheated a couple of days later, making it a favorite recipe of mine to portion into wedges and store in the fridge or freezer.

Let's just get this conversation over with: Yes, we've got a little treif here! I think it's actually the only explicitly nonkosher dish in the book, since I prefer to use beef bacon for the other recipes that call for it. I'm a big believer that while the roots of Jewish food are strictly kosher, as we continue to talk about its evolution when we came to America, that conversation includes a bit of treif. (Hello, Reuben and Rachel sandwiches at so many Jewish delis!) That being said, you can totally swap in a plant-based bacon or sausage fried up in a bit of butter instead!

1. Preheat the oven to 400°F.

2. In a 12-inch cast-iron skillet, lay out the bacon slices in an even layer. Bake for 15 to 17 minutes, until golden brown. Transfer to a cutting board and let cool slightly, then roughly chop. Reserve the skillet and all the rendered bacon fat.

3. In a large bowl, beat the eggs until smooth, then whisk in the milk, maple syrup, salt, and pepper to incorporate. Slowly stir in all but 2 tablespoons of the reserved bacon fat (leave the 2 tablespoons in the skillet). Add the challah, all but ⅓ cup of the grated cheddar, the scallions, and chopped bacon and toss until well incorporated and the liquid is absorbed. Transfer to the skillet and gently press into an even layer, then top with the remaining ⅓ cup grated cheddar.

4. Bake for 25 to 30 minutes, until golden, then serve.

CACIO E PEPE MATZO BREI

Serves 4
Prep Time: 10 minutes
Cook Time: 10 minutes

4 tablespoons (2 ounces)
   unsalted butter
1 medium yellow onion,
   thinly sliced
6 large eggs, at room
   temperature
½ cup finely grated
   Pecorino Romano cheese
2 teaspoons freshly ground
   black pepper
Kosher salt
5 sheets matzo
¼ cup minced fresh chives

Why is it when we talk about matzo brei, we always align ourselves as either team sweet or team savory? There's really no need to choose, since matzo and eggs can take on any flavor you desire! All versions are equally gorgeous and deserve love, but today we're shifting focus to pairing fried onions with tons of black pepper and Pecorino cheese for some cacio e pepe vibes with this Passover breakfast.

Beyond the mix-in debate, whether or not to wet your matzo first can be quite controversial! Many families simply let the crumbled matzo soak in the egg first, which I completely respect. However, I find letting hot water run over the matzo for about 15 seconds helps create the best texture, allowing for both soft matzo and super fluffy eggs. Whatever your taste preferences, I hope this recipe helps you break the matzo brei binary!

1. In a large nonstick skillet, melt the butter over medium-high heat. Add the onion and cook, stirring occasionally, until softened and lightly caramelized, 5 to 6 minutes.

2. Meanwhile, in a large bowl, whisk together the eggs, Pecorino, pepper, and a heavy pinch of salt until smooth.

3. Run each piece of matzo under hot water for 15 to 20 seconds to lightly soak, then crumble into 1-inch pieces and add to the egg mixture, tossing to combine.

4. Once the onion is cooked, reduce the heat to medium and add the egg mixture to the pan. Cook, stirring constantly, until just set, 2 to 3 minutes. Remove from the heat and stir in the chives. Taste and adjust the seasoning with salt, then serve.

WHIPPED AVOCADO-RICOTTA TOAST

Serves 4
Prep Time: 10 minutes

2 ripe avocados

1 cup full-fat ricotta cheese

¼ teaspoon crushed
red pepper

1 lemon, zested and juiced

1 garlic clove, finely grated

Kosher salt

Toasted sourdough or
challah, for serving (see
tips, page 92)

Everything bagel
seasoning, for garnish
(optional)

Over the past few years, I've become known for my videos of avocado toast topped with swirls of sriracha and sprinklings of flaky salt. It's gone as far as the legendary Britney Spears herself posting one of the videos on her Instagram and saying my toast inspired her to take on a new passion in the cooking field, leaving me #shook. This recipe takes my millennial obsession with avo-toast and marries it with a dish I fell in love with at Misi in Brooklyn, New York. Chef Missy Robbins serves her whipped ricotta on toast with roasted peppers in the most luxurious squiggle. Here, avocados and ricotta are pureed into a silky green mousse that gets piped onto griddled sourdough for a rich but surprisingly light breakfast or snack.

You can go as hard as you'd like with the toppings. Some mornings I like a shake of everything bagel seasoning or crushed red pepper, though my favorite option is an everything bagel furikake from a brand called Holy Tshili. When I'm feeling extra, I top the toast with everything from my Sumac-Pickled Onions (page 44) to fried capers to cherry tomatoes dressed with olive oil and herbs. This toast is your canvas; make your own masterpiece!

1. Halve, pit, and scoop the avocados into a food processor. Add the ricotta, crushed red pepper, lemon zest and juice, garlic, and 2 heavy pinches of salt. Process until smooth, then taste and adjust the seasoning with salt.

2. Transfer the mixture to a piping bag and pipe zigzags on the toast to coat. Garnish with everything bagel seasoning, if using, then serve.

BLUEBERRY-LAVENDER BLINTZES

Makes about 16 blintzes
Prep Time: 30 minutes,
plus cooling time
Cook Time: 30 minutes

For the Batter
2¼ cups whole milk
2 cups (270g) all-purpose
  flour
2 tablespoons unsalted
  butter, melted and cooled
1 tablespoon granulated
  sugar
½ teaspoon kosher salt
3 large eggs
Nonstick cooking spray,
  for greasing

For the Filling
2 pounds full-fat ricotta
  cheese
½ cup (100g) granulated
  sugar
1 tablespoon finely grated
  lemon zest (from about 2
  lemons)
½ teaspoon kosher salt

For the Blueberry Sauce
1 teaspoon dried lavender
½ teaspoon kosher salt
2 cups fresh blueberries
½ cup (100g) granulated
  sugar
½ cup water

I always try to be transparent with you, so I'm just going to come clean about this recipe: I became determined to master making blintzes the day I received the intel that they're one of Barbra Streisand's favorite foods. While I'd say my main mission in what I do is preserving and celebrating Jewish culture, I'd be lying if I didn't admit there is a tiny part of me that is just trying to get Babs's attention.

Although I didn't grow up eating blintzes, I became obsessed with them as an adult exploring NYC deli culture. Pockets of sweet cheese wrapped in a buttery crepe and smothered in fruit compote provide an experience that can't be matched by any stack of pancakes. This version is a slight departure from tradition, maintaining the buttery thin pancakes but replacing the classic filling of sweetened farmer cheese with lemon-kissed ricotta for a balance of airy brightness and richness. But the real magic is in the blueberry compote, singing with floral lavender and swirling with the ricotta into a fluorescent purple Jackson Pollock on your plate.

1. Make the batter: In a blender, combine the milk, flour, melted butter, sugar, salt, and eggs. Blend until smooth.

2. Heat a medium nonstick skillet (I use a 10-inch) over medium heat. Grease with nonstick cooking spray. Pour ¼ cup of the batter into the pan and quickly swirl to spread it around the pan to form an 8-inch crepe. Cook until just set, 30 seconds to 1 minute, then gently flip with a spatula. (I will often just use the spatula to lift up one edge of the crepe and then use my hand to pick it up and flip.) Transfer to a sheet pan. Repeat with the remaining batter, greasing with nonstick cooking spray as needed. As the crepes are cooked, stagger them into two piles, alternating between the two to prevent any sticking. You should end up with 16 crepes. Let them cool completely.

3. Meanwhile, make the filling: In a medium bowl, whisk together the ricotta, sugar, lemon zest, and salt to combine.

4. Once the crepes have cooled, place one on the center of a clean work surface. Spoon ¼ cup of the filling along the center of the crepe in a horizontal 4-inch line. Fold the bottom edge of the crepe to cover the filling,

2 tablespoons freshly
squeezed lemon juice

2 tablespoons cornstarch

3 tablespoons unsalted
butter

then fold the left and right edges toward the center. Roll the crepe up toward the top to seal into a 2 × 5-inch blintz. Repeat with the remaining crepes and filling until you have 16 blintzes. Cover with a wet paper towel or plastic while you make the blueberry sauce.

5. Make the blueberry sauce: Using a mortar and pestle or spice grinder, combine the lavender and salt and grind into a fine powder. Transfer to a medium saucepan with the blueberries, sugar, water, lemon juice, and cornstarch, then stir to combine. Place over medium-high heat and cook, stirring constantly, until thickened, 5 to 7 minutes. Keep warm.

6. Finish the blintzes: In a large nonstick skillet, melt 1½ tablespoons of the butter over medium-high heat. Add half of the blintzes and cook, flipping once, until golden, 1 to 2 minutes per side. Transfer to a platter and repeat with the remaining butter and blintzes.

7. Once all the blintzes are golden, spoon the blueberry sauce on top and serve.

CORNED BEEF HASH SPANISH TORTILLA

Serves 4 to 6
Prep Time: 15 minutes,
plus cooling time
Cook Time: 30 minutes

1¼ pounds (3 medium)
   Yukon gold potatoes,
   halved and thinly
   sliced
8 ounces cooked corned
   beef, chopped
2 cups olive oil
2 teaspoons kosher salt
1 medium yellow onion,
   finely chopped
6 large eggs
Freshly ground black
   pepper

While my husband can't ever be found in the kitchen, my brother-in-law Manuel would make the Spanish tortilla he learned from his mother growing up in Madrid. Made of sliced potatoes and onions fried in olive oil before being set in eggs, this omelet can be served at any temperature, any time of day. Though whenever Manuel makes one for us, it never lasts very long.

As a long-time lover of corned beef hash, the second I learned how to make tortilla from Manuel, I began sneaking a bit of corned beef in and fell in love. The keys to success are the same: Simmer the potatoes and onion low and slow until tender; use a good nonstick pan; watch your heat, since you're not looking for a ton of color; have a low-rimmed plate ready for easy flipping. And when you're done, you're also left with the pure liquid gold that is the strained olive oil you simmer the potatoes, beef, and onion in. Save it in the fridge for the next tortilla, or use it for anything from roasting potatoes to making matzo balls.

1. In an 11- or 12-inch nonstick skillet, combine the potatoes, corned beef, olive oil, ½ teaspoon of the salt, and the onion over medium heat. Bring to a simmer and cook, gently stirring occasionally, until the potatoes are tender, 18 to 20 minutes. Meanwhile, place a large metal fine-mesh sieve over a heatproof bowl.

2. In a large bowl, whisk together the eggs with the remaining 1½ teaspoons of salt and 2 heavy pinches of pepper.

3. Once cooked, pour the potato mixture into the sieve to drain. Moving quickly, lightly wipe out the skillet and add 1 tablespoon of the strained oil (see headnote for uses and storage of the remaining oil) over medium heat. Add the drained potato mixture to the beaten eggs and toss to incorporate, then immediately pour the mixture into the pan, smoothing the top with a rubber spatula.

4. Cook, undisturbed, until the edges and bottom are set but not deeply golden, 4 to 6 minutes. Place a low-rimmed plate or platter, slightly larger than the pan, over the tortilla. Remove from the heat and, using a kitchen towel or oven mitts, invert them together quickly, with confidence. Carefully shimmy the flipped tortilla back into the pan, using a rubber spatula to tuck in the edges. Return to the heat and cook until the bottom is set, 4 to 6 minutes more. Transfer to a cutting board. Let cool slightly or completely, then slice and serve.

BEC (BIALY, EGG, AND CHEESE)

Makes 1 sandwich
Prep Time: 10 minutes
Cook Time: 5 minutes

1 bialy, cut in half
1 tablespoon mayonnaise
½ tablespoon unsalted
 butter
1 large egg
Kosher salt and freshly
 ground black pepper
¼ cup grated cheddar
 cheese
Sriracha, to taste

Think of this recipe as more of a technique for a stellar breakfast sandwich you can take in a million different directions. One of my favorite bakers, Melissa Weller, created a bagel grilled cheese at Sadelle's in NYC that inverted the halved bagel so there was a flat surface on the outside to griddle and the bagel toppings would stick to the cheese on the inside. I mean, genius. It inspired me to start using that same technique with a bialy when I make egg and cheese sandwiches, trapping in the onions and poppy seeds without a hole to lose any of the cheese or yolk.

Now, the base for my ideal breakfast sandwich has melty cheddar cheese, a fried egg with a runny yolk, a zip of sriracha, and a fresh bialy brushed with mayo and fried in butter. That being said, you can scramble the egg instead of fry it, or swap in any other cheese, like pepper jack or gouda. From there, throw in bacon, pickled jalapeños, tomato, avocado, sautéed greens, caramelized onions, or whatever your heart desires!

1. On a cutting board, place the bialy halves cut sides up. Spread each cut side with 1½ teaspoons mayonnaise.

2. In a medium nonstick skillet, melt the butter over medium-high heat. Crack the egg directly into the pan and season with a pinch each of salt and pepper. Cook until the bottom is set, about 1 minute. Flip the egg with a spatula, then top it with the grated cheddar and the bottom half of the bialy, cut side up. Cook for 1 minute more, then carefully flip so the egg is on top and the cut-side of the bialy is facedown in the pan. Drizzle the egg with sriracha and place the other half of the bialy on top, cut side up. Continue to cook until the bottom side of the bialy is golden and the cheese is melted, 1 to 2 minutes. Carefully flip again and continue to cook until the other half is golden, 1 to 2 minutes.

3. Transfer to a cutting board and slice in half, then serve.

FRIED CHALLAH PB&J

Makes 1 sandwich

Prep Time: 10 minutes

Cook Time: 5 minutes

2 (½-inch) slices challah

2 tablespoons peanut butter

2 tablespoons jam or jelly

1 tablespoon unsalted butter

1 large egg, beaten

Maple syrup, for serving

Everyone has their late-night snack, and mine is always a PB&J microwaved for exactly 18 seconds to warm through. Setting that intention of gooey-sandwich satisfaction birthed the concept of treating a challah PB&J like this French toast / Monte Cristo hybrid. The whole thing is dipped in egg and pan-fried in butter, which soaks into the challah and adds richness while it caramelizes and warms through the filling. I serve it covered in maple syrup, making this creation just as good for noshing as it is for breakfast or dessert, of course to be eaten with a fork and knife à la *Seinfeld* and Snickers.

I feel like there is nothing more polarizing than how you build a PB&J, which is not what I'm here to wax poetic about . . . it's what I'm here to passionately plead my case over. We need justice for grape jelly. Maybe it's my obsession with Manischewitz, but the floral notes of Concord grape will always take top tier when it comes to marrying with unctuous nut butter. Raspberry is also acceptable when in a pinch, but strawberry jam is not allowed in my house! As for the PB, I truly go both ways when it comes to smooth or chunky. There are moments when you want some bite in your life, while there are times you need pure comfort in the form of a sandwich you can gum down without any resistance. I'll name-drop my allegiance to Fix & Fogg, who makes a crunchy Everything Butter with peanuts, almonds, flax, sesame, chia, and so much more, which I believe makes the ultimate sandwich. As long as we can all agree on crusts off, I think we'll be fine.

1. On a cutting board, lay out the 2 slices of challah. Spread the peanut butter on one slice and the jam or jelly on the other, then sandwich together.

2. In a medium nonstick skillet, melt the butter over medium heat. Add the beaten egg to a shallow bowl or rimmed plate and dip both sides of the sandwich to coat, letting the excess egg drip off. Place the dipped sandwich in the pan and cook, flipping once, until golden, about 2 minutes per side. Transfer to a plate and drizzle with maple syrup, then serve.

4

NOSH
PIT

*This chapter is looking
like a snack.*

Just the Dip

When I think of noshing, I immediately think of dips. They can be first tastes, setting the stage for the meal to come, just as much as they can serve as their own little meal, offering a no-fuss reprieve from hunger. With that, I wanted to create a section of recipes that first and foremost can be companions to a freshly baked loaf of challah on Friday night, ready for ripping and dipping. From there you can take your own journey with these dips, curating crudités platters, bowls of potato chips, warm pita, or any and every type of cracker you can find. It's just as enchanting to throw together a colorful platter for a few friends coming over as it is to grab a bag of baby carrots and a Tupperware of hummus to eat on the couch while you binge *Housewives*. Life is full of both types of moments, and both should be equally delicious.

BARELY-A-RECIPE BAKED BRIE

Serves 6 to 8
Prep Time: 5 minutes
Cook Time: 15 minutes

1 (1-pound) wheel brie
  cheese
⅓ cup fruit preserves
Flaky sea salt, for garnish
Fresh thyme leaves, for
  garnish

I'm sure you could figure this out without a recipe, but when it comes to serving challah on Shabbat, this technique always makes people go wild. The combo of funky creaminess from the brie with the sweetness of the preserves (I mainly reach for raspberry or fig), makes for a classic crowd-pleaser to dip crackers in or schmear on a slice of warm bread. The best part is you can adjust depending on how many people you have. Smaller crowd? Just do this with a smaller wheel of any double-cream cheese and less fruit preserves. You got this, trust me.

1. Preheat the oven to 400°F.

2. On a cutting board, cut off the top rind of the brie and discard. Place the brie in an 8- to 10-inch cast-iron skillet or baking dish, then cover with the fruit preserves.

3. Bake for 15 to 20 minutes, until the brie is melty. Garnish with flaky salt and thyme leaves, then serve.

HONEY-WHIPPED RICOTTA WITH SAGE

Makes about 2½ cups
Prep Time: 15 minutes,
plus cooling time
Cook Time: 5 minutes

6 tablespoons (3 ounces)
    unsalted butter
2 tablespoons minced
    fresh sage
1 pound (2 cups) full-fat
    ricotta cheese
3 tablespoons honey
1 tablespoon freshly
    squeezed lemon juice
Kosher salt and freshly
    ground black pepper
Finely grated lemon zest,
    for garnish

This dip is my love letter to Miss Ada in Brooklyn, one of my favorite Israeli restaurants in NYC. Everything Chef Tomer Blechman cranks out of that kitchen is thoughtful and perfect and will leave you feeling nourished and inspired. One of the first bites I had there that I still think about constantly is their whipped ricotta. Silky smooth and infused with brown butter, honey, and sage, it's everything I want to dip warm pita into. This is my copycat version of that dish, for nights when I want to bring a bit of that scoopable velvet to my Shabbos table. It's just as perfect plain as it is dressed up with lemon zest, extra brown butter, and fried whole sage leaves, if you're feeling ambitious!

1. In a small saucepan, melt the butter over medium-high heat. Cook, stirring continuously, until browned and nutty in aroma, 4 to 6 minutes. Transfer to a small heatproof bowl and stir in the sage, then let cool slightly.

2. Add the warm browned butter to a food processor along with the ricotta, honey, lemon juice, and a heavy pinch each of salt and pepper. Process for about 2 minutes until very smooth, scraping the sides as needed. Taste and adjust the seasoning with salt and pepper.

3. Transfer the dip to a bowl and top with lemon zest, then serve.

SWEET & SMOKY BABA GHANOUSH

Makes about 1 quart
Prep Time: 20 minutes
Cook Time: 15 minutes,
  plus steaming time

2½ pounds (6 small Italian
  or 2 medium standard)
  eggplants
¼ cup olive oil
¼ cup freshly squeezed
  lemon juice
2 garlic cloves, finely grated
3 tablespoons date syrup
  (silan)
1 teaspoon smoked paprika
½ teaspoon ground cumin
Pinch of cayenne pepper
Kosher salt and freshly
  ground black pepper
1/3 cup tahini
½ cup chopped fresh
  parsley

Smoke lovers rejoice! I supercharge this iconic Levantine mezze with smoked paprika for extra smoke and a stunning rust color, while providing the sweet and smoky fantasy thanks to the addition of date syrup. To cook the eggplants, I use the broiler for the sake of my smoke detector, but you can just as easily char them on the open flame of a gas stovetop or on the grill. While the cooking method is flexible, the non-negotiable is using a fork or potato masher to coarsely break up the roasted eggplants, rather than a food processor. The tender bite of the chunky mash you create has so much more depth than a puree, ready to be thickened into a creamy dip by emulsifying in olive oil and tahini.

1. Preheat the broiler with the rack about 6 inches from the top of the oven. Line a sheet pan with aluminum foil.

2. Puncture the eggplants a few times with a fork and place on the prepared pan. Rub with 2 tablespoons of the olive oil. Broil, turning with tongs as needed, until fully charred, 15 to 20 minutes. Transfer to a medium heatproof bowl and cover with plastic wrap. Let steam for 15 minutes.

3. Meanwhile, in a large bowl, combine the lemon juice and garlic. Let sit to take the bite off the garlic.

4. Transfer the eggplants to a cutting board and carefully remove the stems and skins, discarding both. To the garlic mixture, add the peeled eggplants with the date syrup, paprika, cumin, cayenne, and a heavy pinch each of salt and black pepper. Using a fork or potato masher, mash the eggplants to combine. Slowly add the remaining 2 tablespoons of olive oil and the tahini, stirring with a fork to emulsify into a thick, chunky dip, then stir in the parsley. Taste and adjust the seasoning with salt and black pepper, then serve.

SWEET POTATO HUMMUS

Makes about 1½ quarts
Prep Time: 20 minutes,
plus cooling time
Cook Time: 1 hour

2 medium (about
  1½ pounds) sweet
  potatoes
2 (15-ounce) cans
  chickpeas, drained
½ cup tahini
½ cup freshly squeezed
  lemon juice
½ teaspoon sweet or hot
  smoked paprika
2 garlic cloves, smashed
  and peeled
Kosher salt

Ever since I started hosting my giant Shabbat ragers, I've been making sweet potato hummus to serve for the sole reason that it can be made days in advance and stays so gorgeously creamy. The issue with making any good classic hummus is that it should be ephemeral, enjoyed only fresh. The velvety, creamy hummus you labor over disappears the second it goes into the fridge, seizing the tahini into a grainy dip that has lost its luster. By blending in roasted sweet potatoes, you're able to maintain that swoopable texture you desire, while adding welcome color and sweetness. You can take this even further if you want, roasting jalapeños with the potatoes to add heat, or even roasting a whole head of garlic to replace the fresh cloves. I love to garnish it with a drizzle of EVOO and a sprinkling of paprika if I'm entertaining, or I eat it right out of the Tupperware if it's just me noshing.

1.   Preheat the oven to 400°F.

2.   Wash the sweet potatoes, then while still wet, wrap in a double layer of aluminum foil to seal, and place on a sheet pan. Bake for 1 hour, until tender. Let cool completely on the pan, then carefully remove the skins and discard.

3.   Transfer the roasted sweet potatoes to a high-speed blender along with the chickpeas, tahini, lemon juice, paprika, garlic, and 2 heavy pinches of salt. Puree until very smooth, then taste and adjust the seasoning with salt.

4.   Serve immediately, or store in an airtight container in the refrigerator for up to 1 week.

FRENCH ONION SPINACH ARTICHOKE DIP

Serves 6 to 8
Prep Time: 20 minutes,
plus cooling time
Cook Time: 1 hour

2 tablespoons unsalted
   butter
3 medium yellow onions,
   thinly sliced
Kosher salt and freshly
   ground black pepper
1 cup hard cider
6 garlic cloves, minced
1 (14-ounce) can artichoke
   hearts, drained and
   roughly chopped
10 ounces frozen chopped
   spinach, thawed and
   drained
1 (8-ounce) package full-
   fat cream cheese, at
   room temperature
2/3 cup full-fat sour cream
1 teaspoon crushed
   Calabrian chiles (or
   1/2 teaspoon crushed red
   pepper)
8 ounces gruyère cheese,
   coarsely grated (about
   2 cups)
1/2 cup finely grated
   Parmigiano-Reggiano
   cheese
1/4 cup panko bread
   crumbs (optional)
1 tablespoon olive oil

In a world looking for speedy hacks, caramelized onions could not care less. They're an ingredient that forces you to stop everything and give them all your attention for as long as they need (like me), slowly melting into jammy gold (luckily, not like me). I'm a big fan of anything resembling onion dip. It's not revolutionary to give spinach-artichoke dip the allium-heavy treatment, but sometimes the best recipes are the ones most adjacent to your comfort-food fantasies. This dip has become a staple of our game nights, where the players are almost exclusively gay Jews who love to simultaneously eat and scream at each other while playing Catan. And if nobody is willing to trade you any wheat, at least you can stuff your face with this dip.

1. Preheat the oven to 425°F.

2. In a large high-sided skillet or braiser, melt the butter over medium heat. Add the onions and 2 heavy pinches each of salt and black pepper and cook, stirring often, until caramelized, 40 to 45 minutes. After 15 minutes of cooking, begin deglazing the pan as needed with the hard cider, using a few tablespoons at a time every 5 to 10 minutes, until you've used the full cup. After 30 minutes of cooking, stir in the minced garlic, then continue to cook, deglazing with the cider. Once the onions are caramelized, transfer to a large bowl and let cool.

3. To the cooled onions, add the artichoke hearts, spinach, cream cheese, sour cream, chiles, and half of the grated gruyère and Parmigiano-Reggiano. Stir together until well incorporated, then taste and adjust the seasoning with salt and black pepper. Transfer to an 8-inch ovenproof skillet and spread in an even layer.

4. In a small bowl, toss together the remaining half of the grated gruyère and Parmigiano-Reggiano with the bread crumbs, if using. Sprinkle over the dip, then drizzle with the olive oil.

5. Bake for 20 to 25 minutes, until golden and bubbling, then serve immediately.

BAKED FETA & CHERRY TOMATO DIP

Makes about 3 cups
Prep Time: 15 minutes,
plus cooling time
Cook Time: 30 minutes

1 (8-ounce) block feta
    cheese
2 pints (about 1 pound)
    cherry tomatoes
4 garlic cloves, smashed
    and peeled
3 tablespoons olive oil
2 tablespoons balsamic
    vinegar
1 tablespoon honey
2 teaspoons ground sumac
1 teaspoon dried oregano
¼ teaspoon crushed red
    pepper
Kosher salt and freshly
    ground black pepper
1 (8-ounce) package full-fat
    cream cheese, at room
    temperature

If there are two things I can do for hours, they're eating whipped feta and doomscrolling on TikTok, occasionally at the same time. This recipe marries them both, bringing back memories of the feta pasta that everyone and their mothers were making! It's a simple combo of roasted cherry tomatoes and feta, which gets whipped with cream cheese into a creamy, crimson spread that brings just the right tang to balance the richness of this dip. And while no pasta is required in this recipe, warm pita is highly recommended for dipping, as are a garnish of feta crumbles and blistered tomatoes for extra flair.

1. Preheat the oven to 425°F.

2. In a 9 × 13-inch baking dish, place the feta in the center, then scatter the tomatoes and garlic around it. Drizzle with the olive oil, balsamic, and honey, then season with the sumac, oregano, crushed red pepper, and a heavy pinch each of salt and black pepper.

3. Bake for 30 minutes, until the feta is golden and the tomatoes are blistered, then let cool completely in the dish.

4. Transfer the contents of the baking dish to a high-speed blender or food processor along with the cream cheese, then puree until very smooth. Taste and adjust the seasoning with salt and black pepper. Serve immediately, or store in an airtight container in the refrigerator for up to 5 days.

NANNY'S LIPTAUER (SLOVAKIAN CHEESE SPREAD)

Makes about 2 cups
Prep Time: 15 minutes

2 (8-ounce) packages full-
fat cream cheese, at room
temperature
¼ cup blue cheese
crumbles
1 teaspoon finely grated
lemon zest
2 tablespoons freshly
squeezed lemon juice
2 tablespoons minced fresh
parsley
2 tablespoons minced fresh
chives
1 teaspoon onion powder
1 teaspoon sweet or hot
smoked paprika
1 teaspoon drained capers
1 anchovy fillet (optional)
Kosher salt and freshly
ground black pepper

This may be one of the simplest recipes in my book, but this headnote was by far the most difficult to write.

When anyone ever asks me what my goals are, the answer is always the same: I want to be good for the Jews. I want to help reignite passion in preservation of our history, stories, and recipes, as much as I want to be part of the conversation around how we carry our culture through the present and into the future. The last few years, I've been learning more about my family's history, from the towns they were born in to the camps they escaped from to how they rebuilt their lives in America.

As part of this journey, my aunt Susi lent me her mother's (my great-grandmother, known as Nanny) recipe box, a green tin packed with folded newspaper clippings and scribbled index cards. Documented in the Heilberg culinary time capsule is Nanny's recipe for Liptauer, a central European cheese spread laced with herbs and paprika, which entered her recipe Rolodex once the family settled in NYC. But what is so special is there isn't just one recipe noted. She has the original recipe clipping from the *New York Times* as well as index cards covered with her tweaks and variations as she made it her own. This recipe is a version of her wildest, which breaks from tradition by adding blue cheese to the mix, and it just works so well!

As with so much of Jewish history, what may seem to be a simple schmear is so much more. It's a connection to the never-ending story of how our recipes evolve and it just means the world to me to be able to write a small part of it.

In a food processor, combine the cream cheese, blue cheese, lemon zest and juice, parsley, chives, onion powder, paprika, capers, and anchovy, if using. Puree until smooth, then taste and adjust the seasoning with salt and pepper. Serve immediately or store in an airtight container in the refrigerator for up to 5 days.

MATBUCHA

Makes about 3½ cups
Prep Time: 15 minutes,
plus cooling time
Cook Time: 55 minutes,
plus steaming time

2 medium red bell peppers
1 jalapeño
1 red onion, quartered and
    peeled
3 tablespoons olive oil
2 teaspoons smoked
    paprika
4 garlic cloves, minced
1 (28-ounce) can crushed
    tomatoes, preferably fire-
    roasted
Kosher salt and freshly
    ground black pepper

There are few dips as sexy as matbucha, hitting the table like a ruby-red disco ball, shimmering with olive oil and awaiting a torn piece of challah to swoop in. I fell in love with this cooked tomato and pepper salad in Israel. It was brought to the Holy Land by the Jews of Morocco and North Africa, where it's enjoyed with the same fervor as hummus. Every family has their own version to their tastes, covering the spectrum of chunkiness, spiciness, and smokiness. For me, I find that first charring the peppers and onion helps concentrate their flavors and amps up the sweetness before you cook them low and slow with fire-roasted tomatoes. Just be sure to put out some for dipping and save the rest as the base for you next shakshuka.

1. Preheat the broiler with a rack set 6 inches from the heating element. Line a sheet pan with aluminum foil.

2. Place the bell peppers, jalapeño, and red onion on the prepared pan. Broil, turning with tongs as needed, until everything is fully charred, 10 to 12 minutes. Transfer the red onion to a cutting board and let cool, then finely chop. Transfer the jalapeño and bell peppers to a medium heatproof bowl and cover with plastic wrap, then let steam for 15 minutes.

3. Transfer the peppers and jalapeño to the cutting board and carefully remove the stems, skins, and seeds, discarding all three, then finely chop. (If desired, keep the jalapeño seeds intact for more heat.)

4. In a large skillet, heat the olive oil over medium-high heat. Add the onion, peppers, and jalapeño along with the smoked paprika and garlic and cook until softened and fragrant, 4 to 6 minutes. Stir in the crushed tomatoes and 2 heavy pinches each of salt and black pepper, then bring to a simmer. Cook, stirring occasionally and reducing the heat as needed to maintain a light simmer, until thickened, 40 to 45 minutes.

5. Taste and adjust the seasoning with salt and black pepper. Serve immediately, or store in an airtight container in the refrigerator for up to 1 week or in the freezer for up to 6 months.

Let's Make a Toast!

I'm sure you're all perfectly capable of making toast on your own. (Well, most of you at least.) But I did want to share my favorite way to toast bread for a tartine, or really for any application of bread when it comes to noshing. When I worked the line at ABC Kitchen under the iconic chef Dan Kluger, my station was responsible for all the toasts on the menu, which meant I toasted a lot of bread every day. Here's what I learned.

1. **Thickly cut your bread.** You don't want a cracker that will break a tooth. A golden crust that provides support but has a soft interior will always be the goal. I aim for ¾ inch thick with my slices, though give me an inch and I won't complain (with toast, at least). I'd say that 99 percent of my toasting is with sourdough or challah, but really, you do you and use whatever loaf brings you joy.

2. **Use lots of olive oil.** I mean, are you surprised? I typically throw down 2 tablespoons of olive oil in a cast-iron or nonstick skillet over medium-high heat before letting the bread sizzle for 1 to 2 minutes. Then, when I flip, I add another tablespoon of oil to the pan before cooking for another 1 to 2 minutes. The result is crispy, slick toast gleaming like a golden goddess.

3. **A little pressure goes a long way.** You need direct contact between the bread and the pan, though sometimes your slices aren't perfectly flat. A light press with a spatula helps create even color and crunch.

WATERMELON & FETA TARTINES

Serves 4 to 6
Prep Time: 10 minutes

12 ounces watermelon, cut
into ¼-inch cubes (about
2 cups)

8 ounces feta, cut into
¼-inch cubes

2 tablespoons olive oil

2 tablespoons freshly
squeezed lime juice

2 tablespoons minced
fresh mint

2 scallions, thinly sliced

Kosher salt and freshly
ground black pepper

Toasted sourdough slices,
for serving (see tips,
page 92

Summer is tartine season. There's something about the vibrant produce that comes out of the warmer months that should be honored on a throne of crispy bread. And while you can find me eating heirloom tomato toasts for just about any meal, the sweet and salty combo of watermelon and feta belongs on a bed of sourdough. I wish I thought of it, but the idea came from my mother-in-law, Robina, who continues to inspire me with stories of meals from her upbringing across the Middle East. In Iran a common midday snack would be a watermelon and a chunk of feta cut up to be eaten with flatbread, which is what I wanted to create here in a slightly more composed manner. By tossing this iconic duo with citrus and herbs, you get the perfect balance of brightness and sharp bite to round it all out.

You really can go a few different routes with composing these tartines, depending on the vibe you're looking for. Often, I'll build two large toasts for my husband and me to enjoy as a light lunch or summer afternoon snack. However, this recipe also works beautifully when entertaining if you just use smaller pieces of toasted sourdough for a platter of two-bite hors d'oeuvres. I'll just remind you that with such few ingredients, quality is crucial. Make sure you're using fresh bread, ripe watermelon, and a nice block of feta, because you're worth it!

In a large bowl, toss together the watermelon, feta, olive oil, lime juice, mint, scallions, and a heavy pinch each of salt and pepper to combine. Taste and adjust the seasoning with salt and pepper. Using a slotted spoon, spoon over toasted sourdough slices, then serve.

FINGER BEANS

Serves 4 to 6
Prep Time: 20 minutes
Cook Time: 5 minutes

Kosher salt
2 pounds green beans,
  trimmed
3 tablespoons olive oil
2 tablespoons freshly
  squeezed lemon juice
2 garlic cloves, finely grated
Freshly ground black
  pepper
¼ cup minced fresh dill

While everyone confesses their love to chef Eyal Shani for his custardy whole-roasted cauliflower at Miznon (and rightfully so), we need to be spending more time praising his green beans. Blanched and ice-shocked beans are simply dressed with lemon, garlic, and olive oil for the most satisfying crisp-tender bite of vegetal bliss. While I'm sure most use a fork to enjoy their meal, I sit and eat the bag of green beans like potato chips and highly encourage you to follow suit. It reminds me of the bowls of blanched fava beans, a favorite Persian snack, my husband's aunt Diana puts out when she entertains.

This snack was inspired by both dishes, matching the bright lemony-dressed greens beans with chopped dill. When making this dish, there are some key guidelines to ensure all stays green and gorgeous. First, make sure you have a large pot of salted water boiling for blanching. The salt raises the boiling point of the water, meaning that your boiling water is hotter than if you had a pot of boiling unsalted water. By cooking hotter and faster, you're able to help better preserve the color. Same deal with shocking the beans in an ice bath, which helps stop the cooking so your beans don't turn army green. Finally, while you can blanch and shock your beans far in advance of serving, toss them with the dressing only right before they hit the table, since the lemon juice will dull their color over time. Then, just wash your hands and get fingering!

1. Bring a large pot of salted water to a boil and fill a medium bowl with ice and water.

2. Add the green beans to the boiling water and cook until bright green and crisp-tender, 4 to 5 minutes. Transfer the green beans to the bowl of ice water and let cool for 5 minutes, then drain.

3. Meanwhile, in a large bowl, whisk together the olive oil, lemon juice, garlic, and 2 heavy pinches each of salt and pepper. Before serving, add the drained green beans to the dressing along with the dill and toss to coat. Taste and adjust the seasoning with salt and pepper, then serve.

ANNIE'S HONEY-CANDIED WINGS

Serves 6 to 8
Prep Time: 15 minutes
Cook Time: 40 minutes

For the Wings

3½ pounds chicken wings, drumettes and flats separated and patted dry with paper towels

2 tablespoons olive oil

2 teaspoons kosher salt

2 teaspoons garlic powder

2 teaspoons ground sumac

2 teaspoons smoked paprika

1 teaspoon ground ginger

1 teaspoon dry mustard

½ teaspoon cayenne pepper

For the Glaze

½ cup honey

1 teaspoon hot sauce

½ teaspoon kosher salt

1 garlic clove, finely grated

Whenever I get a call from my grandma Annie, I always record it because at some point she'll jump into an oral lecture on some recipe she either used to make or just invented. One call, it was all about how she always bakes wings and smothers them with honey to caramelize in the oven into a shatteringly crisp chicken sensation.

Inspired by Annie's, this recipe first bakes wings in a fragrant spice mix laced with paprika and ginger before getting candied in honey infused with garlic and hot sauce. And while my grandma adamantly disapproves of this version, since she hates all things spicy, they've become an instant hit with the rest of the family.

You can play around with the spice blend using your favorite pantry staples. Feel free to infuse the honey with fresh or dried chiles instead of hot sauce; any herbs you love, like rosemary or sage; or any other aromatics, like fresh ginger or citrus zest. While you could grill these wings, I find it crucial to have the candying portion take place in the oven. The infused honey blends with the chicken juices, making a thick glaze of intense flavor that pools around the wings. It must be saved to drizzle over your finished platter!

1. Preheat the oven to 450°F and arrange two racks in the upper half. Line two sheet pans with aluminum foil.

2. Make the wings: In a large bowl, toss the chicken wings with the olive oil to coat. In a small bowl, stir together the salt, garlic powder, sumac, smoked paprika, ginger, mustard, and cayenne to combine. Sprinkle over the wings and toss to coat.

3. Divide the wings between the prepared sheet pans, arranging them in a single layer. Roast, turning the wings and rotating the pans halfway through the cooking time, for 30 minutes, until lightly golden.

4. Meanwhile, make the glaze: In a small saucepan, combine the honey, hot sauce, salt, and garlic over medium heat. Bring to a simmer, stirring occasionally, then remove from the heat.

5. After the 30 minutes of roasting, drizzle the wings with the honey mixture. Alternatively, you can brush it on with a silicone brush or transfer the wings to a large bowl to toss with the honey. Return the pans to the oven and roast for 10 to 15 minutes more, until the wings are caramelized and crisp. Transfer the wings to a platter and drizzle on any caramelized honey left on the pans, then serve.

KUGEL FRIES

Serves 6 to 8
Prep Time: 30 minutes,
plus cooling and 4-hour
chilling time
Cook Time: 55 minutes

Nonstick cooking spray, for
  greasing
4 pounds russet potatoes,
  peeled and coarsely
  grated
1 medium yellow onion,
  coarsely grated
½ cup matzo meal or bread
  crumbs
3 tablespoons olive oil
2 teaspoons minced fresh
  thyme leaves
2 teaspoons kosher salt,
  plus more as needed
½ teaspoon baking powder
4 large eggs, lightly beaten
4 garlic cloves, minced
Vegetable oil, for frying

Essentially we're making giant Jewish Tater Tots and they're going to blow your mind. Potato kugel—grated potatoes and onion bound with eggs and matzo meal—really is a latke casserole, so the concept of cutting it up and frying it just makes sense. This calls for a little bit more planning, since you must bake and chill the kugel before cutting it into batons and frying, but if you have leftover potato kugel from Seder then half the work is already done. The result is a crispy, golden shell encasing a custardy potato center ready to be assembled into a Jenga platter of fries that will quickly be destroyed.

You can dress up your kugel fries to fit any occasion, sweatpants to black tie. Whatever the fantasy you're trying to create, they'll fit the bill, tasting just as good dipped in ketchup as they are topped with sour cream and salmon roe or caviar. One of my favorite ways to serve them is alongside braised brisket at Seder (they're K4P, of course). That way you can dip the fries into the brisket sauce for a next-level punch of umami.

1. Preheat the oven to 350°F. Grease a 9 × 13-inch pan with nonstick cooking spray and line it with parchment paper.

2. In a large bowl, toss the potatoes and onion with the matzo meal, olive oil, thyme, salt, baking powder, eggs, and garlic until well combined. Transfer to the prepared pan and press into an even layer. Grease a sheet of parchment paper with nonstick cooking spray and press directly on top of the kugel.

3. Bake for 40 to 45 minutes, until the potatoes are very tender, then let cool completely. Chill for at least 4 hours.

4. Once chilled, transfer to a cutting board and discard the parchment. Trim the outer ¼-inch border and discard (or snack on or fry anyway to snack on). Cut in half lengthwise and then across into 1-inch-thick sticks.

5. In a large dutch oven, heat 2 inches of oil to 375°F. Line a sheet pan with paper towels. Working in about three batches, fry the kugel sticks, turning occasionally, until golden brown, 5 to 7 minutes per batch. Transfer to the paper towel–lined sheet pan and immediately season with a pinch of salt. Repeat until all the sticks are fried, then serve (see headnote for serving recommendations).

BINA'S SPINACH BOUREKA ROLLS

Serves 8 to 10
Prep Time: 25 minutes,
plus cooling time
Cook Time: 30 minutes

2 tablespoons olive oil

2 medium yellow onions,
  minced

Kosher salt and freshly
  ground black pepper

2 teaspoons cumin seeds

2 (10-ounce) bags frozen
  chopped spinach, thawed
  and pressed over a sieve
  to drain

1 pound feta, crumbled

All-purpose flour, for
  dusting

2 sheets store-bought
  puff pastry (from one
  17.3-ounce package),
  thawed

1 large egg, lightly beaten

Sesame seeds, for garnish

While bourekas have endless variations spanning the Mediterranean, my mother-in-law, Robina, makes both one of the easiest and most delicious versions whenever we visit. Full sheets of puff pastry are rolled up to lock in a fragrant mixture of cumin-fried onions, chopped spinach, and feta before getting baked into golden, flaky logs. We cut ourselves slice after slice, until it magically disappears, and she vows to make another batch the following day.

I really do make this recipe all the time, so here are my top-line tips. Thaw your frozen spinach and your puff pastry! I typically throw both in the fridge the night before. That way, you can really squeeze out all the moisture from the spinach and roll out the dough without any cracking. Feel free to make the filling in advance! It will hold up to a day in the fridge and still be just as perfect. And of course, let the rolls cool! You want to serve them while still warm, but for clean slices, let the rolls sit for 15 minutes before cutting them.

1. In a large skillet, heat the olive oil over medium-high heat. Add the onions and a heavy pinch each of salt and pepper and cook, stirring often, until softened and caramelized, 5 to 7 minutes. Stir in the cumin seeds and cook until fragrant, 1 minute more. Transfer to a large bowl and let cool completely.

2. Meanwhile, preheat the oven to 400°F. Line a sheet pan with parchment paper.

3. Once the onions are cooled, mix in the drained spinach and feta to combine. Taste and adjust the seasoning with salt and pepper.

4. On a lightly floured work surface, unfold a sheet of the thawed puff pastry with the creases running horizontally. Lightly roll out the dough lengthwise to remove the creases. Spoon half of the spinach mixture along the bottom third of the dough, then roll up to form a tight log, pinching the ends to seal. Place on the prepared pan, then repeat with the remaining dough and filling, spacing the logs 3 inches apart. Brush with the beaten egg and garnish each with a sprinkling of sesame seeds. Using a paring knife, cut three 1-inch slits on the top of each log to allow any steam to vent.

5. Bake for 25 to 30 minutes, until puffed and golden. Let cool slightly, then slice and serve warm.

APRICOT-GLAZED SALAMI TART WITH ARUGULA SALAD

Serves 6 to 8
Prep Time: 20 minutes
Cook Time: 25 minutes

All-purpose flour, for
  dusting
1 (14-ounce) sheet store-
  bought puff pastry,
  thawed
1 (12-ounce) beef salami,
  peeled and thinly sliced
¼ cup dijon mustard
¼ cup apricot preserves
Kosher salt and freshly
  ground black pepper
1 large egg, lightly beaten
2 cups baby arugula
1 tablespoon olive oil
1 tablespoon aged balsamic
  vinegar

It's not a party without a Hasselback salami, period. It's the retro appetizer that never goes out of style. Take a slashed beef salami and slather it with dijon and apricot preserves before baking it to candied perfection. It's sweet and salty, crunchy and juicy, and rich and tangy all at the same time. Put some respect on it! Our friends Ben and Leo made one at their Hanukkah party (I have to clarify: Ben learned it from his mother, Rona), and I distinctly remember being part of the crowd of gay Jews huddled around the salami, gleefully tearing it apart. I wanted to create a tart that caused the same kind of a commotion at any function. This recipe delivers the exact same vibes as the classic but with a little makeover, sporting a crispy puff pastry crust and peppery arugula salad.

I'm particular about my puff pastry in this recipe. You want one single 14-ounce sheet (I use Dufour brand puff pastry) to make this tart, but if you end up buying something else, you can always pivot and make multiple smaller tarts. You could even cut up your puff pastry into squares to make little danish-style salami tarts for entertaining. Get creative, it isn't that deep! It's salami!

1. Preheat the oven to 400°F. Line a sheet pan with parchment paper.

2. On a lightly floured work surface, unfold the puff pastry and lightly roll to remove the creases. Transfer to the prepared sheet pan, and with a paring knife, lightly score a 1-inch border around the dough. Using a fork, prick the dough all around within the border, then shingle the slices of salami on top.

3. In a small bowl, stir together the dijon and apricot preserves with a pinch each of salt and pepper, then brush over the salami. Brush the border of the dough with the beaten egg.

4. Bake for 25 to 30 minutes, until the puff pastry is golden and the salami is caramelized. Let cool slightly.

5. In a medium bowl, toss the arugula with the olive oil, balsamic, and a pinch each of salt and pepper. Top the tart with the arugula salad, then slice and serve warm.

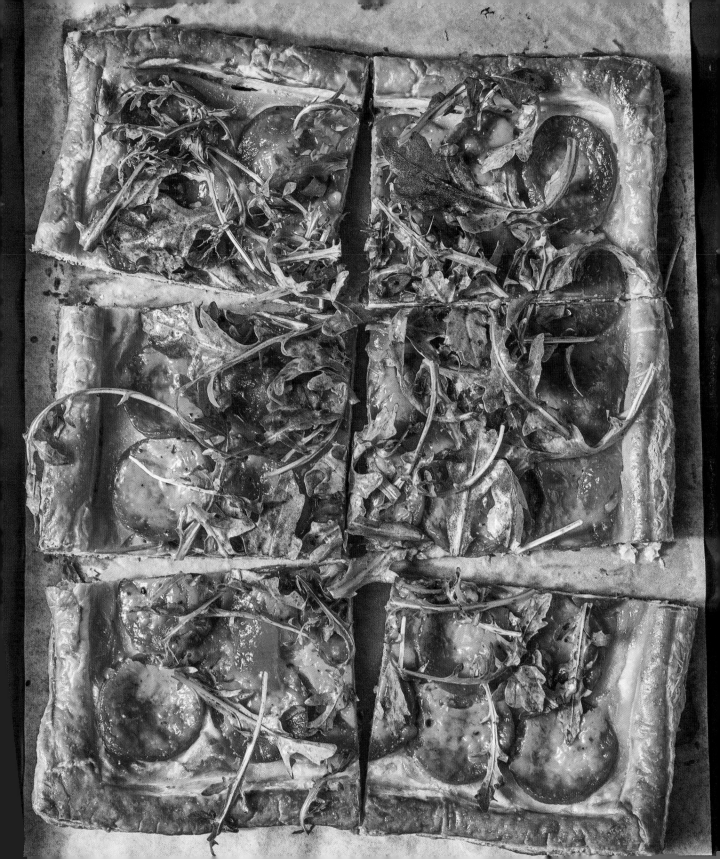

BROCCOLI-CHEDDAR KNISHES

Makes 12 knishes
Prep Time: 30 minutes,
plus chilling and cooling time
Cook Time: 35 minutes

For the Dough

3¼ cups (439g) all-
purpose flour
½ cup water
½ cup vegetable oil
1 tablespoon distilled white
vinegar
1 teaspoon kosher salt
1 large egg

For the Filling

¼ cup vegetable oil
3 garlic cloves, thinly sliced
1½ pounds (3 medium)
russet potatoes, peeled
and cut into ¾-inch
pieces
1 pound (1 medium bunch)
broccoli, cut into 1-inch
florets, stems peeled and
thinly sliced
¾ cup water
Kosher salt and freshly
ground black pepper
4 ounces sharp cheddar
cheese, coarsely grated
(1 cup)
2 tablespoons full-fat sour
cream

Carb-filled carbs! There is no starchier nosh than the almighty knish, which is pretty much just a mashed potato Hot Pocket. I grew up inhaling them at Knish Nosh in Queens, where naturally I'd wash down a plain potato one with a knish dough–wrapped hot dog. My mother, on the other hand, would bring home only broccoli knishes, since she was always working some grift to get us to eat more vegetables. For years, she literally made my sister and me think pizza only came with spinach on it. This recipe is obviously dedicated to her, marrying potatoes and broccoli into the cheesiest, dreamiest filling to be wrapped in a flaky crust.

Rolling and shaping your knishes may be totally new for you, but we're going to walk through it together. First, roll out half of the dough. Next, stuff it with half the filling and roll it up to make a giant log. Then the technique is to twist off each knish like you're making sausage, pinching the dough to separate. And if you have any difficulty, I find twisting the dough and following with a bench scraper to cut through works just as well. Pinch one end closed and bake with the other end facing up and open slightly, to work as a vent for steam, since your knishes can burst open in the oven if totally sealed. Once you get comfortable with the technique, start getting creative with fillings. You can even omit the cheese and sour cream in this recipe if you're looking to keep these pareve. Mashed potatoes are your canvas for infinite knish possibilities!

1. Make the dough: On a clean work surface, place the flour in a pile and make a well in the center. Add the water, vegetable oil, vinegar, salt, and egg to the well. Using a fork, whisk the ingredients in the well together until smooth, slowly incorporating the flour. Once a shaggy dough forms, switch to using your hands to knead together until you have a very smooth ball of dough. This typically takes 4 to 6 minutes. Wrap in plastic and chill for 1 hour.

2. Meanwhile, make the filling: In a medium pot or dutch oven, heat the oil and garlic over medium-high heat. Cook until the edges of the garlic begin to turn golden, about 2 minutes. Add the potatoes, broccoli, water, and 2 heavy pinches each of salt and pepper, then reduce the heat to medium. Cover and cook until the potatoes and broccoli are tender, 12 to 15 minutes. Remove from the heat and mash into a chunky paste, then transfer to a medium bowl and let cool completely. Once cooled, stir in the cheddar and sour cream to combine. Taste and adjust the seasoning with salt and pepper.

All-purpose flour, for
    dusting
1 large egg, lightly
    beaten

3. Assemble and bake your knishes: Preheat the oven to 400°F. Line a sheet pan with parchment paper.

4. On a lightly floured work surface, roll out half of the dough into a 12 × 15-inch rectangle, about 1/8 inch thick and aligned horizontally. Spoon half of the filling in an even layer along the bottom third of the dough, then roll up to form a tight log, pinching the ends to seal. Using the edge of your pinky finger, make indentations to mark the dough into 6 equal pieces. One at a time, twist the dough at the indentations to separate, as if you were making links of sausage, pinching the dough as needed to seal one end, while leaving the other end open about 1 inch. Place the knishes on their sides 2 inches apart on the prepared pan. The sealed ends should be facing down. Repeat this process with the remaining dough and filling. Brush all the knishes with the beaten egg.

5. Bake for 20 to 25 minutes, until golden brown. Let cool slightly, then serve warm.

FRIED PICKLE PLATTER

Serves 4 to 6
Prep Time: 20 minutes
Cook Time: 15 minutes

1¼ cups all-purpose flour
1 teaspoon kosher salt
1¼ cups buttermilk
¼ teaspoon cayenne
  pepper
1 cup plain dried bread
  crumbs
1 cup panko bread crumbs
1 teaspoon garlic powder
½ teaspoon freshly ground
  black pepper
3 to 4 jars assorted pickles,
  including cucumber
  spears or coins, green
  beans, okra, Brussels
  sprouts, and beets,
  drained
Vegetable oil, for frying
Flaky sea salt, for garnish

If there are two things that never fail to amaze me, it's Jewish geography and fried pickles. Most Shabbos mornings, my husband and I fall into our ideal routine of a workout in Williamsburg, Brooklyn, followed by brunch at Gertie, one of our fav Jewish spots. Gertie is owned by our dear friends Nate Adler and Rachel Jackson, who we connected with through Rachel's uncles, our other dear friends and the menschiest mensches, Richie Jackson and Jordan Roth. Well, that settles the geography portion. As for the pickles, I've always been a fan of any fried spear or chip, balancing the crunch and grease of the coating with the tenderness and acidity of a brine-soaked cucumber. But Gertie was the first place where we've experienced the platter venturing beyond cuke, featuring all their house-made pickles, from turmeric-tinted cauliflower florets to earthy slices of tender beets.

From okra and carrots to Brussels sprouts and green beans, there is an incredible variety of different textures and flavors to explore. Experiment and find what brands and types you love the most! I often serve them up with my Spicy Green Sauce (page 43), but I'm not going to stop you from celebrating with your condiment of choice.

1. In a shallow bowl or platter, stir together the flour and ½ teaspoon of the kosher salt. In a second shallow bowl, stir together the buttermilk and cayenne. In a third shallow bowl, stir together both bread crumbs with the garlic powder, black pepper, and the remaining ½ teaspoon kosher salt.

2. Line a sheet pan with parchment paper. Working with one hand for the dry and one for the wet, dredge each pickle in the flour, shaking off any excess, then dip it in the buttermilk, letting any excess drip off, and finally toss it in the bread-crumb mixture, pressing the crumbs against the pickle to completely coat. Arrange the breaded pickles on the prepared pan.

3. Bring a pot with 2 inches of oil to 350°F. Line a sheet pan with paper towels.

4. Working in batches, fry the pickles until golden brown, 3 to 4 minutes. Transfer to the paper towels to drain and immediately season with a pinch of flaky salt. Repeat until all the pickles are fried, then transfer to a platter and serve.

LATKE TARTINES

Makes about 16 latkes
Prep Time: 15 minutes
Cook Time: 20 minutes

2 pounds russet potatoes, peeled
½ medium yellow onion
½ cup matzo meal
2 teaspoons kosher salt
3 large eggs
Vegetable oil, for frying

It's not a party without potato pancakes. I don't make the rules, but I will enforce this one. Instead of the whole applesauce or sour cream conversation, which only serves to divide us, we're just going to pick a vibe for the night and go hard with the toppings. Don't get it twisted, there's nothing wrong with a platter of freshly fried latkes alongside some fancy applesauce or full-fat sour cream and caviar. But tonight, we're setting a mood with some towering latke tartines to pass around at your next soiree, whether it's Hanukkah or not. Latkes can and should be a year-round food!

The only question is, Do you want to go savory or sweet at this very moment (you're allowed to switch teams as many times as you'd like). For savory, my go-to move is to channel the best bagel and lox by layering beet horseradish–stained sour cream with pastrami lox and herbs. For sweet, I've always been obsessed with how often Polish Jews would sprinkle sugar on their latkes, so we're going to toss them with cinnamon sugar and top them with honeycomb and an ingredient called gjetost. Made from caramelized goat milk, this is the wildest Norwegian cheese product. It tastes like butterscotch-flavored Velveeta in a kind of magical way. I'm down with the onion still in the latkes, but you can always sub with peeled Honeycrisp apple instead! These are but two paths you can venture down on your journey of dressing up your latkes. I can't wait to see the combinations you and your family fall in love with!

1. Using a box grater or a food processor fitted with the shredding disc, coarsely grate the potatoes and onion. Transfer to a medium bowl lined with cheesecloth or a thin dish towel and wring the cloth to squeeze out any liquid into the bowl. Set the bowl of liquid aside to sit for 5 minutes. Put the squeezed potatoes and onion in another medium bowl, add the matzo meal, salt, and eggs, and mix until well incorporated.

2. Pour off and discard the reserved liquid from the first bowl, revealing a thin layer of white potato starch stuck to the bottom. Stir the potato starch into the potato mixture.

3. In a large cast-iron or nonstick skillet, heat ¼ inch of oil over medium-high heat until shimmering. Line a sheet pan with paper towels.

4. Working in batches, scoop 4 packed (¼-cup) balls of the potato mixture into the skillet, spacing them 2 inches apart. Using a spatula, smash each ball to flatten. Cook the latkes, flipping once, until golden, 2 to 3 minutes per side. Transfer to the paper towel–lined pan to drain. Repeat with the remaining potato mixture, adding more oil to the skillet between batches and adjusting the heat as needed.

5. Transfer the latkes to a platter and see pages 110–111 for topping guidance.

Savory

Sliced pastrami salmon • Sour cream mixed with beet horseradish, salt, and pepper
Fresh dill • Lemon zest

Sweet

Cinnamon sugar • Sliced gjetost cheese • Fresh honeycomb • Flaky sea salt

As a kid, nothing hit quite as hard as opening the freezer to find a box of Bagel Bites or Stouffer's French bread pizzas, inspiring my life-long obsession with taking any vessel of carbs (whether leavened or not) and baking it with sauce and cheese. Embrace nostalgia! Embrace simplicity!

Pizza Bagel

Embrace pizza-adjacent noshes! Just assemble them on a parchment-lined sheet pan and bake at 425°F for 10 to 15 minutes, until the cheese is melted and golden.

Bagel/matzo • Sauce (marinara/vodka) • Grated low-moisture mozz • Grated parm • Fresh basil • Pickled jalapeños • Honey

Matzo Pizza

5

WE BOTH LOVE SOUP

Gorgeous, gorgeous girls love soup.

These recipes always taste better the next day!
And they all freeze beautifully!

JAKE'S LENTIL STEW

Serves 10 to 12
Prep Time: 20 minutes
Cook Time: 55 minutes

4 garlic cloves, smashed
　and peeled
3 medium carrots, peeled
　and cut into 3-inch pieces
2 celery stalks, cut into
　3-inch pieces
1 medium yellow onion,
　quartered
1 jalapeño, stemmed and
　seeded
3 tablespoons olive oil
Kosher salt
½ teaspoon ground cumin
½ teaspoon ground
　coriander
1 (14.5-ounce) can diced
　tomatoes (preferably fire-
　roasted)
2 cups dried brown lentils
8 cups vegetable stock
2 cups water
Freshly ground black
　pepper
1 bunch (12 ounces) curly
　green kale, stemmed and
　finely shredded

Let's get biblical! We're going to make a lentil stew so delicious that everyone is going to want to sell their birthright for a bowl. (If you're lost, just google "Jacob and Esau lentil stew" for a quick Torah lesson.) Fast forward to current day. When I think of the theme of this book and always being ready to feed those you love, I think of lentil soup. It's the dish my mother always batch cooks and keeps in her freezer, ready to pull out the second anyone is visiting and mentions any hint of hunger. I took her recipe and just amped it up a little by making a sofrito with vegetables charred under the broiler for extra depth. The main takeaway is this technique, but past that feel free to swap any vegetables, spices, or greens to fit your taste.

1. Turn on the broiler with a rack set 4 inches from the heating element. Line a sheet pan with aluminum foil.

2. On the prepared sheet pan, toss the garlic, carrots, celery, onion, and jalapeño with 1 tablespoon of the olive oil and 2 heavy pinches of salt. Broil until well charred, 6 to 8 minutes. Let cool slightly, then transfer to a food processor and pulse to finely chop.

3. In a large pot or dutch oven, heat the remaining 2 tablespoons of olive oil over medium-high heat. Add the chopped vegetables and cook, stirring constantly, until softened, 4 to 5 minutes. Stir in the cumin and coriander and cook until fragrant, 1 minute. Stir in the diced tomatoes and lentils, followed by the stock and water. Season with 2 heavy pinches each of salt and pepper, then bring to a simmer. Cover and cook, adjusting the heat as needed to maintain a simmer, until the lentils are tender, 35 to 40 minutes.

4. Stir in the kale and continue to cook, covered, until tender, 5 to 7 minutes more, then remove from the heat. Taste and adjust the seasoning with salt and pepper, then serve. Leftovers can be stored in an airtight container in the refrigerator for up to 1 week or in the freezer for up to 6 months.

BAHARAT-ROASTED SQUASH SOUP

Serves 10 to 12
Prep Time: 20 minutes, plus cooling time
Cook Time: 1 hour 5 minutes

For the Roasted Squash
1 (3½-pound) kabocha squash, halved and seeded
1 (2½-pound) butternut squash, halved and seeded
2 tablespoons olive oil
2 teaspoons baharat (page 46)
Kosher salt and freshly ground black pepper

For the Soup
2 tablespoons olive oil
4 garlic cloves, thinly sliced
2 medium yellow onions, roughly chopped
1 (1-inch) piece fresh ginger, peeled and minced
Kosher salt and freshly ground black pepper
1 tablespoon minced fresh sage
2 teaspoons baharat (page 46)
4 cups vegetable stock
2 cups water
1 (13.5-ounce) can full-fat coconut milk
1 tablespoon white wine vinegar

This soup tastes like a velvet hug, which we could always use. Baharat is the star of the show and marries the cozy vibes of pumpkin spice with the earthiness of cumin and the heat of cayenne for an Arabic spice blend that warms anything it touches. You'll see it pop up often in this book, but the way it seasons squash is just *chef's kiss.* I'm partial to the combo of kabocha (a magnificent Japanese squash that looks like a green pumpkin) and butternut for the best balance of sweetness and creaminess, but feel free to use all butternut if that's what you have. And as always, this recipe works in stages for not only more flavor but opportunities for easy prep. Roasting the squash helps infuse the baharat and bring out its sweetness while also being a step that you can knock out in advance. Once the squash is roasted and scooped, the rest of the soup comes together in less than 30 minutes!

1. Roast the squash: Preheat the oven to 400°F. Line a sheet pan with aluminum foil.

2. Place the squash halves cut sides up on the prepared pan. Rub the squash with the olive oil, then sprinkle with the baharat and 2 heavy pinches each of salt and pepper. Arrange the squash cut sides down on the pan and roast for 40 to 45 minutes, until tender. Let cool completely on the pan, then scoop out the flesh and discard the skins.

3. Make the soup: In a large pot or dutch oven, heat the olive oil over medium-high heat. Add the garlic, onions, ginger, and a heavy pinch each of salt and pepper and cook until lightly caramelized, 6 to 8 minutes. Add the sage and baharat and cook until fragrant, 1 to 2 minutes. Stir in the roasted squash, then pour in the vegetable stock and water. Season with 2 heavy pinches each of salt and pepper. Bring to a simmer and cook for 15 minutes.

4. Remove from the heat and stir in the coconut milk and vinegar. Using an immersion blender or working in batches in a high-speed blender, puree the soup until smooth. Taste and adjust the seasoning with salt and pepper, then serve. Leftovers can be stored in an airtight container in the refrigerator for up to 1 week or in the freezer for up to 6 months.

CREAMY CAULIFLOWER-POTATO-LEEK SOUP

Serves 8 to 10
Prep Time: 20 minutes
Cook Time: 40 minutes

3 tablespoons olive oil

4 large leeks, white and
 light green parts only
 (about 1 pound), halved,
 rinsed well, and thinly
 sliced

2 pounds (about
 6 medium) russet
 potatoes, peeled and cut
 into 1½-inch pieces

2 pounds (1 medium head)
 cauliflower, cut into
 1½-inch florets, core and
 leaves roughly chopped

8 cups vegetable or chicken
 stock

2 teaspoons fresh thyme
 leaves

1 serrano chile, stemmed,
 seeded if desired, and
 thinly sliced

Kosher salt and freshly
 ground black pepper

½ cup minced fresh dill

½ cup minced fresh
 parsley leaves and stems

½ cup minced fresh chives

1 tablespoon white wine
 vinegar

2 scallions, thinly sliced

In my last book, I claimed that my mother was no Julia Child in the kitchen. (To which she called me, screaming, "What the fuck is that supposed to mean?") But the more headspace I put toward the way I cook, the more I'm able to see her influence on my obsession with soups, even if I stand by my original statement. My mother has this blue ceramic soup bowl with a matching ladle that is mainly decorative, except when I was growing up, she would use it exclusively in the summer to serve her vichyssoise. I've always been obsessed with anything made with potatoes, but the way a cold and creamy potato soup can be the most refreshing summer treat has never ceased to amaze me.

I have built a household that continues to revere the mighty spud, and we are lovers of all potato soups, both hot and cold. With my never-ending goal to reduce our dairy intake, I channeled a trick from my grandmother, who would use cauliflower to make a dairy-free béchamel sauce. By simmering cauliflower with the potatoes and leeks, this soup blends into the silkiest puree, without a drop of cream! While I finish it all off with tons of chopped herbs for a hint of texture, you could also add them before you blend, for a stunning pale-green color.

1. In a large pot or dutch oven, heat the olive oil over medium heat. Add the leeks and cook, stirring often, until softened and jammy, 5 to 7 minutes. Add the potatoes, cauliflower, stock, thyme, serrano chile, and 2 heavy pinches each of salt and pepper, then bring to a simmer. Cover and cook, adjusting the heat as needed to maintain a simmer, until the potatoes and cauliflower are very tender, about 25 minutes. Remove from the heat.

2. Using an immersion blender or working in batches in a high-speed blender, puree the soup until smooth. Stir in the dill, parsley, chives, vinegar, and scallions. Taste and adjust the seasoning with salt and pepper, then divide among bowls and serve. (Alternatively, let cool completely, then chill before serving, thinning out with water if needed.) Leftovers can be stored in an airtight container in the refrigerator for up to 1 week or in the freezer for up to 6 months.

HARISSA TOMATO BISQUE WITH CHALLAH GRILLED CHEESE

Serves 4
Prep Time: 25 minutes
Cook Time: 55 minutes

For the Soup

3 pounds ripe plum
   tomatoes, quartered
¼ cup harissa
¼ cup minced fresh basil
2 tablespoons olive oil
1 tablespoon honey
4 garlic cloves, smashed
   and peeled
1 medium red onion, finely
   chopped
Kosher salt and freshly
   ground black pepper
½ cup heavy cream

For the Grilled Cheese

8 (½-inch-thick) slices
   challah
8 ounces sharp cheddar
   cheese, coarsely grated
4 tablespoons butter

Ok, we're going to pop a famotidine and a Lactaid and just try to enjoy one of my favorite soup-sammy combos of all time. The challah grilled cheese was born long before this soup, as a super cozy way to use up leftover challah. The sweetness from the bread just pairs so well with the sharpness of the cheddar. It's no surprise I wanted to pair it with a bowl of creamy tomato soup for dipping.

To add an extra layer to this classic, I roast the tomatoes and aromatics with harissa paste—a powerhouse North African spiced pepper paste—for a whisper of smoky heat that permeates every bowl. Every brand of harissa is different, with varying levels of heat and spices, so start to play with which one fits your taste. More importantly, try to get ripe tomatoes! If your haul is a little less juicy, you may need to thin your soup out with a touch of water.

1. Make the soup: Preheat the oven to 400°F.

2. On a sheet pan, toss together the tomatoes, harissa, basil, olive oil, honey, garlic, onion, and 2 heavy pinches each of salt and pepper to combine. Roast for 40 minutes, until the tomatoes are softened and caramelized. Transfer to a high-speed blender along with the heavy cream and puree until smooth. Taste and adjust the seasoning with salt and pepper. Keep warm either in the blender with the lid on or by transferring it to a medium saucepan over low heat.

3. Make the grilled cheese: On a cutting board, lay out 4 of the challah slices. Divide the grated cheddar among them, then sandwich with the remaining 4 challah slices.

4. In a large nonstick skillet, melt 2 tablespoons of the butter over medium heat. Add 2 of the sandwiches and cook, pressing firmly with a spatula and flipping once, until golden brown and the cheese has melted, about 3 minutes per side. Transfer to the cutting board and repeat with the remaining 2 tablespoons of butter and sandwiches. Slice each grilled cheese in half diagonally.

5. Divide the soup among four bowls and serve each with a grilled cheese on the side.

MISO MUSHROOM BARLEY SOUP

Serves 10 to 12
Prep Time: 20 minutes
Cook Time: 1 hour,
plus steeping time

4 cups water
5 dried shiitake
    mushrooms
3 tablespoons olive oil
1 pound mixed fresh
    mushrooms, such as
    oyster, shiitake, cremini,
    and royal trumpet, torn
    into ½-inch pieces
4 scallions, whites and
    greens sliced and
    separated
1 medium yellow onion,
    finely chopped
Kosher salt and freshly
    ground black pepper
8 cups beef stock
1¼ cups pearled barley
2 tablespoons barley miso
    paste
1 tablespoon rice vinegar
4 celery stalks, chopped
8 ounces snap peas, ends
    trimmed and sliced
    ¼ inch thick
1 cup fresh or frozen peas
½ cup minced fresh chives

We focus so much on soups for fall and winter that I wanted to give you a recipe that tastes like spring! Mushrooms and barley are the perfect combination for that, providing a backdrop of earthiness that always plays so well with other verdant flavors. But to really step up the umami levels, I add a bit of barley miso (because we're using barley, of course, but any miso will do). Then on the other end, sliced snap peas, green peas, and chives bring a pop of green that just brightens up the whole soup. It's a hearty soup that's still surprisingly light. I'm partial to the richness beef stock adds, though if you swap it for vegetable stock you'll end up with a great vegan soup. Same goes with the vegetables! You can mix and match your favorite spring produce—asparagus and fennel would work just as well. If you're a fan of all types of shrooms, I know you're going to have a good time.

1. In a medium saucepan, combine the water and dried mushrooms and bring to a boil. Remove from the heat and let steep for 10 minutes. Strain the broth through a fine-mesh sieve into a clean bowl. Transfer the rehydrated mushrooms to a cutting board and finely chop, then return to the mushroom broth. Set aside.

2. In a large pot or dutch oven, heat the olive oil over medium-high heat. Add the fresh mushrooms, scallion whites, onion, and 2 heavy pinches each of salt and pepper and cook until softened and lightly caramelized, 10 to 12 minutes. Add the reserved mushroom broth and chopped rehydrated mushrooms along with the beef stock, barley, miso, vinegar, celery, and another 2 heavy pinches each of salt and pepper and bring to a simmer. Cover and cook, stirring occasionally and reducing the heat as needed to maintain a simmer, until the barley is tender, about 30 minutes.

3. Stir in both peas and continue to simmer until tender, about 5 minutes more. Remove from the heat and stir in the scallion greens and chives. Taste and adjust the seasoning with salt and pepper, then serve. Leftovers can be stored in an airtight container in the refrigerator for up to 1 week or in the freezer for up to 6 months. (The barley will soak up the broth like a sponge over time, so thin out the soup with a little water when reheating, if needed.)

BROCCOLI SPLIT PEA SOUP WITH CHICKEN SAUSAGE

Serves 8 to 10
Prep Time: 20 minutes
Cook Time: 1 hour 10 minutes

3 tablespoons olive oil
12 ounces chicken sausage, cut into ½-inch pieces
1 pound (1 medium bunch) broccoli, cut into 1-inch florets, stems separated, peeled, and roughly chopped
4 garlic cloves, thinly sliced
3 medium carrots, chopped
3 celery stalks, chopped
1 medium yellow onion, finely chopped
1 tablespoon fresh thyme leaves
Kosher salt and freshly ground black pepper
8 cups vegetable or chicken stock
2 cups (1 pound) dried green split peas
½ cup minced fresh parsley

This one's for my gloop lovers. There's no other way to describe split pea soup, a texture thicker than the average puree, bordering on porridge territory. And I can't get enough! I won't elaborate on the subject, but as a kid in Hebrew school, I always imagined manna from heaven to resemble the consistency of split pea soup. With that in mind, I wanted to share my version of an old-Jewish-man staple.

Sautéed chunks of chicken sausage set the base of flavor, later serving as the textural Easter eggs (I guess the Jewish version would be afikomen?) hidden throughout the soup. But my true obsession is the addition of broccoli, which adds not only flavor but a pop of vibrant green color to distract from the typical shade of, well, you know. And while I've never tried it, as I write this headnote, I imagine you could replace the chicken sausage with chunks of pastrami for a reimagined soup-sandwich combo!

1. In a large pot or medium dutch oven, heat the olive oil over medium-high heat. Add the chicken sausage and cook, stirring often, until golden and crisp, 5 to 6 minutes. Using a slotted spoon, transfer to a bowl and set aside.

2. To the pot, add the chopped broccoli stems, garlic, carrots, celery, onion, thyme, and 2 heavy pinches each of salt and pepper and cook, stirring often, until softened, 3 to 4 minutes. Add the stock, split peas, and another 2 heavy pinches each of salt and pepper, then bring to a simmer. Cover and cook, stirring occasionally and reducing the heat as needed to maintain a simmer, until the peas are tender, about 40 minutes. Stir in the broccoli florets, then cover and cook until tender, 10 minutes more. Remove from the heat.

3. Using an immersion blender or working in batches in a high-speed blender, puree the soup until mostly smooth, with a few chunks remaining. Stir in the reserved sausage and the parsley. Taste and adjust the seasoning with salt and pepper, then serve. Leftovers can be stored in an airtight container in the refrigerator for up to 1 week or in the freezer for up to 6 months.

BORSCHT WITH FLANKEN & SAUERKRAUT

Serves 10 to 12
Prep Time: 25 minutes
Cook Time: 2 hours 55 minutes

3 tablespoons vegetable oil
1½ pounds beef flanken (crosscut short ribs)
Kosher salt and freshly ground black pepper
2 medium yellow onions, thinly sliced
1 (15-ounce) can diced tomatoes
½ teaspoon ground allspice
8 cups beef stock
2 cups water
1 cup drained sauerkraut
½ cup sauerkraut brine
1 pound (2 medium) red beets, peeled and coarsely grated
4 medium carrots, cut into ½-inch pieces
4 celery stalks, cut into ½-inch pieces
3 garlic cloves, finely grated
2 medium Yukon gold potatoes, cut into ¾-inch pieces
1 pound (½ small head) green cabbage, cored and thinly sliced
½ cup minced fresh parsley

Like so many dishes in this book, borscht has endless variations, each one reflecting a unique culinary narrative from families spanning across Eastern Europe and Northern Asia. While it's a dish that touches almost every region my family comes from (Ukraine, Poland, Russia, and Lithuania), the first time I ever got to cook it was under the guidance of my dear friend and prolific Ukrainian cookbook author Olia Hercules. I was testing her duck borscht with fermented tomatoes for a feature in *Saveur* magazine and luckily had her in town to teach me her ways of making a flavorful broth and balanced soup. Her passion for celebrating and honoring tradition while making it her own was infectious, and you could taste it in her food. I wanted to bring that same passion to this borscht recipe, highlighting some staple ingredients from the Ashkenazi kitchen.

The base of this version is a beef broth fortified with flanken, the German and Yiddish term for crosscut beef short ribs. This cut provides not just the chunks of meat for the soup. Since it's cut across the bones, the exposed bone marrow helps infuse fat and collagen into the broth for extra body. And while you'll find tons of herbs and chunks of potatoes in this beet-stained soup, my secret is using both fresh and fermented cabbage. I simmer the broth with sauerkraut and its brine for tang and finish the borscht with shredded green cabbage for a toothsome bite. It's a mélange of powerhouse flavors that you'd think would compete for dominance, but instead they work together, when cooked low and slow, to share the spotlight.

1. In a large pot or dutch oven, heat the vegetable oil over medium-high heat. Season the flanken with a heavy pinch each of salt and pepper, then sear, flipping once, until golden brown, 3 to 4 minutes per side. Transfer to a plate.

2. Add the onions along with a heavy pinch of salt and pepper to the pot and cook, stirring often, until softened and lightly caramelized, 5 to 7 minutes. Stir in the diced tomatoes and allspice and cook until the tomatoes begin to break down, about 2 minutes. Add the beef stock, water, sauerkraut, brine, seared flanken, and 2 heavy pinches each of salt and pepper and bring to a simmer. Cover and cook, reducing the heat as needed to maintain a simmer, until the meat is tender, about 2 hours.

½ cup minced fresh dill

2 tablespoons red wine
vinegar

3. Add the beets, carrots, celery, garlic, and potatoes, then cover and cook until the vegetables are tender, 25 to 30 minutes.

4. Transfer the flanken to a bowl and let cool slightly, then separate the meat from the bones, roughly chopping the meat and discarding the bones.

5. Meanwhile, add the cabbage to the pot and cook until just tender, 7 to 10 minutes more. Stir in the parsley, dill, vinegar, and chopped meat. Taste and adjust the seasoning with salt and pepper, then serve, though this soup is always best the next day. Leftovers can be stored in an airtight container in the refrigerator for up to 1 week or in the freezer for up to 6 months.

The Brothel

We're looking to make soup.

I wanted to do a deeper dive into the world of chicken soup because it really is my life force. It's the dish I need when I'm sick. It's the dish I need when I'm sad. It's the dish I need to cook for anyone I love who's feeling sick or sad. The issue is, there couldn't be just one master recipe. Instead, I'm going to guide you in making your stock, broth, and mix-ins so you can build the pot of soup that brings you the most comfort.

CHICKEN STOCK

**Makes about 3 quarts
of stock**
Prep Time: 15 minutes
Cook Time: 2 hours 50
minutes

3 pounds chicken wings,
  legs, or drumsticks
  (whatever is on sale/
  cheapest!)
1 pound carrots, cut into
  3-inch pieces
8 ounces parsnips, cut
  into 3-inch pieces
4 celery stalks, cut into
  3-inch pieces
2 medium yellow
  onions, skins on,
  ends trimmed, and
  quartered
2 tablespoons olive oil
Kosher salt
16 cups water
2 teaspoons black
  peppercorns
6 sprigs thyme
3 sprigs parsley
3 sprigs dill
3 fresh or dried bay
  leaves

If you want good soup, you need good stock. I roast a combo of chicken and vegetables to start building up flavor, as well as avoid any scum or cloudiness that forms from simmering raw chicken. The main thing to remember is that you're looking to transfer every bit of flavor into the water. That means the stock is done when all the solids are flavorless, which is why we don't save any of them. (Though I do love to snack on the mushy carrots for some reason.) Feel free to add in any other vegetable scraps you have saved up from the week, and you can supplement the chicken with any carcasses saved from breaking down a whole bird (I stockpile them in the freezer) or even use exclusively chicken bones if you can get them from your butcher. I've included some of my favorite flavor combos below this recipe to inspire whatever soup journey you're looking to take!

1.   Preheat the oven to 450°F.

2.   On a sheet pan, combine the chicken, carrots, parsnips, celery, and onions. Drizzle with the olive oil and season with 2 heavy pinches of salt, then toss to coat. Roast for 25 to 30 minutes, until the chicken and vegetables are golden.

3.   Transfer the roasted chicken and vegetables to a large stockpot along with the water, peppercorns, thyme, parsley, dill, and bay leaves. Bring to a simmer over medium heat and cook, adjusting the heat as needed to maintain a low simmer, for 2 hours. Remove from the heat and, using a ladle, skim off any fat from the top of the liquid and discard. Strain the stock into another pot or large bowl, discarding all of the solids. Use immediately to make Jewish Penicillin (page 132), or let cool and store in airtight containers in the refrigerator for up to 5 days or in the freezer for up to 6 months.

Flavors of Love!

**To add with the chicken and vegetables
before roasting:**
- 2 bulbs fennel, quartered
- 1 medium rutabaga, cut into 8 wedges
- 1 (3-inch) knob fresh ginger, thinly sliced
- 1 bunch scallions, cut into 3-inch pieces
- 1 head garlic, halved crosswise
- 1 to 2 fresh chiles, halved

To add with the herbs and water:
- Any other herbs you love/have
- 2 teaspoons coriander seeds
- 2 teaspoons hawaij, baharat (page 46), or
  ground turmeric
- ½ teaspoon saffron threads
- 4 whole dried black Persian limes
- 2 preserved lemons (page 49), halved

JEWISH PENICILLIN

Serves 10 to 12
Prep Time: 20 minutes
Cook Time: 1 hour

2½ pounds (4 medium) whole chicken legs

1 tablespoon olive oil

Kosher salt and freshly ground black pepper

12 cups chicken stock (page 131)

4 cups water

4 medium carrots, peeled and diced

4 celery stalks, sliced on an angle ¼ inch thick

3 medium parsnips, peeled and diced

¼ cup minced fresh dill

¼ cup minced fresh parsley leaves and stems

There is no physical or mental ailment that doesn't leave me desperate for a bowl to revive my body and soul. If you've already made your stock, then the hard part is done. Now we're just fortifying that stock with more chicken, carrots, celery, and parsnips to create a flavor-packed broth. Unlike in the stock, we're simmering them until just cooked, which is why these become the tender, flavorful chunks of meat and veg that will get ladled into your bowl. Finally, don't skimp on the dill, as my mother has always preached that the dill makes it!

1. Preheat the oven to 400°F. Line a sheet pan with aluminum foil.

2. Place the chicken legs on the prepared sheet pan, drizzle with the olive oil, and season with 2 heavy pinches each of salt and pepper. Roast for 20 minutes, until lightly golden.

3. Meanwhile, in a large pot or dutch oven, combine the chicken stock and water and bring to a light simmer. Once roasted, add the chicken legs to the pot and simmer until cooked through and tender, 20 minutes more. Transfer the chicken to a clean sheet pan to cool slightly. When the chicken is cool enough to handle, use two forks to shred the meat and discard the skin and bones. Set the meat aside.

4. While the chicken cools, add the carrots, celery, and parsnips to the pot and simmer until tender, 10 to 12 minutes. Remove from the heat.

5. Once shredded, stir the chicken into the soup along with the dill and parsley. Taste and adjust the seasoning with salt and pepper, then serve.

The Mix-Ins

JAKE'S FLUFFY BALLS

Makes about 14 matzo balls
Prep Time: 20 minutes,
plus 1 hour chilling time
Cook Time: 1 hour,
plus 15 minutes resting time

2 cups matzo meal

½ cup fat, such as melted
   schmaltz, melted duck
   fat, or any neutral oil

2 tablespoons minced fresh
   herbs, such as dill, chives,
   parsley, tarragon, or
   cilantro

2 teaspoons kosher salt,
   plus more as needed

6 large eggs, beaten

½ cup seltzer water

Everyone loves my balls! This is a more customizable version of my famous recipe because I want you to feel comfortable playing with your food. First off, you don't have to buy matzo meal. I make it all the time by throwing my extra matzo sheets into the food processor, and the texture often comes out even better this way. Then, I'm giving you permission to experiment with your fat and herbs. Schmaltz is the golden standard, but if you don't want to make it or can't find any, there are so many alternatives. I tend to gravitate toward duck fat, but any oil will work. And don't sleep on infused oils (not that kind of infused), like the leftover oil from my Corned Beef Hash Spanish Tortilla (page 68) or from my Sweet & Salty Onion Crunch (page 44), for an extra layer of flavor. I even adjusted the seltzer amount to ensure your mixture is easy to roll no matter what fat you choose, but if you're looking for more of a sinker vibe just omit the seltzer altogether. As for the herbs, whatever green you're choosing, lean into it. I had Shabbat with Joan Nathan (iconic name drop) and she made her matzo balls by simmering them with an entire bunch of dill in the pot, a technique I loved! After you've used enough herbs for the balls and your soup, throw the rest of the bunch in the pot for extra flavor when simmering your balls. Joan knows best!

1. In a large bowl, stir together the matzo meal, fat, herbs, salt, and eggs until smooth. Gently stir in the seltzer until incorporated. Cover and refrigerate for 1 hour.

2. Bring a large pot of salted water to a boil. Scoop the chilled matzo mixture into ¼-cup balls, using wet hands to roll them until smooth. You should have about 14 matzo balls. Gently add the matzo balls, one at a time, to the boiling water. Reduce the heat to maintain a simmer, cover, and cook until fluffy and tender, about 1 hour. Remove from the heat, cover, and let sit for 15 minutes, then keep warm until the soup is ready.

GONDI (PERSIAN CHICKEN & CHICKPEA DUMPLINGS)

Makes about 15 gondi
Prep Time: 20 minutes,
plus 1 hour chilling time
Cook Time: 20 minutes

1 (15-ounce) can chickpeas

1½ teaspoons kosher salt,
plus more as needed

½ teaspoon ground
cardamom

½ medium yellow onion,
roughly chopped

1 pound ground chicken

1 cup chickpea flour

These ground chicken and chickpea meatball-adjacent dumplings can best be described as the Persian Jewish equivalent of matzo balls, served in chicken soup on Shabbat. They weren't going to be a part of this book until, on a recent trip to Tel Aviv, I was inspired by the most sensational lunch at HaBasta in the Carmel Market with some friends. Everything we ordered had arrived except for their gondi, which we were going to skip since we were running late. Just as we were about to leave, the bowl hit the table and I decided to take a single bite, already standing and ready to run. I immediately sat back down and inhaled this soup in a frenzy. They served one giant fluffy gondi, as if it were a matzo ball, floating in a golden chicken broth and adorned with chopped dill. The only way I can describe it is that this one bowl tasted like the family Alex and I have built, a blend of Ashkenazi and Mizrahi cultures that honors both the past and future of Jewish food. It was a true *Ratatouille* moment. This recipe, served in my Jewish Penicillin, has become a hit with both Alex and my family, and hopefully it will be with yours, too. Oh, and it's extra special if you're gluten free or a superfan of sinkers.

1. Drain the chickpeas, saving ¼ cup of the aquafaba liquid. Add the chickpeas and aquafaba to a food processor along with the salt, cardamom, and onion. Process until smooth. Add the ground chicken and chickpea flour, then pulse until just incorporated. Scrape into a bowl and cover, then refrigerate for 1 hour.

2. Bring a large pot of salted water to a boil. Scoop the chilled gondi mixture into ¼-cup balls, using wet hands to roll them until smooth. You should have about 15 balls. Gently add the gondi, one at a time, to the boiling water. Reduce the heat to maintain a simmer, cover, and cook until fluffy and tender, about 20 minutes. Remove from the heat and keep warm until the soup is ready.

KREPLACH

Makes about 3 dozen kreplach

Prep Time: 1 hour 30 minutes, plus cooling and resting time

Cook Time: 30 minutes

For the Dough

3 cups (405g) all-purpose flour, plus more as needed

4 large (210g) eggs

2 tablespoons water

1 tablespoon olive oil

For the Filling

2 tablespoons olive oil

4 garlic cloves, minced

1 medium yellow onion, minced

Kosher salt and freshly ground black pepper

1 pound ground beef (preferably 80% lean)

¼ cup minced fresh dill

¼ cup minced fresh parsley leaves and tender stems

While I didn't grow up with these Ashkenazi meat-filled dumplings, they became integral to my diet after my husband and I began a weekly date-night ritual at Sarge's Deli, which was around the corner from our first apartment in NYC. We'd each get their soup special—which came in a giant bowl of broth with a matzo ball, egg noodles, and a kreplach—and proceed to slurp it down like the old Jewish men we are destined to be. Luckily my dear friend and pasta aficionado Meryl Feinstein (@PastaSocialClub) has taught me everything I know about making good pasta, including kreplach. This dough is an adaptation of the dough she taught me, made a little softer so you can roll it out completely by hand. After boiling in water, I recommend you let the kreplach sit in the hot soup for at least 30 minutes before serving, to really let them soak up the broth, and they honestly taste even better the next day.

1. Make the dough: On a clean work surface, place the flour in a pile and make a well in the center. Add the eggs, water, and olive oil to the well. Using a fork, whisk the ingredients in the well together until smooth, slowly incorporating the flour. Once a shaggy dough forms, switch to using your hands to knead it together until you have a very smooth ball of dough. This typically takes 6 to 10 minutes. Cover and let rest at room temperature for 1 hour.

2. Meanwhile, make the filling: In a large skillet, heat the olive oil over medium-high heat. Add the garlic, onion, and a heavy pinch each of salt and pepper and cook, stirring often, until softened and lightly caramelized, 5 to 6 minutes. Add in the ground beef and another heavy pinch of salt and pepper. Stir often to break up the beef into small crumbles, until it is no longer pink and beginning to brown, 5 to 7 minutes. Remove from the heat and stir in the dill and parsley. Taste and adjust the seasoning with salt and pepper. Transfer to a bowl to cool completely.

3. Line a sheet pan with parchment paper and lightly dust with flour. Divide the dough into quarters. Using a rolling pin, roll out 1 piece of the dough on a counter, dusting with flour as needed, until ⅛ inch thick. Transfer the pasta sheet to the prepared sheet pan and loosely cover with plastic wrap to prevent

it from drying out. Repeat with the remaining dough until all the pasta is rolled out. (You can stack the dough sheets, just be sure to dust each sheet with flour to prevent sticking.)

4. Use a 3-inch round cutter to cut out as many circles as you can from all the sheets of dough. Stack the circles into piles, covering them with a damp cloth or paper towel. Knead the scraps lightly into a ball and repeat the rolling process once more to get as many circles of dough as you can. You should have about 3 dozen.

5. Working one at a time, place a dough circle on a clean work surface. Spoon 1 scant tablespoon of the cooled filling in the center. Fold 3 edges of the circle toward the center to meet, forming a tetrahedron (triangular pyramid). Pinch firmly to seal the edges. With fresh pasta dough, there shouldn't be any issue sealing the edges, but if your dough isn't sticking (that can happen with excess dusting of flour), brush the edges with a little water before folding. Transfer the kreplach to the parchment-lined pan. Repeat until you've used all the dough and filling. (If you're not looking to cook all the kreplach at once, freeze the ones you want to save for later on a parchment-lined pan for 1 hour, then transfer to a sealable plastic bag and freeze for up to 3 months. I typically will cook half and freeze the other half for my next soup since they cook beautifully from frozen.)

6. Bring a large pot of salted water to a boil. Gently add half of the kreplach and boil until tender, 10 to 12 minutes. Using a large metal spider or slotted spoon, transfer the kreplach directly to the pot of hot soup. Repeat with the remaining half of the kreplach, then let them sit in the soup for at least 30 minutes before serving.

6

I JUST WANT A BIG SALAD

Become a master salad tosser.

ICEBERG SLICE SALAD WITH GRILLED CHICKEN

Serves 2 to 4
Prep Time: 20 minutes,
plus 30 minutes
marinating time
Cook Time: 15 minutes

4 (4- to 6-ounce) boneless,
  skinless chicken thighs
1 cup Susi's Dressing
  (page 45)
12 ounces cherry tomatoes,
  halved
4 red radishes, thinly sliced
1 English cucumber, cut
  into ½-inch pieces
1 avocado, diced (optional)
Kosher salt and freshly
  ground black pepper
1 head iceberg, cored and
  sliced into 1-inch-thick
  rounds

We need to stop it with the wedge salads. I love iceberg lettuce with all my heart, but you know deep down that it just doesn't work. The dressing never penetrates the wedge, leaving you with some lettuce bare and some sopping wet with dressing. I'm going to suggest my alternative: The Iceberg Slice. By cutting the head into round slices, you have the perfect cross-section that can catch all the dressing in its nooks and crannies. Instead of blue cheese dressing, this is my salad of choice to highlight the magic of my aunt Susi's dressing, a tangy and citrusy concoction with the perfect kick from dijon and raw garlic.

To really get the most of its flavor, I love to dress the veggies and let them sit in the dressing for a bit, to start to get juicy before spooning over the iceberg (a technique that you'll also see in my High Holiday Apple & Endive Salad, page 150). But don't stop there! As memories flood in of my mom marinating every piece of chicken she bought with Wish-Bone Italian dressing, I must tell you Susi's Dressing is one of my all-time favorite marinades! I frequently marinate boneless, skinless chicken thighs, but you could swap in salmon, tofu, steak, or portobello mushrooms instead.

1. In a medium bowl, toss the chicken thighs with ⅓ cup of the dressing to coat. Cover and let sit on the counter for 30 minutes to marinate.

2. Right before you're ready to grill, in a medium bowl, toss the tomatoes, radishes, cucumber, and avocado, if using, with the remaining ⅔ cup dressing to coat. Set aside.

3. Heat a cast-iron grill pan over medium-high heat. Add the chicken and cook, flipping once, until charred and cooked through, 4 to 5 minutes per side. Transfer to a cutting board and let rest for 5 minutes, then slice.

4. Taste the vegetable mixture and adjust the seasoning with salt and pepper. Shingle the iceberg slices on a platter and spoon the vegetable mixture on top. Top with the sliced chicken, then serve.

BEET & TURNIP CAPRESE

Serves 4 to 6
Prep Time: 15 minutes,
plus cooling time
Cook Time: 45 minutes

1 pound (3 medium) red
　beets, peeled
1 pound (3 medium)
　turnips, peeled
1 tablespoon distilled white
　vinegar
Kosher salt
1 to 2 balls Burrata
½ cup kalamata olives,
　roughly chopped
3 tablespoons freshly
　squeezed orange juice
3 tablespoons olive oil
2 scallions, thinly sliced
Aged balsamic vinegar, for
　drizzling
Freshly ground black
　pepper
Flaky sea salt, for garnish

Alex and I spent three months of quarantine living with his parents, his sister, and her girlfriend in Florida and it brought us closer together than we could have ever imagined. One of the greatest gifts during a challenging year was the conversations I had with my mother-in-law. Everyone else in the family had claimed a different room of the house to work, so Robina and I were stationed together in the kitchen. My days would be interspersed with the vibrant recounting of her upbringing between Iran and Israel, from joyous stories of holiday traditions and the foods they ate to the more difficult moments of her family fleeing Tehran during the revolution and leaving everything behind. This dish was just the first of the many recipes inspired by these conversations.

A common nosh for her in Iran would be beets and turnips boiled together, turning the turnips a blushing pink color, and seasoned simply with salt. It influenced what has become an equally colorful winter take on a caprese salad. Instead of tomatoes, thin slices of the humble boiled beets and turnips get all dressed up with creamy Burrata and a briny olive salad. It's a delectable reminder to call or visit someone you love and let them recollect bits of their past for you to preserve.

1.　In a medium saucepan, add the beets and turnips and cover with 2 inches of water. Season with the vinegar and 2 heavy pinches of kosher salt, then bring to a boil over medium-high heat. Cover and cook, adjusting the heat to maintain a simmer, until the vegetables are tender when pierced with a paring knife, 45 to 50 minutes. Remove from the heat and let them cool completely in their cooking liquid, then transfer to a cutting board (place a sheet of parchment paper on top to prevent staining). Thinly slice the beets and turnips into ¼-inch-thick coins.

2.　On a platter, shingle the slices, alternating between beet and turnip. Lightly tear open the Burrata and place in the center of the platter. In a small bowl, toss the olives, orange juice, olive oil, scallions, and a heavy pinch of kosher salt to combine. Spoon the mixture over the beets, turnips, and Burrata. Drizzle with aged balsamic and garnish with freshly ground black pepper and flaky salt, then serve.

QUINOA CHOPPED SALAD

Serves 6 to 8
Prep Time: 20 minutes,
plus cooling time
Cook Time: 25 minutes

2 cups water
1 cup quinoa, rinsed and
    drained
Kosher salt
2 medium red bell peppers
1½ pounds (1 dry quart)
    cherry tomatoes, halved
1 pound Persian
    cucumbers, cut into
    ¼-inch pieces
½ medium red onion,
    finely chopped
½ cup minced fresh
    parsley leaves and tender
    stems
½ cup torn fresh basil
½ cup freshly squeezed
    lemon juice
½ cup olive oil
1 teaspoon ground sumac
Freshly ground black
    pepper

Wherever you go in the Levant, no meal is complete without some type of tomato-cucumber salad on the table. It's simplicity at its best, marrying juicy, acidic tomatoes with cool, crunchy cucumbers in the brightest of dressings with a little zip from red onions. The only issue is that if you have any leftovers, by the next day they're practically gazpacho. I started adding in cooked quinoa to add some extra protein as well as serve as a buffer to soak up any extra liquid so the salad lasts for a couple of days instead of hours.

This version is inspired by some of the variations my mother-in-law, Robina, makes to her Shirazi salad (the Persian tomato-cuke number), mainly her addition of chopped bell peppers and basil. While I can get behind the basil, I'm not the biggest fan of raw bell peppers, so I roast mine. I think roasting them adds the perfect whisper of smoke to the salad, but if you're looking to cut back on steps, feel free to go raw.

1. In a medium saucepan, bring the water to a boil, then add the quinoa and a heavy pinch of salt. Cover and cook, adjusting the heat as needed to maintain a simmer, until all the liquid is absorbed and the quinoa is tender, about 15 minutes. Remove from the heat and let sit for 10 minutes, covered, then fluff with a fork and let cool completely. Transfer to a large bowl.

2. Meanwhile, preheat the broiler with a rack set 6 inches from the heating element. Line a sheet pan with aluminum foil and place the bell peppers in the center. Broil, turning as needed with tongs, until well charred, 7 to 9 minutes. Alternatively, you can char the peppers directly over the flame of a gas stovetop. Transfer to a bowl and cover with plastic wrap to steam, then let cool completely.

3. Once cooled, transfer to a cutting board. Remove and discard the stems and seeds, then use the back of a knife to scrape off the charred skins and discard. Finely chop the roasted red peppers and add to the bowl with the quinoa.

4. To the bowl, add the tomatoes, cucumbers, red onion, parsley, basil, lemon juice, olive oil, sumac, and 2 heavy pinches each of salt and black pepper. Toss to coat, then taste and adjust the seasoning with salt and black pepper. Serve immediately.

HEALTH SALAD

Serves 6 to 8
Prep Time: 30 minutes

For the Dressing
2 cups (1 bunch) packed
    fresh parsley leaves and
    tender stems, roughly
    chopped
6 tablespoons sunflower oil
¼ cup minced fresh chives
¼ cup white wine vinegar
¼ cup toasted pine nuts
3 tablespoons maple syrup
2 garlic cloves, peeled
Kosher salt and freshly
    ground black pepper

For the Salad
2 pounds (1 medium) green
    cabbage, quartered,
    cored, and thinly sliced
2 red bell peppers,
    stemmed, seeded, and
    thinly sliced
2 medium carrots, peeled
    and julienned
1 English cucumber,
    julienned

No NYC bagel shop is complete without a giant bowl of health salad in the deli case. Coleslaw's mayo-less sister, it's just a simple cabbage slaw dressed with oil, vinegar, and lots of sugar, of course. When I was an adolescent swept up in diet culture, health salad was always my accompaniment of choice for a whole wheat flagel with low-fat schmear (and a diet peach Snapple on the side). While I've moved away from some of my more questionable eating habits, I'm still always going to find a way to eat an entire green cabbage.

The glow-up of that recipe takes the crisp combo of cabbage, carrots, cucumber, and bell peppers (I know I said I hate raw bell peppers, but I love them here for some reason) and tosses it with an electric-green parsley dressing, packed with garlic and maple syrup. (Major shout-out to Melissa Ben-Ishay, the founder of Baked by Melissa, whose Lizzo-approved green goddess chopped cabbage video paved the way for this recipe!) It's a crunch-lover's dream, and lasts for days in the fridge, ready whenever you need a little roughage.

1. Make the dressing: In a blender, combine the parsley, sunflower oil, chives, vinegar, pine nuts, maple syrup, garlic, and 2 heavy pinches each of salt and black pepper. Puree until smooth.

2. Assemble the salad: In a large bowl, toss the cabbage, bell peppers, carrots, and cucumber with the dressing to coat. Taste and adjust the seasoning with salt and black pepper, then serve.

HIGH HOLIDAY APPLE & ENDIVE SALAD

Serves 6 to 8
Prep Time: 20 minutes
Cook Time: 5 minutes

For the Candied Walnuts
½ cup walnuts, roughly
  chopped
1 tablespoon date syrup
  (silan) or honey
2 teaspoons olive oil
Pinch of ground cinnamon
Pinch of smoked paprika
Kosher salt and freshly
  ground black pepper

For the Salad
¼ cup freshly squeezed
  lemon juice
1 tablespoon honey
2 teaspoons whole grain
  mustard
1 garlic clove, finely grated
Kosher salt and freshly
  ground black pepper
¼ cup olive oil
2 Honeycrisp apples, cored
  and cut into
  ¼-inch pieces
12 ounces (3 medium
  heads) endive, ends
  trimmed and leaves
  separated
1 small head radicchio,
  halved and thinly sliced
¼ cup fresh parsley leaves
4 ounces blue cheese,
  crumbled

Jews love some edible symbolism! This recipe is not only the perfect fall and winter salad but it can and should sneak onto your Passover and Rosh Hashanah menus. A bed of chicories is topped with a sweet apples-and-honey dressing, candied walnuts, and blue cheese for a combo of tang, sweetness, funk, and bitterness that always has me coming back for seconds. Obviously the dressing plays into bringing a sweet New Year, but the holiday references do not stop there! The walnuts are candied in date syrup, which is a play on the typical Iraqi charoset served at Passover. Oh, and endive and radicchio 100 percent could count as chazeret (the second bitter herb on the Seder plate). What is Jewish food if not a jumping-off point for thoughtful and introspective conversation about our past, present, and future?!

And if symbolism wasn't enough, this salad is a favorite of mine because it's so easy to prep in advance! Go ahead and candy your nuts whenever. Then, any time the day you're serving, lay out all the endive, radicchio, and parsley on a platter and cover with damp paper towels and plastic to hold in the fridge. Even the dressing can be made hours ahead, and that includes the apples, which can be added in to prevent them from turning brown. And since this book is about noshing, this recipe pivots seamlessly into a finger food when you're in need of hors d'oeuvres. Just assemble the components in individual leaves of endive.

1. Make the candied walnuts: In a small saucepan, combine the walnuts, date syrup, olive oil, cinnamon, smoked paprika, and a heavy pinch each of salt and pepper over medium heat. Cook, stirring constantly, until the date syrup caramelizes and glazes the walnuts, 3 to 5 minutes. Transfer to a bowl and let cool slightly.

2. Assemble the salad: In a medium bowl, whisk together the lemon juice, honey, mustard, garlic, and 2 heavy pinches each of salt and pepper. Slowly whisk in the olive oil until incorporated. Taste and adjust the seasoning with salt and pepper. Add the chopped apples and toss to coat.

3. On a large platter, toss the endive leaves, radicchio, and parsley to mix and arrange in an even layer. Spoon the apple mixture over the salad and top with the crumbled blue cheese and candied walnuts, then serve.

KALE-TAHINI CAESAR

Serves 4 to 6
Prep Time: 20 minutes

For the Dressing
1 teaspoon finely grated
    lemon zest
2 tablespoons freshly
    squeezed lemon juice
2 teaspoons dijon mustard
½ teaspoon granulated
    sugar
3 anchovy fillets, mashed
    into a paste
2 garlic cloves, finely grated
1 large egg yolk
Kosher salt and freshly
    ground black pepper
¼ cup tahini
¼ cup neutral oil
2 tablespoons warm water
¼ cup finely grated
    parmesan cheese

For the Salad
1 bunch (about 8 ounces)
    lacinato kale, stemmed
    and thinly sliced
5 ounces baby kale
Kosher salt and freshly
    ground black pepper
½ cup finely grated
    parmesan cheese
1 cup Za'atar Bread Crumbs
    (page 47)

I don't even care if you make this whole salad, you just need to experience the dressing. The way tahini plays with the garlic and anchovies (non-negotiable ingredient!) adds a deep nutty richness to this caesar dressing that blows away all other versions. If and when you do make it, most of your work will be done since the rest of the salad is incredibly straightforward. For the kale, I'm all about the adult-baby combo, pairing hearty lacinato shreds with tender baby leaves to give your jaw and digestive tract a little break. Yes, you should massage your adult kale, but don't get weird and give it a full deep tissue. Just do it for like a minute to soften. I recommend starting with half of the dressing and building from there, since I don't know you! My husband likes his salad drenched, while I prefer it on the dewier side. Once your salad is tossed, it's time to top. (Oy, these are just too easy.) Hopefully you've already made a batch of Za'atar Bread Crumbs to sprinkle on top (I always keep a bag in the freezer for just this), but you can always swap them out for any kind of crouton, or even some toasted panko bread crumbs. Then, just make it rain parm and say, "Open sesame!"

1. Make the dressing: In a medium bowl, whisk together the lemon zest and juice, dijon, sugar, anchovy paste, garlic, egg yolk, and a heavy pinch each of salt and pepper until smooth. Whisk in the tahini, followed by the oil and warm water until a thick dressing forms. Stir in the grated parmesan, then taste and adjust the seasoning with salt and pepper. Makes about 1 cup of dressing.

2. Make the salad: In a large salad bowl, add the lacinato kale and half of the dressing and massage with your hands for about 1 minute to soften. Toss in the baby kale, adding more tahini caesar dressing as desired to coat. Taste and adjust the seasoning with salt and pepper. Top with the grated parmesan and Za'atar Bread Crumbs, then serve.

EVERYTHING BAGEL PANZANELLA

Serves 6 to 8
Prep Time: 25 minutes,
plus cooling time
Cook Time: 15 minutes

**For the Everything
Bagel Croutons**
3 everything bagels, cut into
    1-inch pieces
2 tablespoons olive oil
Kosher salt and freshly
    ground black pepper

For the Blistered Corn
2 tablespoons olive oil
4 garlic cloves, minced
1 jalapeño, seeded and minced
2 cups (10 ounces) fresh corn
    kernels
Kosher salt and freshly
    ground black pepper

For the Salad
12 ounces cherry tomatoes,
    halved
4 Persian cucumbers,
    smashed and roughly torn
1 medium shallot, thinly
    sliced
2 tablespoons olive oil
2 limes, zested and juiced
Kosher salt and freshly
    ground black pepper
¼ cup fresh cilantro leaves
    (or fresh basil leaves)
2 avocados, diced

Family is complicated. This probably isn't a revelation for anyone coming from a Jewish household with a hefty dose of inherited trauma. But still, above all else, I'm a family man. It's the color behind every recipe I cook and every headnote I write. In my last book, I had the privilege of sharing my late great-great-aunt Lotte's meringue cookies and a little bit of her story surviving the war to help build our family in America. At her shiva, I met her granddaughter, my cousin Karen, for the first time, and I found out she not only lived in Brooklyn but ran a catering company. Whatever the reason was that kept us apart so long, we made the decision that it shouldn't any longer. While plans got pushed a year because of the pandemic, we finally gathered to have dinner at her home, where I got to meet her children, watch her husband manage to set a moderately large fire on the grill, and begin building a relationship. Karen served this everything bagel panzanella among a cheese board representative of a master nosher. It was both summery and Jewish in the best way possible, combining toasted chunks of everything bagels with sweet corn, tomatoes, and avocados. Hopefully it's just the beginning of many new recipes inspired by our meals together.

1. Make the croutons: Preheat the oven to 400°F.

2. On a sheet pan, toss the bagel pieces with the olive oil and a heavy pinch each of salt and pepper. Bake for 10 to 12 minutes, until golden and crisp. Let cool.

3. Meanwhile, cook the corn: In a large skillet, combine the olive oil, garlic, and jalapeño over medium-high heat. Cook until the garlic begins to turn golden, 2 to 3 minutes, then stir in the corn and a heavy pinch each of salt and pepper. Cook, stirring often, until the corn is tender and lightly golden, 2 to 3 minutes more. Transfer to a bowl and let cool.

4. While the croutons and corn cool, assemble the salad: In a large bowl, toss the tomatoes, cucumbers, and shallot with the olive oil, lime zest and juice, and 2 heavy pinches each of salt and pepper. Let sit at room temperature for 10 minutes to marinate.

5. Add the bagel croutons, corn, cilantro, and avocados to the bowl with the tomato mixture and gently toss to combine. Taste and adjust the seasoning with salt and pepper, then serve.

COBB-ISH SALAD WITH SMOKED SALMON

Serves 4 to 6
Prep Time: 30 minutes,
plus cooling time
Cook Time: 10 minutes

For the Dressing
½ cup plain full-fat Greek
  yogurt
¼ cup blue cheese crumbles
3 tablespoons water
2 tablespoons olive oil
2 tablespoons white wine
  vinegar
2 tablespoons minced chives
1 tablespoon maple syrup
1 garlic clove, finely grated
Kosher salt and freshly
  ground black pepper

For the Salad
3 large eggs, at room
  temperature
1 pound (2 medium) romaine
  hearts, sliced or torn
8 ounces cherry tomatoes,
  halved (about 1½ cups)
4 ounces hot-smoked salmon,
  flaked
¼ cup blue cheese crumbles
1 small shallot, thinly sliced
1 medium watermelon radish
  (or 3 to 4 red radishes),
  halved and thinly sliced
1 avocado, diced

This recipe is an expression of love for anyone who's picky about their mix-ins and likes their dressing on the side. Of course, it's my book, so I'm partial to everything in this salad being an absolute dream combo and don't think you should change a thing! Lines of jammy eggs, hot-smoked salmon, and crunchy veg meet a cool and piquant yogurt–blue cheese dressing for a definite Cobb vibe that's still uniquely in a league of its own. And before you flip the page because of the blue cheese, I promise I developed this salad with that aversion in mind, creating a gateway recipe for my husband to fall in love with it like I have. But as always, you're the master of your own domain. Embrace the "-ish" and make it your own!

1. Make the dressing: In a medium bowl, whisk together the yogurt, blue cheese, water, olive oil, vinegar, chives, maple syrup, garlic, and 2 heavy pinches each of salt and pepper until mostly smooth with a few chunks. Taste and adjust the seasoning with salt and pepper.

2. Make the salad: Bring a medium saucepan of water to a boil and fill a medium bowl with ice and water.

3. Using a slotted spoon, lay the eggs carefully on the bottom of the pan of boiling water. Reduce the heat to maintain a simmer and cook for 8 minutes. Using the slotted spoon, transfer the eggs to the bowl of ice water and let cool for 5 minutes, then drain. Peel the eggs and slice each into quarters.

4. On a platter, lay out the romaine, then top with rows of the eggs, cherry tomatoes, flaked salmon, blue cheese, shallot, radish, and avocado. Serve with the dressing for drizzling or tossing.

7

I'LL HAVE WHAT SHE'S HAVING

Let's get you a sandwich.

PICKLED CELERY TUNA SALAD

Makes 1 scant quart
Prep Time: 20 minutes,
plus 1 hour pickling time
Cook Time: 5 minutes

For the Pickled Celery
4 celery stalks, diced
½ cup white wine vinegar
½ cup water
3 tablespoons granulated
   sugar
2 teaspoons kosher salt
½ teaspoon fennel seeds

For the Tuna Salad
3 (6-ounce) cans tuna in
   water, drained
1 cup mayonnaise
¼ cup minced light yellow
   celery leaves
¼ cup minced fresh
   parsley leaves and tender
   stems
¼ cup minced fresh dill
1 teaspoon finely grated
   lemon zest
1 tablespoon freshly
   squeezed lemon juice
1 large shallot, minced
Kosher salt and freshly
   ground black pepper

If there is one takeaway you get from this entire book, it's that there is no greater sandwich combo than tuna fish on a cinnamon raisin bagel. Before you grab your phone to cyberbully me, you must promise me you'll try it. So many tuna salad recipes already call for raisins; I'm just saying to save them for your bagel! The hint of sweetness just works, and I'll be campaigning for this sandwich combo forever. Beyond the bagel controversy, this tuna salad recipe also happens to be a game changer. Instead of adding fresh celery, we're going to lightly pickle it first, providing just the right amount of tang to match the brightness of lemon and fresh herbs. It's so light and fresh, you'll never have too much tuna!

1. Make the pickled celery: Place the celery in a medium heatproof bowl or glass mason jar. In a small saucepan, combine the vinegar, water, sugar, salt, and fennel seeds. Bring to a boil over medium-high heat and cook to dissolve the sugar and salt, 1 to 2 minutes. Pour over the celery and let pickle at room temperature for 1 hour. Strain out the celery, reserving 1 tablespoon of the pickling liquid. (I like to save the remaining pickling liquid and use it for salad dressings or future pickling projects.)

2. Make the tuna salad: In a large bowl, combine the drained pickled celery and reserved 1 tablespoon of the pickling liquid with the tuna, mayonnaise, celery leaves, parsley, dill, lemon zest and juice, shallot, and a heavy pinch each of salt and pepper. Use a fork to mix until just incorporated. Taste and adjust the seasoning with salt and pepper. Serve immediately, or store in an airtight container in the refrigerator for 3 to 5 days.

Get Those G(r)ains!

One of my favorite ways to incorporate some extra protein is adding in 1 cup of cooked quinoa. It adds a lovely texture and stretches your tuna to get an extra sandwich or two out of this recipe!

HILLEL CHICKEN SALAD

Makes 1 scant quart
Prep Time: 20 minutes,
plus cooling time and
12 hours chilling time
Cook Time: 15 minutes

For the Poached Chicken
2 large (about 1 pound
    2 ounces) boneless,
    skinless chicken breasts
4 cups water
4 dried bay leaves
2 garlic cloves, smashed
    and peeled
2 teaspoons kosher salt
½ teaspoon freshly ground
    black pepper

For the Chicken Salad
½ cup mayonnaise
½ cup minced fresh
    parsley leaves and tender
    stems
2 to 3 tablespoons drained
    prepared horseradish
1 tablespoon honey
1 teaspoon apple cider
    vinegar
1 teaspoon dried tarragon
    (or minced fresh)
2 celery stalks, finely
    chopped
1 Honeycrisp apple, cored
    and finely chopped
1 garlic clove, finely grated
Kosher salt and freshly
    ground black pepper

We're going to take a Passover tradition and bring it out of yontif. I'm a big fan of the Hillel sandwich at Seder, where you make a little matzo sandwich with some horseradish and charoset. It's a reference to Hillel the Elder, a Jewish sage and scholar, who during temple times would do the same with matzo, bitter herbs, and the paschal lamb. Beyond the important commemoration of our Exodus from Egypt, it's quite a tasty combo of sweet heat year-round. Since I adore a bit of apple in my chicken salad for sweetness (big fan of raisins, too, if you want to throw a handful in!), I decided to go full Hillel and match it with some prepared horseradish for a kick. To hold up to all this flavor, I poach my chicken breasts to ensure they're super juicy, though you can always substitute leftover roasted chicken if you have it. It's going to make a mean sandwich, whether your bread is leavened or not!

1. Poach the chicken: In a medium saucepan, combine the chicken, water, bay leaves, garlic, salt, and pepper over medium-high heat. Bring to just under a simmer (a few lazy bubbles), then reduce the heat to medium-low and cook until the chicken reaches an internal temperature of 165°F, about 15 minutes. Transfer it to a heatproof bowl and cover with plastic wrap. Let cool completely, then use two forks to coarsely shred the chicken.

2. Make the chicken salad: In a large bowl, toss the shredded chicken with the mayonnaise, parsley, horseradish, honey, apple cider vinegar, tarragon, celery, apple, garlic, and a heavy pinch each of salt and pepper until well combined. Taste and adjust the seasoning with salt and pepper, then transfer to an airtight container. Store in the refrigerator for at least 12 hours before serving and up to 5 days.

No Grain, No Gain!

Just like with the tuna salad, I love to add some extra protein by throwing in 1 cup of cooked quinoa. It adds a tender bite and stretches your chicken to get an extra sandwich or two out of this recipe!

SABICH EGG SALAD

Makes 1 heaping quart
Prep Time: 25 minutes,
plus cooling time
Cook Time: 20 minutes

1 pound (1 medium)
   eggplant, cut into
   ½-inch pieces
2 tablespoons olive oil
Kosher salt and freshly
   ground black pepper
8 large eggs
¾ cup mayonnaise
¼ cup amba
2 tablespoons minced fresh
   dill
2 tablespoons minced sour
   pickles
1 Persian (or ¼ English)
   cucumber, finely chopped
½ medium red onion,
   finely chopped

While I've always been a tuna boy, my husband, Alex, has a deep devotion to egg salad. When he requested some to have in the fridge for noshing, it took me all of two seconds to visualize this masterpiece, putting an Iraqi Jewish twist on the original. If you're unfamiliar, *sabich* is an otherworldly Israeli dish, taking the traditional Iraqi Jewish Shabbat breakfast of fried eggplant, hard-boiled eggs, chopped salad, and amba (a spicy pickled mango sauce) and stuffing it all in a pita with tahini. To accomplish the same fantasy, I toss hard-boiled eggs and roasted eggplant with crunchy pickles, cucumber, and red onion, all dressed in a lip-smacking amba mayo. Your shopping list will be pretty standard, except for the amba. While I've actually made it from scratch before (it's a project!), you can find jars of it in many specialty spice stores, or easily online from La Boîte or Amazon. Stock up on it now, because the second I opened Pandora's box by serving this version to Alex, there was no going back!

1. Preheat the oven to 400°F with a rack set 6 inches from the heating element.

2. On a sheet pan, toss the eggplant with the olive oil and 2 heavy pinches each of salt and pepper. Roast until tender and lightly golden, 15 to 18 minutes. (For more color, feel free to then broil for 2 to 3 minutes more.) Let cool completely on the pan.

3. Meanwhile, bring a medium pot of water to a boil and fill a medium bowl with ice and water.

4. Using a slotted spoon, lay the eggs carefully on the bottom of the pot of boiling water. Reduce the heat to maintain a simmer and cook for 12 minutes. Using the slotted spoon, transfer the eggs to the bowl of ice water and let cool for 5 minutes, then drain. Peel the eggs and chop into roughly ¼-inch pieces.

5. In a large bowl, combine the cooled eggplant and chopped eggs with the mayonnaise, amba, dill, pickles, cucumber, and onion, then toss to combine. Taste and adjust the seasoning with salt and pepper. Serve immediately, or store in an airtight container in the refrigerator for up to 5 days.

TURK-ISH LEEK BURGERS

Makes 8 burgers
Prep Time: 30 minutes,
plus cooling time
Cook Time: 25 minutes,
plus time to heat the grill

For the Burgers
2 tablespoons olive oil, plus
    more for grill
4 large leeks, white and
    lightgreen parts only
    (about 1 pound), halved,
    rinsed well, and thinly
    sliced
Kosher salt
¼ teaspoon cayenne
    pepper
2 pounds ground beef
    (preferably 80% lean)
¼ cup plain dried bread
    crumbs or matzo meal
Freshly ground black
    pepper

For Assembly
8 Burger Buns, halved
    (page 33)
Sandwich Schmear (page
    46)
Sumac-Pickled Onions
    (page 44)
Torn butter lettuce
Sliced tomatoes

While my mother-in-law is an Iraqi Jew raised between Iran and Israel, her cooking is also inspired by her time living in Turkey with her first husband. His family was part of the large community of Sephardic, Ladino-speaking Jews that settled in the Ottoman Empire after their expulsion from Spain. Just as I have learned so much from cooking with Robina, she picked up a great deal from her time in the kitchen with her ex-mother-in-law. Most notably, Robina has a fondness of adding tons of leeks to whatever she's cooking, inspired by the *keftes de prasa* (fried leek and beef patties) they would make. It just made so much sense to give my burgers the same treatment, and I'll never go back to grilling them any other way!

1. Make the burgers: In a large skillet, heat the olive oil over medium-high heat. Add the leeks with a heavy pinch of salt and cook, stirring often, until jammy and caramelized, 12 to 15 minutes. Remove from the heat and stir in the cayenne. Let cool completely.

2. In a large bowl, combine the cooled leek mixture with the ground beef and bread crumbs. Mix with your hands until just combined, then form into 8 burger patties about 1 inch thick, and make a very light indentation with your thumb in the center of each.

3. Start a charcoal fire or heat a gas grill to high. Dip a rolled-up paper towel in olive oil and, using tongs, brush the grates of the grill to grease. Season both sides of each patty with a heavy pinch of salt and black pepper. Place the patties on the grill and cook undisturbed until golden, 3 to 4 minutes, then flip with a metal spatula and continue to cook for another 3 to 4 minutes for medium-rare. Transfer to a platter and let rest for 5 minutes.

4. For assembly: Serve on the challah buns, with sandwich schmear, sumac-pickled onions, lettuce, and tomatoes.

WHITE BEAN & QUINOA VEGGIE BURGERS

Makes about 8 burgers
Prep Time: 25 minutes,
plus cooling time
Cook Time: 50 minutes

For the Veggie Burgers
¼ cup olive oil
¼ cup hulled sunflower
 seeds
2 garlic cloves, minced
¼ teaspoon crushed red
 pepper
2 cups water
1 cup dry quinoa, rinsed
 and drained
1 pound mixed chopped
 vegetables, fresh or
 frozen, such as broccoli
 florets, carrots, zucchini,
 and peas
2 (15-ounce) cans
 cannellini beans, drained
Kosher salt and freshly
 ground black pepper
1 cup plain dried bread
 crumbs
½ cup minced fresh herbs,
 such as parsley, basil,
 and/or chives

For Assembly
8 Burger Buns, halved
 (page 33)
Sandwich Schmear (page
 46)
Sliced avocado
Torn butter lettuce
Sliced tomatoes

Most people don't know this, but I was a vegetarian for almost a decade. It all began at the age of eight, when I saw the animated children's movie *Ice Age* and there was a scene depicting the lead woolly mammoth's parents being killed by hunters. While for most kids it probably just made them sad, I became distraught over the ethics around where our meat came from and made the choice on the spot. Shortly before I gave up vegetarianism to go to culinary school, these veggie burgers were born. They're like my version of a savory protein bar, packing quinoa, veggies, and beans together into a hearty patty that can be adored by vegetarians, vegans, and omnivores alike! As always, it's infinitely customizable. Find the right blend of veggies you love, either fresh or frozen and thawed, and even switch up the beans. This recipe bakes the patties for a healthier option, but I've been known to pan-fry them in olive oil when I'm feeling a little more decadent.

1. Make the veggie burgers: Preheat the oven to 425°F. Line a sheet pan with parchment paper.

2. In a 4-quart saucepan, heat the olive oil over medium heat. Add the sunflower seeds, garlic, and crushed red pepper and cook until lightly golden, about 2 minutes. Stir in the water and quinoa, followed by the chopped vegetables, beans, and 2 heavy pinches each of salt and black pepper, then bring to a boil over medium-high heat. Cover and cook, adjusting the heat as needed to maintain a simmer, until all the liquid is absorbed and the quinoa and vegetables are tender, about 15 minutes. Remove from the heat and let sit for 10 minutes, covered, then transfer to a large bowl. Using a potato masher, mash into a chunky paste, then let cool slightly.

3. Add the bread crumbs and herbs and use your hands or a rubber spatula to stir until well combined. The mixture should hold together when a handful is lightly squeezed. Taste and adjust the seasoning with salt and black pepper.

4. Scoop 1-cup-sized patties, shaping with wet hands to make them about 1 inch thick, and place on the prepared sheet pan. Bake, flipping once, for 30 minutes, until golden.

5. For assembly: Serve on the challah buns, with sandwich schmear, sliced avocado, lettuce, and tomatoes.

SCHNITZEL CHALLAH SANDWICHES WITH CELERY ROOT REMOULADE

Makes 8 sandwiches

Prep Time: 30 minutes, plus 30 minutes marinating time

Cook Time: 20 minutes

For the Remoulade

2 pounds celery root, peeled and coarsely grated

¾ cup mayonnaise

2 tablespoons freshly squeezed lemon juice

2 tablespoons minced fresh parsley

2 tablespoons minced fresh tarragon

2 teaspoons minced drained capers

2 teaspoons dijon mustard

½ teaspoon granulated sugar

Kosher salt and freshly ground black pepper

For the Schnitzel

4 medium boneless, skinless chicken breasts

1 cup pickle brine

1 cup plain dried bread crumbs

1 cup panko bread crumbs

2 tablespoons herbes de Provence

2 teaspoons kosher salt

When I tell you my husband is my muse, I'm not exaggerating. Alex literally has difficulty turning on the stove, but still is constantly challenging me with flavors or ingredients he wants me to incorporate into my recipes. It makes me think in new ways that lead to such wondrous creations.

To inspire this recipe, he requested that celery root remoulade, one of his favorite snacks as a child growing up in Switzerland, make a cameo somewhere in this book. It's kind of like French coleslaw, a classic salad of shredded raw celery root in a tangy mayo dressing. Of course, he mentioned this out of the blue, right as I was struggling to figure out what direction I wanted to take this schnitzel sandwich. I went full Francophile, adding herbes de Provence to the schnitzel breading and tons of chopped cornichons, and it was an instant hit.

For a Shabbos centerpiece, I save one of my two challot to slice up (untoasted to contrast the crispy chicken). The remoulade and sandwich schmear can be made days in advance and chilled in the fridge. As for the schnitzel, I fry them right before my guests arrive and rest on a wire rack–lined sheet pan, ready to flash in the oven. But like so much of this book, this recipe isn't just for entertaining! You can meal-prep all the components so you just have to reheat your schnitzel in the oven and build a treat-yourself nosh any time of day.

1. Make the remoulade: In a medium bowl, stir together the celery root, mayonnaise, lemon juice, parsley, tarragon, capers, dijon, sugar, and 2 heavy pinches each of kosher salt and black pepper to combine. Taste and adjust the seasoning with kosher salt and black pepper, then cover and chill until you're ready to assemble the sandwiches.

2. Make the schnitzel: Line a sheet pan with parchment paper and a second sheet pan with paper towels.

3. On a silicone cutting board, slice each chicken breast crosswise in half on an angle to form 2 equal-sized pieces. Using a meat mallet or the bottom of a small saucepan, pound each piece to ¼ inch thick.

4. In a medium bowl, toss the chicken with the pickle brine, then cover with plastic and let sit on the counter for 30 minutes.

¼ teaspoon cayenne
  pepper
1 cup all-purpose flour
3 large eggs, lightly
  beaten
Vegetable oil, for frying
Flaky sea salt

For Assembly
16 slices challah bread
Mayonnaise or
  Sandwich Schmear
  (page 46)
Sliced cornichons
Torn butter lettuce

5. Meanwhile, in a shallow bowl, whisk together both bread crumbs with the herbes de Provence, kosher salt, and cayenne. Place the flour in another shallow bowl and the eggs in a third shallow bowl.

6. Drain the chicken, discarding the pickle brine. Dredge each piece in the flour, shaking off any excess, then dip it in the beaten egg, letting any excess drip off, and finally toss it in the bread crumb mixture, pressing the crumbs against the chicken to completely coat. Arrange the breaded chicken on the parchment-lined sheet pan.

7. In a large cast-iron or nonstick skillet, heat ¼ inch of oil over medium-high heat until shimmering. Working in batches, fry the schnitzel, flipping once, until golden brown and crisp, about 3 minutes per side. Transfer to the paper towel–lined sheet pan to drain and immediately season with a pinch of flaky salt. Continue to fry the chicken, adding more oil to the pan as needed between batches (be sure to let the oil get hot before adding the next batch), until all the schnitzel has been fried.

8. Assemble the sandwiches: Serve the schnitzel alongside the sliced challah, mayonnaise or sandwich schmear, cornichons, lettuce, and celery root remoulade for your guests to build their own sandwiches.

The Art of the Turkey Club

Something about a double-decker, two-handed club is just my gold-standard sandwich. You get what you put into it, so don't skimp on quality when it comes to this centerfold. The taller the sandwich, the closer to G-d!

Sourdough pullman slices

More flavor in the square shape we're looking for. I always use the broiler when toasting, to help get a super quick golden crust while keeping the center of every slice soft and warm. Just don't walk away from the oven.

Beef bacon or regular bacon

Whether you're kosher or not, beef bacon needs to enter your culinary repertoire. It's like little crispy bits of unctuous pastrami and I can't get enough. Porter Road sells a stunning thick-cut version online and Jack's Gourmet is a great kosher option.

Shallots cooked in rendered fat

Once you render all that fat, don't waste it! Use it to caramelize shallots (or any allium you've got) to throw on in.

Sandwich Schmear (page 46)

Flavored mayo or bust. Do the most, be the most.

Honey or pastrami turkey

You're on your own at the deli counter, but honey and pastrami are my ride-or-dies. What you're going to do is first get at least five different sample slices to choose from.

Sliced heirloom tomatoes

Only the juicy ones and don't forget to season them with a little S&P!

Torn butter lettuce

Just a leaf or two, we're not making a salad.

Sliced avocado

Ripe and ready to show off your knife skills.

8

I ONLY HAVE TIME FOR A QUICKIE

*Give me one hour and
I'll show you a good time.*

Kasha for Every Season!

If you have one back-pocket dinner recipe you're always stocked on, it should be kasha varnishkes. It's Ashkenazi comfort food at its best, tossing chewy buckwheat groats and bow-tie pasta in a simple, yet enchanting buttery sauce of fried onions or mushrooms. It's nice enough for company, yet still screams *shtetl*! I've taken some liberties with my kasha varnishkes, shifting the flavors I add to the pot every season to match what's fresh and always stocked in my kitchen.

But before we get into the mix-ins, I must share a shortcut I discovered that blew my mind. Instead of cooking the kasha separately like a pilaf, in an act of laziness, I tried adding it to the boiling water with the pasta. The result was perfectly tender and fluffy buckwheat, ready in the exact time it took the pasta to become al dente. I'll never make it any other way, and you shouldn't either.

While low and slow caramelized onions and mushrooms are still an iconic way to serve this dish, I wanted to give you powerhouse recipes that come together in a hurry for a pasta party any night of the week. From pesto and asparagus in spring to roasted cherry tomatoes in summer, brown butter cauliflower in fall, and lemony cabbage in winter, these combos are just jumping-off points for a love affair with kasha varnishkes with endless possibilities. You'll be feeling your groats all year long!

Spring Kasha

PISTACHIO PESTO KASHA VARNISHKES WITH ASPARAGUS AND PEAS

Serves 4 to 6
Prep Time: 20 minutes
Cook Time: 15 minutes

For the Pesto
1 cup packed fresh basil leaves
1 cup packed fresh parsley leaves
  and tender stems
½ cup toasted pistachios
¼ cup finely grated
  parmesan cheese
¼ cup olive oil
2 tablespoons lemon juice
2 tablespoons packed fresh
  mint leaves
¼ teaspoon crushed red pepper
3 garlic cloves, smashed and peeled
Kosher salt and freshly ground
  black pepper

For the Kasha Varnishkes
Kosher salt
1 pound dried farfalle (bow-tie)
  pasta
1 cup kasha (toasted whole
  buckwheat groats)
2 tablespoons olive oil
1 pound asparagus, ends trimmed
  and sliced on an angle ½ inch
  thick
Freshly ground black pepper
1¼ cups frozen peas, thawed
4 ounces goat cheese, crumbled

1. Bring a large pot of water to a boil.

2. Make the pesto: In a food processor, add the basil, parsley, pistachios, parmesan, olive oil, lemon juice, mint leaves, crushed red pepper, garlic, and 2 heavy pinches each of salt and black pepper. Process until smooth, stopping to scrape the sides of the bowl as needed. Taste and adjust the seasoning with salt and black pepper.

3. Make the kasha varnishkes: Season the boiling water liberally with salt, then add the pasta and kasha. Cook, stirring occasionally, until the pasta is al dente and the buckwheat is tender, 10 to 11 minutes, then drain, reserving 1 cup pasta water.

4. Meanwhile, in a large pot or dutch oven, heat the olive oil over medium-high heat. Add the asparagus with a heavy pinch each of salt and black pepper. Cook, stirring often, until tender and lightly golden, 4 to 5 minutes. Add in the peas and cook for 1 minute to warm through, then remove from the heat. Add the drained pasta and kasha with the reserved pasta water, the pesto, and goat cheese. Stir until the pesto and goat cheese melt into a creamy sauce that coats the pasta. Taste and adjust the seasoning with salt and black pepper, then serve.

Summer Kasha

CHARRED CHERRY TOMATO KASHA VARNISHKES

Serves 4 to 6
Prep Time: 15 minutes
Cook Time: 15 minutes

Kosher salt
1 pound dried farfalle
   (bow-tie) pasta
1 cup kasha (toasted whole
   buckwheat groats)
2 pounds cherry tomatoes,
   halved
¼ cup olive oil
2 tablespoons balsamic
   vinegar
1 tablespoon honey
1 teaspoon dried oregano
1 teaspoon dried thyme
½ teaspoon crushed red
   pepper
6 garlic cloves, thinly sliced
1 medium shallot, minced
Freshly ground black
   pepper
½ cup torn fresh basil
   leaves

1. Preheat the broiler with a rack set 6 inches from the heating element.

2. Bring a large pot of salted water to a boil. Add the pasta and kasha to the water and cook, stirring occasionally, until the pasta is al dente and the buckwheat is tender, 10 to 11 minutes, then drain.

3. Meanwhile, on a sheet pan, toss the tomatoes with the olive oil, vinegar, honey, oregano, thyme, crushed red pepper, garlic, shallot, and 2 heavy pinches each of salt and black pepper. Broil until the tomatoes are blistered and softened, 7 to 9 minutes.

4. Off the heat, return the drained pasta and kasha to the pot and add the roasted tomato mixture. Let sit for 2 minutes to allow the tomato juices to be absorbed, then stir in the basil. Taste and adjust the seasoning with salt and black pepper, then serve immediately.

Fall Kasha

CAULIFLOWER-CAPER KASHA VARNISHKES

Serves 4 to 6
Prep Time: 15 minutes
Cook Time: 30 minutes

1 large head (about 2
    pounds) cauliflower, cut
    into small florets, leaves
    and core finely chopped
3 tablespoons drained
    capers
2 tablespoons olive oil
2 tablespoons sherry
    vinegar
¼ teaspoon crushed red
    pepper
8 garlic cloves, thinly sliced
Kosher salt and freshly
    ground black pepper
1 pound dried farfalle
    (bow-tie) pasta
1 cup kasha (toasted whole
    buckwheat groats)
6 tablespoons (3 ounces)
    unsalted butter
½ cup minced fresh
    parsley leaves and tender
    stems

1.   Preheat the oven to 450°F with a rack set 6 inches from the heating element.

2.   On a sheet pan, toss the cauliflower with the capers, olive oil, vinegar, crushed red pepper, garlic, and 2 heavy pinches each of salt and black pepper. Roast for 20 to 25 minutes, until the cauliflower florets are tender, then turn on the broiler and broil until lightly charred, about 3 minutes.

3.   Meanwhile, bring a large pot of salted water to a boil. When you are about 10 minutes away from the cauliflower being cooked, add the pasta and kasha to the water and cook, stirring occasionally, until the pasta is al dente and the buckwheat is tender, 10 to 11 minutes, then drain, reserving 1 cup pasta water.

4.   While the is pasta cooking, in a small saucepan, melt the butter over medium-high heat. Cook, stirring constantly, until browned and nutty in aroma, 5 to 7 minutes.

5.   Add the browned butter to the empty pasta pot over medium-high heat along with the drained pasta and kasha, the reserved pasta water, and the roasted cauliflower. Cook, stirring constantly, until a glossy, loose sauce forms, about 2 minutes. Remove from the heat and let sit for 2 to 3 minutes to allow the sauce to be absorbed, then stir in the parsley. Taste and adjust the seasoning with salt and black pepper, then serve immediately.

Winter Kasha

DILLY CABBAGE KASHA VARNISHKES

Serves 4 to 6
Prep Time: 15 minutes
Cook Time: 15 minutes

Kosher salt
1 pound dried farfalle
   (bow-tie) pasta
1 cup kasha (toasted whole
   buckwheat groats)
6 tablespoons (3 ounces)
   unsalted butter
1 medium yellow onion,
   finely chopped
½ medium head (about 1½
   pounds) green cabbage,
   cored and cut into 1-inch
   pieces
¼ cup minced fresh dill
3 tablespoons freshly
   squeezed lemon juice
1 teaspoon poppy seeds
   (optional)
Freshly ground black
   pepper

1. Bring a large pot of salted water to a boil. Add the pasta and kasha to the water and cook, stirring occasionally, until the pasta is al dente and the buckwheat is tender, 10 to 11 minutes, then drain, reserving 1 cup pasta water.

2. Meanwhile, in a large pot or dutch oven, melt the butter over medium-high heat. Add the onion and cabbage with 2 heavy pinches of salt and cook, stirring often, until softened and lightly caramelized, 8 to 10 minutes. Add the drained pasta and kasha with the reserved pasta water and cook, stirring constantly, until a glossy, loose sauce forms, about 2 minutes. Remove from the heat and let sit for 2 to 3 minutes to allow the sauce to be absorbed, then stir in the dill, lemon juice, and poppy seeds, if using. Taste and adjust the seasoning with salt and pepper, then serve immediately.

MA'ACARONI IN A POT

Serves 4 to 6
Prep Time: 15 minutes
Cook Time: 25 minutes

2 tablespoons olive oil
4 garlic cloves, thinly sliced
1 medium yellow onion,
   finely chopped
Kosher salt
1 pound ground beef
   (preferably 80% lean)
2 teaspoons Osem
   consommé
2 teaspoons sweet paprika
1 teaspoon baharat
   (page 46)
¼ teaspoon cayenne
   pepper
1 (28-ounce) can crushed
   tomatoes
3½ cups water
1 tablespoon red wine
   vinegar
1 pound dried elbow
   macaroni
Sliced scallions, for garnish

I mainly named the recipe this because my mother-in-law taught it to me right when "WAP" came out and I haven't been able to shake the association! Loosely, it's an Arabic hamburger helper—pasta in a quick meat sauce flavored with Middle Eastern spices. I'm using elbow macaroni, but that's my own substitution from what would typically be spaghetti. The term *ma'acaroni* is just what any type of pasta is called in Arabic, but again, Cardi B's influence is almost as strong as Robina's. The sauce separates itself from the average ragu with fried beef and onions, paprika, and baharat, for a warmth that perfumes your kitchen. But you can season to your heart's content! Robina often just raids her spice cabinet, swapping baharat for *advieh polo* (a Persian spice blend for rice with very similar vibes) or even sometimes just ground cumin. The only constant in her cooking is a healthy sprinkling of Osem consommé powder, which is the Israeli equivalent of how my mother always popped a Knorr bouillon cube into every pot on her stove. And if it wasn't already easy enough, I made it into a one-pot pasta so you can throw it all together at a moment's notice, just as intended!

1. In a large pot or dutch oven (preferably a 5½-quart dutch oven), heat the olive oil over medium-high heat. Add the garlic, onion, and a heavy pinch of salt and cook, stirring often, until softened and lightly caramelized, 5 to 7 minutes. Add in the ground beef and another heavy pinch of salt and cook, stirring often to break up the beef into small crumbles, until no longer pink and beginning to brown, 6 to 8 minutes. Stir in the Osem, paprika, baharat, and cayenne and cook until fragrant, 1 minute.

2. Stir in the crushed tomatoes, water, and vinegar, followed by the macaroni with 2 heavy pinches of salt. Cook, stirring often, until the pasta is al dente and the sauce has thickened, 10 to 12 minutes. It should be very saucy. Remove from the heat and let sit for 2 minutes for the sauce to be soaked up, then taste and adjust the seasoning with salt. Divide among bowls, garnish with sliced scallions, and serve.

HONEY-MUSTARD BROILED SALMON WITH ROASTED POTATOES, BROCCOLI & FENNEL

Serves 4
Prep Time: 20 minutes
Cook Time: 35 minutes

For the Vegetables
1 pound baby creamer
  potatoes, halved
1 pound (1 medium bunch)
  broccoli, cut into 1-inch
  florets, stems peeled and
  thinly sliced
2 medium bulbs fennel, each
  cut into 8 wedges
2 tablespoons olive oil
2 tablespoons lemon juice
2 tablespoons water
Kosher salt and freshly
  ground black pepper

For the Salmon
4 (8-ounce) salmon fillets,
  skin on
2 tablespoons olive oil
2 tablespoons dijon mustard
2 tablespoons whole grain
  mustard
1½ tablespoons honey
1 teaspoon minced fresh
  thyme leaves
2 teaspoons finely grated
  lemon zest
Kosher salt and freshly
  ground black pepper

For Serving
Minced fresh dill
Lemon wedges

Jews love broiled salmon because it ticks every box. Easy? Beyond. Quick? Ready in minutes. Cleanup? You practically only have to throw away some foil. Healthy? You know you need your omega-3s. I grew up with my aunt Susi making a version of this broiled honey-mustard salmon in her toaster oven (long before Sonja Morgan graced *RHONY*), and it always came out super juicy with a golden crust. I made a couple of little tweaks to the sauce and added some roasted veg to make it a meal, but the goal was simplicity at its best. The combo of smooth dijon and whole grain mustard provides the same sharpness but with little pops of mustard seeds that caramelize under the broiler, though you can always use just one or the other if it's all you have. And of course, you're an adult, so vegetables are negotiable! This lemony trio goes so well with the salmon, but feel free to follow your own inspiration for sides. (I'll often make it with one of my kasha varnishkes recipes!)

1. Roast the vegetables: Preheat the oven to 450°F. Place a rack 6 inches from the top of the oven and another in the lower half of the oven.

2. On a sheet pan, combine the potatoes, broccoli, fennel, olive oil, lemon juice, water, and 2 heavy pinches each of salt and pepper. Toss to coat. Roast on the top rack, tossing halfway through, for 25 to 30 minutes, until tender and lightly golden.

3. Meanwhile, line another sheet pan with aluminum foil and place the salmon fillets, skin side down, on it. In a small bowl, whisk together the olive oil, both mustards, honey, thyme, lemon zest, and 2 heavy pinches each of salt and pepper. Spoon over the salmon to coat.

4. Once the vegetables are cooked, remove the pan from the oven and turn on the broiler. Place the salmon on the top rack and broil for 6 to 8 minutes, until golden and cooked through. Place the pan of vegetables on the bottom rack for the last few minutes to keep warm.

5. For serving: Divide the vegetables and salmon among plates, then garnish with dill and serve with lemon wedges.

POMEGRANATE-GLAZED LAMB MEATBALLS WITH HERBY ISRAELI COUSCOUS

Serves 4
Prep Time: 20 minutes
Cook Time: 15 minutes

For the Herb Blend

1 cup minced fresh parsley
 leaves and tender stems
¾ cup minced fresh
 cilantro leaves and tender
 stems
2 tablespoons minced fresh
 mint leaves

For the Meatballs

1 pound lean ground lamb
¼ cup plain dried bread
 crumbs or matzo meal
1 teaspoon kosher salt
½ teaspoon garlic powder
½ teaspoon ground
 cinnamon
½ teaspoon ground cumin
½ teaspoon ground
 coriander
½ teaspoon freshly ground
 black pepper
2 small shallots, minced

For the Couscous

2¼ cups water
1½ cups Israeli or pearled
 couscous (ptitim)
Kosher salt

Nothing becomes a staple recipe in my kitchen like an evergreen weeknight dinner that morphs to every season. Spiced lamb with tart pomegranate molasses and tons of herbs provides just as much warmth in winter as it does brightness in summer. I developed it because of my passion for Israeli couscous. Also sold as pearled couscous, it's not actually couscous at all but little pellets of pasta invented in Israel during a rice shortage. There you'll find it only under its real name, *ptitim*. Here, you'll find it soaking up all the rendered fat and juices from the meatballs, a technique inspired by our dedicated patronage to Persian kebab houses. No matter what you order, the platter of skewers will be lined with a layer of lavash flatbread that becomes saturated in the meat juices, so you get to enjoy every last drop. Same deal here, with the welcomed addition of pomegranate molasses and herbs to round out this bed of carbs. Start to finish, it takes about 35 minutes, but you can always prep your herb blend and have your meatball mixture ready to scoop in advance if you want to shave off about half the time. Let's ball out!

1. Make the herb blend: In a small bowl, toss together the parsley, cilantro, and mint to combine.

2. Make the meatballs: In a medium bowl, combine the lamb, bread crumbs, salt, garlic powder, cinnamon, cumin, coriander, black pepper, shallots, and 3 tablespoons of the herb blend and use your hands to mix until just incorporated. Scoop into 3-tablespoon-sized balls, rolling with your hands to smooth, then place on a plate.

3. Cook the couscous: In a medium saucepan, bring the water to a boil. Add the couscous and 2 heavy pinches of salt, then reduce the heat to medium low. Cover, with the lid slightly ajar, and cook until the liquid is absorbed and the couscous is tender, 12 to 15 minutes. Remove from the heat and let steam, covered completely, for 5 minutes, then fluff with a fork.

4. While the couscous cooks, cook the meatballs: In a large cast-iron

For Cooking and Serving

2 tablespoons olive oil

3 tablespoons
  pomegranate molasses

Kosher salt and freshly
  ground black pepper

1 celery stalk, thinly sliced
  on an angle

Pomegranate seeds
  (optional)

Fresh parsley, cilantro, and
  mint leaves

skillet, heat the olive oil over medium-high heat. Add the meatballs and cook, turning as needed with tongs, until golden brown, 6 to 8 minutes. Reduce the heat to medium and pour the pomegranate molasses over the meatballs. Cook, shaking the pan often, until the pomegranate molasses has caramelized, 2 to 3 minutes more. Remove from the heat and transfer to a plate.

5. Add the cooked couscous and the remaining herb blend to the skillet and stir to coat the couscous with the pan drippings and herbs. Taste and adjust the seasoning with salt and pepper, then return the meatballs to the skillet and place them over the couscous. Garnish with the sliced celery, pomegranate seeds, if using, and herbs, then serve.

CHICKEN TAGINE POT PIE

Serves 4 to 6
Prep Time: 20 minutes
Cook Time: 30 minutes

1 (14-ounce) sheet store-
    bought puff pastry, thawed
    and trimmed into a 12-
    inch circle

1 large egg yolk, lightly
    beaten

3 tablespoons olive oil

1¼ pounds boneless,
    skinless chicken thighs,
    cut into 1-inch pieces

3 garlic cloves, minced

2 medium carrots, cut into
    ½-inch pieces

1 medium yellow onion,
    finely chopped

Kosher salt and freshly
    ground black pepper

1 teaspoon smoked paprika

½ teaspoon ground cumin

½ teaspoon ground
    cinnamon

2 cups chicken stock

½ cup dried apricots,
    roughly chopped

½ cup pitted Castelvetrano
    olives, roughly chopped

1 whole preserved lemon
    (page 49), minced

¾ cup couscous

½ cup minced fresh parsley
    leaves and tender stems

So many of my recipes have their origin stories at Shabbat, where I give myself free rein to explore whatever random ideas pop inside my head. This creation was for Friday night dinner with Alex's aunt Diana and her family. I was craving something with an air of a North African tagine to add to the Persian feast awaiting us. I began in the more traditional pot pie format, making a roux of olive oil and flour to turn the cooking liquid into a thick and creamy sauce studded with chunks of preserved lemon, olives, and dried apricots. The flavor was on point, but I've come to terms with the fact that no matter how incredible the crust is, pot pies do not have the proper filling-to-carb ratio! Luckily there was no shortage of rice at Diana's, which saved the day. After stepping away from it for a few months (something I do often, waiting for that lightbulb "aha" moment), it dawned on me to try using couscous as the sole thickener for the braising liquid, which gave me the consistency and carb ratio I wanted. And because the couscous absorbs the liquid so fast, I go ahead and bake off a puff pastry crust separately, cutting down the total cook time to around 30 minutes!

1. Preheat the oven to 425°F. Line a sheet pan with parchment paper.

2. Transfer the puff pastry circle to the prepared sheet pan and brush with the egg yolk to coat. Using a paring knife, cut slits in the puff pastry at 12, 3, 6, and 9 o'clock. Bake for 12 to 15 minutes, until golden brown, then set aside.

3. Meanwhile, in a 12-inch cast-iron or ovenproof skillet, heat the olive oil over medium-high heat. Add the chicken, garlic, carrots, onion, and 2 heavy pinches each of salt and pepper and cook, stirring often, until the chicken is no longer pink and the vegetables are beginning to brown, 5 to 7 minutes. Stir in the paprika, cumin, and cinnamon and cook until fragrant, 1 minute. Add the chicken stock, apricots, olives, and preserved lemon. Cover and cook until the chicken is cooked through, 8 to 10 minutes.

4. Remove from the heat and stir in the couscous and parsley. Let sit, covered, for 5 minutes, then taste and adjust the seasoning with salt and pepper. Place the baked puff pastry on top, then serve.

GHORMEH SABZI PANEER

Serves 4 to 6
Prep Time: 20 minutes
Cook Time: 40 minutes

3 tablespoons olive oil
1 pound paneer, cut into
   ¾-inch cubes
Kosher salt and freshly
   ground black pepper
2 medium yellow onions,
   finely chopped
1 teaspoon dried fenugreek
   leaves
1 teaspoon ground
   turmeric
4 cups packed fresh parsley
   leaves and tender stems
   (from 2 bunches), minced
4 cups packed fresh
   cilantro leaves and tender
   stems (from 2 bunches),
   minced
6 scallions, minced
2 (15-ounce) cans dark red
   kidney beans, drained
3 cups vegetable stock
2 teaspoons ground dried
   black Persian limes
1 teaspoon Osem
   consommé (optional)
Cooked rice, preferably
   tahdig, for serving

When I fell in love with Alex, I fell in love with ghormeh sabzi. It's his (and now my) favorite Persian stew, filled with tender kidney beans, pungent dried limes, and bouquets of herbs. And while I adore a relaxed braise packed with tender meat, I was determined to create an abbreviated version that also just happened to be vegetarian. The first iteration of this recipe used extra-firm tofu, a great alternative to take this recipe vegan, but it seemed to be missing a textural component only a seared chunk of the Indian cheese could provide.

Iraqi Jewish food has a huge influence from Indian cuisine due to Iraqi Jews' role in managing trade between India and the Middle East. When this community, like Alex's family, arrived in Iran after exile in the early 1950s, they brought their own culinary traditions, which naturally blended with the Persian dishes and ingredients of their new home. My mother-in-law makes so many Persian dishes with Iraqi flair and vice versa, all uniquely authentic to her family's experience. It's part of the delicious Diasporic narrative of how Jewish food evolves!

1. In a medium dutch oven or pot, heat the oil over medium-high heat. Season the paneer with a heavy pinch each of salt and pepper. Sear the paneer, turning it as needed, until golden brown, 6 to 8 minutes. Transfer the seared paneer to a bowl.

2. Add the onions to the pot and cook, stirring often, until softened and lightly caramelized, 3 to 4 minutes. Stir in the fenugreek and turmeric and cook until fragrant, about 1 minute. Add the parsley, cilantro, and scallions to the pot and cook, stirring continuously with a wooden spoon and scraping up any browned bits on the bottom of the pot, until the herbs are dark green in color, 4 to 5 minutes.

3. Add the seared paneer, beans, stock, ground dried lime, Osem, if using, and 2 heavy pinches each of salt and pepper, then bring to a light simmer, reducing the heat as needed. Cover, with the lid slightly ajar, and cook until the flavors have blended and the liquid has slightly thickened, about 20 minutes. Remove from the heat and let sit for 5 minutes to allow the beans to further soak up some of the cooking liquid.

4. Taste and adjust the seasoning with salt and pepper, then serve with rice.

STEAK "FRITES" WITH GARLIC WHIP

Serves 4
Prep Time: 20 minutes
Cook Time: 40 minutes

For the Frites
2½ pounds (4 medium)
    russet potatoes, each cut
    into 8 wedges
3 tablespoons vegetable oil
1 teaspoon garlic powder
1 teaspoon smoked paprika
Kosher salt and freshly
    ground black pepper

For the Garlic Whip
1 large head garlic (about 13
    cloves), smashed, peeled,
    and roughly chopped
⅔ cup vegetable oil
2 tablespoons freshly
    squeezed lemon juice
1 tablespoon water
2 teaspoons dijon mustard
Kosher salt

For the Steak
2 tablespoons vegetable oil
2 (1½-inch-thick) boneless
    rib eye or strip steaks
    (about 2½ pounds)
Kosher salt and freshly
    ground black pepper
2 tablespoons unsalted
    butter or vegan butter
4 sprigs thyme

If you're invited for steak night, that means I really love you. We began the tradition as a way to celebrate any small occurrence in our lives that required a bit of gratitude via expensive cuts of meat shared with our nearest and dearest. And it always works the same way: four people max, two super thick steaks, an abundance of crispy potato wedges, and this life-changing, garlic-breath-inducing sauce. It's inspired by toum, a mayo-adjacent sauce from the Levant that consists of raw garlic, lemon, and oil. The only difference here is that I add dijon for a little extra tang and some of the steak pan drippings to share a bit of all that flavor you build up with your steaks. It comes together super quickly with an immersion blender (please invest in one if you haven't), so you can focus all your attention on the potatoes and steak!

Everyone has their potato tricks, but I believe the secret to the best oven-baked fries is the delicate dance of rotating the pan to different racks. I start on the middle rack to help create a nice sear on the bottom of the potato wedges. Only when this happens will the fries release from the pan, which is why you do not touch them for the first 30 minutes. Then, after a scrape with a metal fish spatula to toss, I move them up to the top rack for the final 10 to 15 minutes to crisp up. It's foolproof and leaves you with the crunchiest fries, every time.

As for the steaks, my first step is always to open all the windows in my apartment, so I don't set off the smoke detector. Past that, just follow the recipe! Cooking steak shouldn't be scary. Preheat your pan, pat the steaks dry, and use your thermometer, and you'll get a result worthy of a steak night celebration itself.

1. Roast the frites: Preheat the oven to 450°F with racks in the middle and top of the oven.

2. On a sheet pan, toss the potato wedges with the vegetable oil, garlic powder, smoked paprika, and 2 heavy pinches each of salt and pepper. Spread in an even layer, then roast on the middle rack for 30 minutes, until lightly golden. Toss the potatoes (I prefer using a fish spatula for this) and return to the oven, this time on the top rack. Roast for another 10 to 15 minutes, until deeply golden and crisp.

3. Meanwhile, make the garlic whip: In a quart container or glass wide enough to fit an immersion blender, add the chopped garlic followed by the oil, lemon juice, water, dijon, and 2 heavy pinches of salt. Using an immersion blender, blend the mixture until smooth and thick, starting at the bottom and slowly lifting up to incorporate all of the oil. Transfer to a heatproof bowl and cover.

4. Once you've returned the potatoes to the oven on the upper rack, cook the steak: In a large cast-iron skillet, heat the oil over medium-high heat until it begins to shimmer. Pat the steaks dry with paper towels and season both sides of each steak with a heavy pinch each of salt and pepper.

5. Sear the steaks, flipping once, until golden brown and a thermometer inserted into the center reads 125°F (for medium-rare), about 4 minutes per side. Add the butter and thyme to the pan and

cook, basting the steaks constantly for 1 minute. Transfer the steaks to a cutting board to rest for 5 minutes.

6. To the garlic whip, slowly whisk in ¼ cup of the steak pan drippings until incorporated. Taste and adjust the seasoning with salt and pepper.

7. Carve the steaks and transfer to a platter with the roasted frites. Serve with the garlic whip on the side.

ROAST CHICKEN WITH SCHMALTZY GREEN BEANS & ONE-POT MASHED POTATOES

Serves 4 to 6
Prep Time: 20 minutes
Cook Time: 40 minutes

For the Chicken
1 (5- to 6-pound) chicken, broken down into 8 pieces
2 tablespoons olive oil
2 tablespoons Master Meat Rub (page 45)

For the Green Beans
Kosher salt
2 pounds green beans, stems trimmed
2 tablespoons olive oil
2 medium leeks, white and light green parts only, halved, rinsed well, and thinly sliced into half-moons
Freshly ground black pepper
¼ cup white wine or chicken stock

For the Mashed Potatoes
¼ cup olive oil
6 garlic cloves, thinly sliced
1 tablespoon minced fresh rosemary leaves
¼ teaspoon crushed red pepper

The winner of chicken dinners, this recipe serves up the main, side, and vegetable all in an hour flat, and using only one sheet pan and one 4-quart pot. It's my Rachael Ray spin on an Ina Garten date night, if that makes sense. The chicken gets its oomph from the Master Meat Rub, which infuses a light pastrami vibe with a hint of brown sugar to get the skin extra crispy. The green beans are tossed with leeks and white wine to serve as an edible roasting rack for the chicken, catching all the schmaltzy juices while becoming flawlessly tender. And for the potatoes, we're making a one-pot mash, simmering them with chicken stock and a spicy rosemary-infused olive oil. If you're kosher or sensitive to dairy, these spuds are for you! If not, you'll stir in a little sour cream for extra richness!

1. Preheat the oven to 425°F. Bring a 4-quart pot of water to a boil.

2. Prep the chicken: Pat the chicken dry with paper towels, then transfer to a large bowl. Toss with the olive oil, followed by the meat rub to coat. Set aside.

3. Prep the green beans: Season the boiling water liberally with salt. Add the green beans and cook for 2 minutes. They should be vibrant green but still quite crisp. Drain and transfer to a sheet pan. Add the olive oil, leeks, and 2 heavy pinches each of salt and black pepper. Using tongs, toss to incorporate. Pour the white wine over the green beans.

4. Place the seasoned chicken over the green beans, skin side up. Roast for 30 to 35 minutes, until the chicken is golden and reaches an internal temperature of 165°F.

5. Meanwhile, make the mashed potatoes: In the same pot you blanched the green beans, add the oil, garlic, rosemary, and crushed red pepper over medium-high heat. Cook until the mixture begins to sizzle and the edges of the garlic turn golden, 1 to 2 minutes. Add the potatoes, chicken stock,

2½ pounds (4 large) russet potatoes, peeled and cut into 1-inch pieces
2 cups chicken stock
Kosher salt and freshly ground black pepper
¼ cup full-fat sour cream (optional)

and two heavy pinches each of salt and black pepper, then bring to a simmer. Cover and cook until the potatoes are tender, 12 to 14 minutes. Remove from the heat and mash with a potato masher. Stir in the sour cream, if using. Taste and adjust the seasoning with salt and black pepper, then keep warm.

6. Transfer the chicken and green beans to a platter and serve with the mashed potatoes.

KITCHRI (IRAQI JEWISH LENTIL RICE) WITH GARLICKY YOGURT

Serves 4 to 6
Prep Time: 15 minutes
Cook Time: 25 minutes

For the Kitchri
3 tablespoons olive oil
4 garlic cloves, minced
1 medium yellow onion,
    finely chopped
Kosher salt and freshly
    ground black pepper
1 (6-ounce) can tomato
    paste
2 teaspoons curry powder
1½ teaspoons ground
    cumin
2 cups long grain basmati
    rice, rinsed
1 cup dried red lentils,
    rinsed
4 cups water

For the Yogurt Sauce
1 cup plain full-fat yogurt
1 to 2 garlic cloves, finely
    grated
Kosher salt

For Serving (optional)
Fried eggs
Sliced serrano chiles
Sliced scallions

This is one of the best examples of the influence of Indian cuisine on Iraqi Jewish cooking. Derived from Indian kitchari, a creamy rice and mung bean dish, this Middle Eastern version uses red lentils and a fragrant tomato sauce with fried garlic and cumin. My mother-in-law, Robina, remembers it as one of her mother's favorite dishes to serve at break fast on Yom Kippur, with yogurt to stir in. Here, we're building on it for the full grain-bowl treatment, topping your kitchri with a biting garlicky yogurt, fried egg, sliced chiles, and scallions. It's a quick and pantry-heavy vegetarian meal that's easy to knock out when hunger strikes, whether you're fasting or not!

1. Make the kitchri: In a medium saucepan (I typically use a 3- or 4-quart pot), heat the olive oil over medium heat. Add the garlic, onion, and a heavy pinch each of salt and pepper and cook until softened and lightly caramelized, 6 to 8 minutes. Add in the tomato paste, curry powder, and cumin and cook, stirring constantly, until the spices are fragrant and the tomato paste begins to caramelize, about 2 minutes. Then stir in the rice and lentils to coat. Add the water and 2 heavy pinches each of salt and pepper and bring to a simmer. Cover and cook, reducing the heat as needed to maintain a simmer, until the rice and lentils are tender and all the liquid is absorbed, 15 to 18 minutes. Remove from the heat and let steam, covered completely, for 5 minutes, then fluff with a fork.

2. Meanwhile, make the yogurt: In a bowl, whisk together the yogurt, garlic, and a heavy pinch of salt, then thin out the mixture with a few tablespoons of water so you can drizzle the sauce over the rice. Taste and adjust the seasoning with salt.

3. To serve, divide the kitchri among bowls and drizzle with the garlicky yogurt. Top each bowl with a fried egg, sliced chiles, and scallions, if using, then serve.

SOUPLESS CHICKEN SOUP

Serves 4
Prep Time: 20 minutes
Cook Time: 35 minutes

3 tablespoons olive oil
1 (4- to 4½-pound)
    chicken, broken down
    into 8 pieces and patted
    dry with paper towels
Kosher salt and freshly
    ground black pepper
1 pound carrots, cut into
    ¾-inch pieces
1 pound parsnips, cut into
    ¾-inch pieces
1 pound (5 medium) celery
    stalks, cut into ¾-inch
    pieces
2 garlic cloves, smashed
    and peeled
¾ cup white wine or
    chicken stock
6 sprigs thyme
Chopped fresh parsley and
    dill, for garnish

Brilliantly named by my husband, of course, this is a one-skillet chicken for the soul. One of my most frequented recipes during the cold months, you get all the cozy feelings of Jewish penicillin in golden pieces of chicken roasted on a bed of the same vegetables you'd find floating in your bowl. Just remember, any good Jewish deli will serve slices of challah on the side of their chicken soup, for dipping, so be sure to do the same with this skillet. You'll want to sop up all those pan drippings!

I call for a medium-sized chicken in this recipe, but it's not the end of the world if your chicken falls out of that range. If you happen to get a smaller bird, just start temping the breasts after 10 minutes in the oven to make sure you don't overcook them. But more likely, you'll end up buying a supersized chicken, and you'll need to roast it longer to reach a 165°F internal temperature. Depending on the weight, you may need to add an extra 5 to 10 minutes. If the chicken pieces no longer fit in your skillet (I'm bringing this up since it has happened to me), just grab a 9 × 13-inch baking dish! Follow the recipe as is, and once you pour in the wine or stock, dump all the contents of the skillet into the baking dish with the thyme before topping with the seared chicken and roasting.

1. Preheat the oven to 425°F.

2. In a large cast-iron or ovenproof skillet, heat the olive oil over medium-high heat. Season the chicken pieces with 2 heavy pinches each of salt and pepper. Working in two batches, sear the chicken, starting skin side down and turning as needed, until golden, 6 to 8 minutes per batch. Transfer to a plate or sheet pan.

3. To the skillet, add the carrots, parsnips, celery, garlic, and 2 heavy pinches each of salt and pepper and cook until lightly softened and caramelized, 5 to 7 minutes. Pour in the wine, then nestle the thyme in the skillet. Place the chicken over the vegetables, skin side up, then transfer the skillet to the oven.

4. Roast for 15 to 20 minutes (see headnote about roasting times!), until the chicken reaches an internal temperature of 165°F. Garnish with chopped parsley and dill, then serve.

THERE WILL BE LEFTOVERS

*If there aren't leftovers,
did you even make enough?*

JEW-MAMI BRAISED BRISKET

Serves 10 to 12

Prep Time: 30 minutes, plus cooling time and overnight chilling

Cook Time: 4 hours, plus reheating time

1 (5- to 6-pound) beef brisket, fat cap intact

Kosher salt and freshly ground black pepper

3 tablespoons vegetable oil

2 pounds sweet onions, thinly sliced

1 pound cremini mushrooms, thinly sliced (2½ cups)

6 garlic cloves, smashed and peeled

1 (6-ounce) can tomato paste

2 cups dry red wine

1 (28-ounce) can crushed tomatoes

¼ cup soy sauce or liquid aminos (see headnote)

¼ cup balsamic vinegar

1 pound carrots, scrubbed and cut into 1-inch pieces

4 fresh or dried bay leaves

4 sprigs thyme

2 sprigs rosemary

Perfection is an illusion! I can be very proud and satisfied with the recipes I share with you, while constantly working to improve them. I think the best example of that is my Jewish braised brisket, which is the masterpiece that will never be finished. Both recipes in my last book are triumphs, but over the past few years, I took my favorite aspects of both and created a new braise with some unexpected ingredients. To fortify the punch of umami, a base of caramelized onions, mushrooms, and tomato paste is deglazed with red wine, balsamic vinegar, and soy sauce (or swap the soy with an equal amount of liquid aminos if avoiding *kitniyot* during Passover). After bubbling away in the oven, the tender beef is hugged by an ultrasavory sauce, balanced with the perfect tinge of acidity and sweetness.

Remember that scene in *White Chicks* when they're helping each other squeeze into a pair of jeans a couple of sizes too small? Well, that's too often what happens in the kitchen when you're trying to pick the right pot. For searing and braising a brisket, you need a ton of surface area to really make sure everything gets golden rather than steams and then can cook evenly as it bubbles away in the oven. I typically use a 7.25-quart round dutch oven, which works when shimmying the brisket around, but I will always recommend an oval-shaped one for the best result. Let's say Hanukkah is far away and you just don't have a pot that works: It is totally kosher to halve your brisket crosswise for ease; just be sure both halves are covered in sauce when braising.

The greatest reward for your hard work is that this recipe lasts for days and only gets better after you've cooked it. This makes it my ideal candidate for stocking in the fridge, even outside of the High Holidays, ready to reheat whenever you want. Yes, it's irresistible with potatoes, whether roasted, mashed, or turned into Kugel Fries (page 98). But I think the boss-level move is always to serve it with pasta, letting that sultry sauce work its magic on any noodle you love. Braise be!

(cont.)

1. Preheat the oven to 325°F.

2. Season each side of the brisket with 2 heavy pinches each of salt and pepper. In a large dutch oven (see headnote), heat the vegetable oil over medium-high heat. Sear the brisket, turning it as needed, until golden brown on all sides, 15 to 20 minutes. Transfer the brisket to a platter.

3. Reduce the heat to medium, then add the onions, mushrooms, and garlic to the pot. Cook, stirring often, until softened and lightly caramelized, 10 to 15 minutes. Add the tomato paste, stirring to coat all the vegetables, and cook until lightly caramelized, 2 to 3 minutes. Add the wine, then stir continuously with a wooden spoon for 1 minute to scrape up any browned bits on the bottom of the pot.

4. Stir in the crushed tomatoes, soy sauce, vinegar, carrots, and 2 heavy pinches each of salt and pepper, then return the brisket to the pot. Tie together the bay leaves, thyme, and rosemary with a small piece of butcher's twine (tying is optional, but makes it much easier to remove the herbs after cooking) and nestle the herb bundle in the pot. Bring to a simmer, then cover the pot and transfer to the oven. Cook for 3 to 3½ hours, until the brisket is very tender when pierced with a fork. Remove from the oven and let cool completely, then refrigerate overnight.

5. The next day, skim off and discard any fat, if desired, and discard the herbs. Transfer the brisket to a cutting board and cut it across the grain (perpendicular to the fibers you'll see running through the brisket) into ¼-inch-thick slices. Return the meat to the sauce and heat over medium heat until warmed through. Taste and adjust the seasoning with salt and pepper, then serve. Store leftovers in an airtight container in the refrigerator for up to 5 days.

CHOLENT BOURGUIGNON

Serves 8 to 10

Prep Time: 30 minutes, plus soaking time

Cook Time: 2 hours 50 minutes

2 ounces beef bacon or regular bacon, sliced into ¼-inch strips

2 tablespoons vegetable oil

3 pounds boneless short ribs, cut into 2-inch pieces and patted dry with paper towels

Kosher salt and freshly ground black pepper

1 pound cremini mushrooms, sliced

8 garlic cloves, smashed and peeled

1 medium yellow onion, finely chopped

¼ cup tomato paste

1 tablespoon honey

2 teaspoons minced fresh rosemary leaves

1 teaspoon smoked paprika

1 (750-ml) bottle pinot noir

4 cups beef stock

2 cups water

1 cup pearled barley

1 cup dried navy beans, soaked and drained (see Note)

This cholent strangely begins at the Surf Club in Miami, where I took my grandmother Annie out for a fancy dinner. I've been trying to take as many opportunities as I can to preserve our family history, jotting down everything I learn in my notes app. A true gourmand, she enjoyed oysters Rockefeller and lobster thermidor while she told me everything: where her parents were born, what their life was like before and after the war in Europe, and their journey to NYC. Naturally the conversation turned to food, spanning stories of her mother cooking fresh gefilte fish from a bathtub carp and simmering pots of Shabbos cholent. I was shocked to hear she grew up with the Ashkenazi stew, since my mother had never heard of it when I first made it for her. Annie blamed my grandfather, who she claims tempted her away from her more religious upbringing with a Cuban sandwich. Since she was no longer kosher or keeping Shabbat, she felt no need to cook cholent.

I wanted to bring it back into our family in a way that felt authentic to us. Having grown up in Belgium, Annie always cooked with Gallic flair, so I thought a cholent mash-up with boeuf bourguignon seemed fitting. While this recipe leans heavily toward the traditional French braise, the addition of barley and beans is what brings it to the next level of nourishment. And in true grandma fashion, you should make it in advance so you're always ready to heat up a bowl!

1. In a large dutch oven, add the bacon and vegetable oil over medium-high heat. Cook until the fat has rendered and the bacon is crisp, 8 to 9 minutes. Using a slotted spoon, transfer to a medium bowl. Season the short rib pieces with 2 heavy pinches each of salt and pepper. Working in two batches, sear the short rib pieces, turning them as needed, until golden brown, 8 to 10 minutes per batch. Transfer the seared meat to the bowl with the crispy bacon.

2. Add the mushrooms, garlic, and chopped onion to the pot and cook, stirring often, until softened and lightly caramelized, 8 to 10 minutes. Stir in the tomato paste, honey, rosemary, and paprika and cook until fragrant and the tomato paste is lightly caramelized, 2 minutes.

(cont.)

1 pound small red potatoes,
    halved
1 pound carrots, cut into
    2-inch pieces
1 cup frozen pearled
    onions, thawed
1 tablespoon red wine
    vinegar
¼ cup minced fresh
    parsley leaves and tender
    stems

3. Slowly pour in the wine, scraping up any browned bits on the bottom of the pot with a wooden spoon, then pour in the stock and water. Stir in the seared short rib pieces and bacon with the barley, beans, potatoes, carrots, and 2 heavy pinches each of salt and pepper, then bring to a simmer. Cover and cook, adjusting the heat as needed to maintain a low simmer, for 2 hours, until the beef and beans are extremely tender.

4. Stir in the pearled onions and vinegar and cook for 5 minutes more to warm through, then remove from the heat and stir in the parsley. Taste and adjust the seasoning with salt and pepper, then serve. Store leftovers in an airtight container in the refrigerator for up to 5 days.

Super Soaker

If I'm just cooking beans, I typically don't do any soaking and just let them bubble away, low and slow, until tender. But when coordinating cook times with other items like in a cholent, the soak is super important! I try to soak them covered in at least 2 inches of cool water at room temperature for about 12 hours if possible. However, often I forget or just have no patience for that. In that case, I find that a quick soak works totally fine for this recipe. If you're joining me on this route, before anything else, throw your beans in a saucepan covered in 2 inches of water and bring to a boil. Cook for 5 minutes, then turn off the heat and let sit for 45 minutes to 1 hour. While your beans are cooling, you can prep the rest of the ingredients and then be ready to party.

HAMIS E POTATA WITH GRENPIS (IRAQI CURRIED CHICKEN & POTATO STEW WITH PEAS)

Serves 8 to 10
Prep Time: 20 minutes
Cook Time: 55 minutes

3 tablespoons olive oil
6 scallions, white and
    green parts separated
    and thinly sliced
2 medium yellow onions,
    finely chopped
2 teaspoons curry powder
1 teaspoon ground cumin
2 pounds boneless, skinless
    chicken thighs, cut into
    1½-inch pieces
Kosher salt and freshly
    ground black pepper
1 pound (about 3 medium)
    Yukon gold potatoes, cut
    into ½-inch pieces
1 pound (about 5 medium)
    carrots, cut into ½-inch
    pieces
1 pound (½ medium head)
    cauliflower, cut into
    1-inch florets
1 (28-ounce) can tomato
    puree
4 cups chicken stock
2 teaspoons Osem
    consommé (optional)
1 cup frozen peas, thawed
½ cup minced fresh
    parsley
Cooked rice, for serving

There is never a visit to Alex's parents that does not involve a giant Tupperware of this Iraqi stew in the fridge, awaiting our arrival. It embodies the full vibe of this book and noshing. It's an easy recipe that Robina throws together in advance so she'll always have something ready to throw in the microwave without sacrificing quality! Past it being a logistical marvel, this recipe is also just delightful—simmering chunks of chicken and vegetables in a spiced tomato broth. It's extremely filling yet falls on the lighter side of the spectrum of stews, making it an evergreen choice for dinner any season. I took the liberty of adding cauliflower, and you should also play around with whatever vegetables you feel like throwing into the pot!

1. In a large pot or dutch oven (this recipe will fill up a 7-quart-ish Le Creuset), heat the olive oil over medium-high heat. Add the scallion whites and onions and cook until softened and lightly caramelized, 7 to 9 minutes. Stir in the curry powder and cumin and cook until fragrant, 1 minute. Add the chicken and season with 2 heavy pinches each of salt and pepper, then cook, stirring constantly, until no longer pink, 4 to 5 minutes.

2. Stir in the potatoes, carrots, and cauliflower, followed by the tomato puree, chicken stock, Osem consommé, if using, and 2 heavy pinches each of salt and pepper. Cover, with the lid slightly ajar, and cook, stirring occasionally, until the vegetables and chicken are very tender, 40 to 45 minutes.

3. Remove from the heat and stir in the scallion greens, peas, and parsley. Taste and adjust the seasoning with salt and pepper, then serve with rice. Store leftovers in an airtight container in the refrigerator for up to 5 days.

PINEAPPLE-MUSTARD CORNED BEEF WITH ROASTED CABBAGE

Serves 6 to 8
Prep Time: 25 minutes
Cook Time: 3 hours 20 minutes

Kosher salt
1 tablespoon black peppercorns
1 tablespoon juniper berries
4 dried bay leaves
1 (3½-pound) corned beef
1 small green cabbage, cut into 8 wedges
1 cup minced fresh pineapple
¼ cup dijon mustard
3 tablespoons packed light brown sugar
1 garlic clove, finely grated
Freshly ground black pepper
2 tablespoons olive oil

If you ask my mother, my sister loved her corned beef. My mother made it often when we were kids, topping it with dijon, brown sugar, and canned pineapple rings before throwing it into the oven to caramelize. And while the truth is that my sister only loved to pick off the roasted pineapple, I will give my mother credit for a great corned beef. I mean, she took salty meat and covered it in tons and tons of sugar. What could be bad? I decided to revive her recipe, maintaining the same feel but with some fresh pineapple and cabbage. Roasted all on one sheet pan, this version is so popular with the fam, my sister will even eat the corned beef itself!

I played around with corning my own beef and I highly recommend it for anyone passionate about curing meats, but it just wasn't for me. It requires time and pink curing salt and faith that you won't poison yourself and your loved ones (I don't have too much of any of these things). However, my confidence in what to do with an already-corned beef is at an all-time high!

1. Bring a large pot of salted water to a boil with the peppercorns, juniper berries, and bay leaves, then add the corned beef. Cover and cook, adjusting the heat as needed to maintain a simmer, until tender, 2½ to 3 hours. Using tongs, carefully transfer the corned beef to a sheet pan, leaving the water in the pot.

2. About 30 minutes before the corned beef is ready, preheat the oven to 425°F.

3. Return the water to a boil and add the cabbage. Cook for 5 minutes, then use a slotted spoon or tongs to carefully transfer the boiled cabbage wedges to the sheet pan, nestling them around the corned beef.

4. In a small bowl, stir together the pineapple, dijon, brown sugar, garlic, and a heavy pinch each of salt and pepper. Spoon over the corned beef in an even layer. Drizzle the olive oil over the cabbage wedges and season each with a pinch of salt and pepper.

5. Roast for 45 to 55 minutes, until the pineapple is caramelized and the cabbage is golden and tender. Carefully transfer the corned beef to a cutting board and cut it across the grain (perpendicular to the fibers you'll see running through the beef) into ¼-inch-thick slices. Transfer to a platter with the roasted cabbage wedges and serve. Store leftovers in an airtight container in the refrigerator for up to 5 days.

DATE-ROASTED VEGETABLE TAHCHIN

Serves 8 to 10
Prep Time: 30 minutes
Cook Time: 1 hour 45 minutes

For the Filling

1 pound mixed mushrooms, roughly torn
12 ounces cauliflower florets
12 ounces Brussels sprouts, halved
8 ounces diced butternut squash
¼ cup date syrup (silan)
3 tablespoons olive oil
2 tablespoons rice vinegar
1 teaspoon ground sumac
¼ teaspoon Aleppo pepper or crushed red pepper
2 shallots, thinly sliced
Kosher salt and freshly ground black pepper
½ cup plain full-fat Greek yogurt
½ cup minced fresh cilantro leaves and tender stems

For the Rice

3 cups basmati rice, rinsed
3 tablespoons kosher salt
½ cup boiling water
¼ teaspoon saffron threads, finely ground with a mortar and pestle

Alex and I have a minor obsession with his aunt Diana's friend Janet. She's Persian Jewess perfection, sporting cascading curls, piercing blue eyes, and an almost melodic accent that she uses to speak in riddles whenever she wants Diana to secretly smoke a cigarette with her outside. If that wasn't enough for us, she also makes the best tahchin.

The casserole counterpart of crispy Persian rices, tahchin typically consists of yogurt-coated rice layered with chicken and tart, dried barberries, then baked in the oven until golden and ready to be flipped out in front of your guests. However, Janet, like many Persian Jews who have adapted Iranian classics to meet kosher guidelines, uses mushrooms in place of the chicken. We love Janet's version so much that I ran with it to make a veggie-lover's tahchin packed with mushrooms, cauliflower, Brussels sprouts, and squash. Roasted with date syrup for sweetness, and plenty of sumac for tang, the vegetables in this filling would be just as popular as a side dish as they are stuffed into golden saffron rice.

Leftovers are a blessing for reheating, but when serving this recipe the first time, I prefer to have it land on the table straight from the oven. For prep, I'll typically make the vegetable filling up to a full day in advance to just have it out of the way. Same goes with the Sweet & Salty Onion Crunch, a pantry staple of mine that is a mandatory topping for this dish and any rice you make! Then, the day I'm serving I'll parboil my rice and assemble it in the baking dish a few hours in advance, holding in the fridge until ready to bake. Pop it in the oven 45 minutes before guests are set to arrive so it's perfectly golden by the time any fashionably late diners have made their entrance.

1. Make the filling: Preheat the oven to 450°F.

2. On a sheet pan, toss the mushrooms, cauliflower, Brussels sprouts, squash, date syrup, olive oil, rice vinegar, sumac, Aleppo pepper, shallots, and 2 heavy pinches each of salt and black pepper to combine. Spread in an even layer and roast, tossing halfway through, for 30 minutes, until caramelized and tender. Transfer the vegetables to a medium bowl, then add

(cont.)

4 ounces (1 stick) unsalted
  butter, melted
1 cup plain full-fat Greek
  yogurt
1 large egg yolk
Nonstick cooking spray, for
  greasing

For Serving
Sweet & Salty Onion
  Crunch (page 44)
Fresh parsley leaves, for
  garnish

the yogurt and cilantro and toss to coat. Taste and adjust the seasoning with salt and black pepper. Reduce the oven temperature to 400°F.

3. While the vegetables are roasting, prepare the rice: In a large bowl, cover the rice with 2 inches of cold water and 1 tablespoon of the salt. Stir to combine, then let soak for 30 minutes.

4. In a 2-cup liquid measuring cup, combine the boiling water and ground saffron. Let bloom for 2 minutes, then whisk in the butter and another tablespoon of the salt.

5. In a large bowl, whisk the yogurt and egg yolk with half of the saffron butter until smooth.

6. Bring a large pot of water to a boil. Season the water with the remaining 1 tablespoon of salt. Drain the soaked rice and add it to the pot. Cook for 4 minutes, then drain.

7. Grease a 9 × 13-inch glass baking dish with nonstick cooking spray. Gently stir 4 cups of the parboiled rice into the yogurt-egg mixture until the rice is well coated. Spread the coated rice over the bottom of the greased baking dish and 1½ inches up the sides. Gently top with the roasted vegetables, followed by the remaining parboiled rice. Drizzle the remaining saffron butter over the top.

8. Cover the baking dish with 2 layers of aluminum foil, then bake for 1 hour 15 minutes, until the sides and bottom are golden. Remove from the oven and discard the foil, then run an offset spatula around the sides of the dish to ensure the rice doesn't stick. Place a platter over the baking dish and carefully but quickly invert them together, then remove the baking dish so the crispy rice is on top. Top with the onion crunch and parsley leaves, then serve. Store leftovers in an airtight container in the refrigerator for up to 5 days.

T'BEET (IRAQI BAKED CHICKEN & RICE)

Serves 8 to 10
Prep Time: 20 minutes
Cook Time: 2 hours 20 minutes

3 cups long grain basmati rice, rinsed

Kosher salt

¼ cup vegetable oil

4 whole (about 3 pounds) chicken legs

Freshly ground black pepper

1 medium yellow onion, finely chopped

¼ cup tomato paste

2 tablespoons baharat (page 46)

1 (15-ounce) can diced tomatoes

3 cups chicken stock

This is one of the first recipes I learned how to make from Alex's aunt Diana. At the time, I was writing my first book proposal for a cookbook I was calling *Helwa*, both Alex's great-grandmother's name and the Arabic word for "sweet" or "beautiful." I wanted to document his family's recipes, creating a preservation of Iraqi Jewish cooking for not only them but the entire community. And it was rejected by every single publisher. Each rejection came with a heartfelt note of how beautiful and important this cookbook would be, but it was too niche, and they didn't see a broad audience interested in it. Fast-forward to *Jew-ish*—the Iraqi roasted salmon and *hadji bada* (Iraqi almond cookies) became some of the most cooked and adored dishes from the book. It's why in this book you'll find even more Iraqi Jewish representation, introducing you to new recipes I know you'll love that deserve the spotlight as much as any other dish from the Diaspora!

Much like Ashkenazi cholent, *t'beet* is a dish created to provide a hot Shabbat lunch, cooking baharat-spiced chicken and rice overnight. When I made it with Diana, we followed her more traditional recipe, where you stuff a whole chicken with a tomato-tinted rice mixture packed with the chicken gizzards, and then nestle it in more red rice. After hours of cooking low and slow, the entire apartment filled with the most enchanting aroma of schmaltzy baharat. The fragrant rice was slightly mushy in the best way possible, with a perfectly golden crust along the pan, while the chicken was literally spoon tender.

Over the years, I've made a few adjustments to Diana's dreamy recipe, but it still never fails to bring those homey Shabbos vibes any night of the week. I swap the whole chicken for just legs, which makes it easy to sear to build up some more flavor while staying a bit juicier after the long cook time. And instead of using a giant rice cooker like Diana does (the equivalent of making cholent in a slow cooker), I'm partial to a shorter bake in the oven. I've found using a cast-iron braiser is ideal for a golden crust, but if you use an ovenproof nonstick pot, you could even flip out your *t'beet* onto a platter for extra showmanship!

(cont.)

1. Preheat the oven to 300°F.

2. In a medium bowl, cover the rice with cool water and stir in 1 tablespoon of salt. Set aside.

3. In a large cast-iron braiser or wide, ovenproof nonstick pot (I use a 5-quart Le Creuset braiser), heat the oil over medium heat. Season the chicken with a heavy pinch each of salt and pepper and sear, starting skin side down and flipping once, until golden, 5 to 7 minutes per side. Transfer to a plate.

4. To the pot, add the onion and cook, stirring often, until softened and lightly caramelized, 4 to 5 minutes. Stir in the tomato paste and baharat and cook until fragrant, 1 to 2 minutes, then stir in the diced tomatoes.

5. Drain the rice and add to the pot along with the chicken stock and 2 teaspoons of salt. Stir gently to combine, then nestle the chicken legs in the rice, skin side up. Bring to a simmer over medium-high heat.

6. Cover and bake for 2 to 2½ hours, until the rice and chicken are very tender and the edges of the rice are golden. Serve immediately, or it also holds well to be reheated before serving. Store leftovers in an airtight container in the refrigerator for up to 5 days.

BINA'S BURGHUL B'SENIYEH

Serves 8 to 10
Prep Time: 20 minutes
Cook Time: 45 minutes

4 cups cracked bulgur
4 cups chicken stock
2 cups water
½ cup vegetable oil
1 medium yellow onion,
 finely chopped
1 garlic clove, minced
1 pound ground beef
 (preferably 80% lean)
3 tablespoons baharat
 (page 46)
Kosher salt
1 cup pine nuts
1 cup dried currants or
 raisins
Chopped fresh parsley,
 for garnish

This is another one of my mother-in-law's American adaptations of a childhood favorite, cutting every corner she can while still creating an absolute showstopper. A Levantine staple, burghul b'seniyeh is one of the variations of kubbeh (a boiled or fried meat-stuffed dumpling), specifically *kubbeh burghul*, which uses a dough of fine bulgur instead of semolina or rice. (The Iraqi Jewish style is typically a flat patty shape that is boiled and pan-fried as opposed to the commonly found fried torpedo shape.) *B'seniyeh*, meaning "in a tray," is the baked version, which sandwiches the meat in between two layers of bulgur, and is then sliced and served straight from the dish.

Bina's burghul b'seniyeh takes cracked bulgur and blends it in with the beef filling and the traditional Iraqi garnish of fried pine nuts and currants or raisins. You can build on it to make a full meal, but when hunger strikes, Bina knows a simple bowl of this is the cure.

1. Preheat the oven to 425°F.

2. Place the bulgur in a large heatproof bowl. In a medium saucepan, bring the stock and water to a simmer. Remove from the heat and pour over the bulgur. Let sit for 20 minutes.

3. Meanwhile, in a large pot or dutch oven, heat ¼ cup of the oil over medium-high heat. Add the onion and garlic and cook, stirring often, until softened and lightly caramelized, 5 to 7 minutes. Add the beef and season with 2 tablespoons of the baharat and 2 heavy pinches of salt. Cook, stirring often to break up the beef into small crumbles, until lightly golden, 6 to 8 minutes.

4. While the beef cooks, in a small saucepan, combine the remaining ¼ cup oil with the pine nuts, currants, the remaining 1 tablespoon baharat, and a heavy pinch of salt. Cook, stirring occasionally, over medium-high heat until golden, 3 to 4 minutes.

5. Add the soaked bulgur and the pine nut mixture to the beef mixture. Cook, stirring to combine, until all the liquid is absorbed and the bulgur is glossy in appearance, 2 to 3 minutes. Taste and adjust the seasoning with salt.

6. Transfer the mixture to a 9 × 13-inch baking dish and drag a fork over the top to make grooves. Bake for 25 to 30 minutes, until golden. Top with chopped parsley, then serve.

BAKED EGGPLANT PARM WITH VODKA SAUCE

Serves 6 to 8
Prep Time: 20 minutes
Cook Time: 55 minutes

1 cup all-purpose flour

Kosher salt

4 eggs, lightly beaten

1½ cups plain dried bread crumbs

1½ cups panko bread crumbs

2 teaspoons dried oregano

2 teaspoons garlic powder

¼ teaspoon cayenne pepper

3 pounds (2 large elongated) eggplants, sliced into ½-inch-thick disks

¼ cup olive oil

¾ cup grated parmesan cheese

4 cups Spicy Vodka Sauce (page 47), plus more for pasta if desired

1 cup cherry tomatoes, halved

8 ounces shredded low-moisture mozzarella cheese

Fresh basil leaves, for garnish

Pasta, for serving

Other than Jewish deli, if there's one type of food I could eat every day, it's Italian food. Not the super authentic stuff, but the NYC Italian American gold, made by someone who talks with their hands as much as I do. Luckily I found myself a husband who also needs pasta for dinner multiple times a week, so this recipe has become a staple for any family gathering. Instead of pan-frying the eggplant, it's breaded and baked until crispy, ready to get layered with vodka sauce and cheese for a second round in the oven. It's definitely lush, but by no means greasy or heavy, leaving you with plenty of room for seconds.

1. Preheat the oven to 450°F. Line two sheet pans with parchment paper.

2. In a shallow bowl, stir together the flour with 1 teaspoon of salt. In a second shallow bowl, add the beaten eggs. In a third shallow bowl, stir together both bread crumbs with the oregano, garlic powder, cayenne, and 1 teaspoon of salt.

3. Working with one hand for the dry and one for the wet, dredge each eggplant slice in the flour, shaking off any excess, then dip it in the eggs, letting any excess drip off, and finally toss it in the bread crumb mixture, pressing the crumbs against the eggplant to completely coat. Arrange the breaded eggplants on the prepared pans.

4. Drizzle the eggplants with 3 tablespoons of the olive oil and sprinkle on ¼ cup of the parmesan cheese. Bake, rotating the pans halfway through the cooking time, for 25 to 30 minutes, until golden. Reduce the heat to 400°F.

5. In a 9 × 13-inch baking dish, spread 2 cups of the vodka sauce in an even layer. Shingle the eggplant slices over the sauce, then spoon the remaining 2 cups of sauce over the eggplants. Scatter the cherry tomatoes and sprinkle the shredded mozzarella and remaining ½ cup grated parmesan on top. Season with a pinch of salt, and drizzle with the remaining tablespoon of olive oil.

6. Bake for 20 to 25 minutes, until golden brown and bubbling. Garnish with basil, then serve alongside your favorite pasta tossed with more vodka sauce or whatever sauce you like.

BIG A** VEGETABLE LASAGNA

Serves 10 to 12
Prep Time: 1 hour,
plus cooling time
Cook Time: 2 hours

For the Dough
3 1/3 cups (450g) "00" flour
4 large eggs, plus 2 large
  yolks (255g)

For the Sauce
3 tablespoons olive oil
1 pound cremini
  mushrooms, thinly sliced
6 garlic cloves, thinly sliced
2 medium yellow onions,
  diced
1/4 teaspoon crushed red
  pepper
Kosher salt and freshly
  ground black pepper
1 cup dry red wine
2 (24.5 ounce) jars tomato
  puree (passata)
2 teaspoons dried oregano

For the Roasted Veggies
2 medium zucchini,
  ends trimmed and cut
  lengthwise into 1/4-inch-
  thick slices
1 medium eggplant,
  ends trimmed and cut
  lengthwise into 1/4-inch-
  thick slices

Here we have another product of the culinary TED Talks my grandmother gives me whenever she calls. A believer in making gargantuan dishes to portion and freeze, my grandmother Annie never sounds as giddy as when I catch her in the process of making a few trays of lasagna, packed with an equal abundance of vegetables and cheese. This recipe is the Jake-ified version, layering fresh pasta sheets with a hearty mushroom-tomato sauce, basil-kissed ricotta, slices of roasted zucchini and eggplant, and tons of mozzarella. I've made it for her many times and confirm it is grandma approved.

I've become a true believer that fresh pasta is what takes any lasagna from good to great, but I understand that it might not be in the cards for you. I find that Ina Garten's trick of soaking dried lasagna sheets (a 1-pound box is all you need) in hot tap water for 20 minutes is the best alternative. Once you're ready to assemble, use my guide (page 229) for a visual on how to build this massive lasagna!

1. Make the dough: On a clean work surface, place the flour in a pile and make a well in the center. Add the whole eggs and yolks to the well. Using a fork, whisk the ingredients in the well together until smooth, slowly incorporating the flour. Once a shaggy dough forms, switch to using your hands to knead it together until you have a very smooth ball of dough. This typically takes 6 to 10 minutes. Cover and let rest at room temperature for 1 hour.

2. Meanwhile, make the sauce: In a large pot or dutch oven, heat the olive oil over medium-high heat. Add the mushrooms, garlic, onions, crushed red pepper, and 2 heavy pinches each of salt and black pepper and cook, stirring occasionally, until softened and lightly caramelized, 10 to 12 minutes. Add the wine, then stir continuously with a wooden spoon for 1 minute to scrape up any browned bits on the bottom of the pot. Stir in the tomato puree, oregano, and another 2 heavy pinches each of salt and black pepper, then bring to a simmer. Cover, with the lid slightly ajar, and cook, reducing the heat as needed to maintain a simmer, for 30 minutes. Remove from the heat, then taste and adjust the seasoning with salt and black pepper. Let cool completely. Makes about 6 cups.

(cont.)

3 tablespoons olive oil

Kosher salt and
freshly ground black
pepper

For the Ricotta Filling

1 pound part-skim
ricotta cheese

1 cup packed fresh
basil leaves and
stems

1/2 cup finely grated
parmesan cheese

1 teaspoon finely
grated lemon zest

2 garlic cloves, thinly
sliced

Kosher salt and
freshly ground black
pepper

For Assembly

Olive oil, for greasing
and drizzling

"00" flour, for dusting

1 1/2 pounds shredded
low-moisture
mozzarella cheese

1 cup finely grated
parmesan cheese

3. Meanwhile, roast the veggies: Preheat the oven to 375°F. Line two sheet pans with parchment paper.

4. Lay out the zucchini and eggplant on the prepared pans in a single layer, then drizzle with the olive oil and season each pan with a heavy pinch each of salt and black pepper. Roast for 15 to 20 minutes, until just tender. Let cool.

5. Make the ricotta filling: In a food processor, combine the ricotta, basil, parmesan, lemon zest, garlic, and a heavy pinch each of salt and black pepper. Puree until smooth, then taste and adjust the seasoning with salt and black pepper. Set aside.

6. Assemble the lasagna: Grease an ovenproof 9 × 13-inch baking dish with olive oil.

7. Line a sheet pan with parchment paper and lightly dust with flour. Divide the dough into quarters. Using a rolling pin, roll out 1 piece of the dough as thin as you can. Switch to a pasta roller and, starting at the thickest setting and rolling twice on each setting before moving to the next, roll the dough until 1/8 inch thick (#2 setting). Cut crosswise into 4 equal pieces and transfer the pasta sheet to the prepared pan, then loosely cover with plastic wrap to prevent it from drying out. Repeat with the remaining dough until all the pasta is rolled out.

8. In the prepared baking dish, spread 1 1/2 cups (a quarter) of the sauce on the bottom. Place 4 of the pasta sheets across the bottom, overlapping slightly to cover. Spread half of the ricotta mixture over the sheets, then sprinkle on a third of the shredded mozzarella and grated parmesan. Shingle the roasted zucchini over the cheese, then place another 4 pasta sheets on top. Spread 1 1/2 cups of the sauce over the pasta, then shingle the roasted eggplant on top and spread another 1 1/2 cups of the sauce over it. Place another 4 pasta sheets over the sauce and spread the remaining half of the ricotta mixture on top, then sprinkle on another third of the shredded mozzarella and grated parmesan. Place the remaining 4 pasta sheets over the cheese, then spread on the remaining 1 1/2 cups of the sauce. Sprinkle the remaining third of the shredded mozzarella and grated parmesan, then drizzle with a tablespoon of olive oil.

9. Grease the shiny side of a sheet of aluminum foil with oil and cover the lasagna with it, greased side down. Place the dish on a sheet pan. Bake for 45 minutes, then remove the foil and continue to bake for 30 minutes more, until the cheese is golden brown and bubbling. Let cool for at least 20 minutes, then slice and serve.

Some Assembly Guidance for Visual Learners!

TOP

⅓ of the shredded mozzarella (8 ounces) and grated parmesan (⅓ cup)

¼ of the sauce (1½ cups)

¼ of the pasta (4 sheets)

⅓ of the shredded mozzarella (8 ounces) and grated parmesan (⅓ cup)

½ of the ricotta (1 cup)

¼ of the pasta (4 sheets)

¼ of the sauce (1½ cups)

All of the roasted eggplant

¼ of the sauce (1½ cups)

¼ of the pasta (4 sheets)

All of the roasted zucchini

⅓ of the shredded mozzarella (8 ounces) and grated parmesan (⅓ cup)

½ of the ricotta (1 cup)

¼ of the pasta (4 sheets)

¼ of the sauce (1½ cups)

BOTTOM

10

WHO DOESN'T SERVE CAKE AFTER A MEAL?

Just a sliver, please.

ANY-FRUIT POPPY STREUSEL COFFEECAKE

Makes 1 (9-inch) square cake
Prep Time: 20 minutes,
plus cooling time
Cook Time: 55 to 65 minutes

For the Streusel

¾ cup (101g) all-purpose
flour
½ cup packed (107g)
light brown sugar
1 tablespoon poppy seeds
½ teaspoon kosher salt
6 tablespoons (3 ounces)
unsalted butter, cold and
cubed

For the Cake

8 ounces (1 scant cup) full-
fat sour cream
½ cup olive oil
½ cup packed (107g) light
brown sugar
½ cup (100g) granulated
sugar
1 teaspoon vanilla extract
1 teaspoon finely grated
lemon zest
2 large eggs
2½ cups (338g)
all-purpose flour
¼ cup poppy seeds
1 teaspoon baking soda
1 teaspoon baking powder
1 teaspoon kosher salt
¼ teaspoon freshly grated
nutmeg

This recipe began as a pear-poppy coffeecake, since I have a passion for both pear desserts and alliterations. However, long past its season, I was still craving that scrumptious crumb. That's when I started testing it out with other fruit and discovered this batter is sturdy enough to take a pound of anything ripe, allowing you to mix and match depending on the season. That means I've explored strawberries and rhubarb in spring; peaches, blueberries, and cherries in summer; and apples and pears through fall and winter. Whatever fruity path you take, you'll be using the same poppy-packed sour cream batter and crisp streusel topping and adjusting only baking time. I use nutmeg for a bit of warmth, which translates well to whatever you choose to throw in, but use this opportunity to spice up your life any way you'd like. Every variation pairs just as well with a cup of coffee and a fork.

1. Preheat the oven to 350°F. Line a 9-inch square cake pan with parchment paper, leaving overhang on all sides.

2. Make the streusel: In a medium bowl, whisk together the flour, brown sugar, poppy seeds, and salt to combine. Add the cubed butter and, using your fingers, pinch the butter into the dry ingredients until a mixture reminiscent of clumpy wet sand forms. (There should not be any loose flour in your streusel.) Set aside.

3. Make the cake: In a large bowl, whisk together the sour cream, olive oil, both sugars, vanilla, lemon zest, and eggs until smooth. Add the flour, poppy seeds, baking soda, baking powder, salt, and nutmeg. Using a rubber spatula, gently stir together the dry ingredients piled above the wet ingredients a few times before folding together into a smooth batter. Add the fruit and fold in until just incorporated, then transfer to the prepared pan, smoothing the top with a rubber or offset spatula. Sprinkle the streusel over the top of the cake in an even layer.

4. Bake for 55 to 65 minutes, until golden brown and the cake reaches an internal temperature of 190°F. If you use firmer fruit like apples and pears, it will take closer to 55 minutes. If you use juicier fruit like berries

1 pound fresh fruit, cut into ½-inch pieces (see headnote for recommendations)

or peaches, it will take closer to 65 minutes. Let cool completely in the pan, then use the parchment overhang to transfer to a cutting board. Slice, then serve. Store leftovers in an airtight container on the counter or in the refrigerator (I like it cold) for up to 5 days.

PRESERVED LEMON & OLIVE OIL LOAF CAKE

Makes 1 loaf
Prep Time: 20 minutes,
plus cooling time
Cook Time: 40 minutes

For the Cake
1¾ cups (236g) all-purpose
 flour
1 teaspoon baking powder
½ teaspoon baking soda
1 cup (200g) granulated
 sugar
⅓ cup (75g) chopped
 preserved lemon (page
 49)
½ cup plain full-fat Greek
 yogurt
½ cup olive oil
1 teaspoon vanilla extract
2 large eggs, at room
 temperature

For the Glaze
¾ cup (90g) confectioners'
 sugar
2 tablespoons freshly
 squeezed lemon juice

It's an Entenmann's lemon loaf cake, all grown up! Instead of fresh lemons, this cake uses entirely preserved lemons, incorporating that salty tang you get from pickling citrus, while also allowing you to use the whole fruit, rind and all. If you made the lemons yourself, great! If not, just buy a jar from the store. I won't be hurt either way, I'm just grateful you turned on your oven for this recipe! The batter comes together with one blender and one bowl, pureeing the lemons with olive oil and yogurt for a pop of acidity and a ridiculously tender crumb. I finish the loaf with a bright fresh lemon glaze, but you can always sneak in a little of the preserved lemon brine for some extra pizazz.

1. For the cake: Preheat the oven to 350°F. Line a 9 × 5-inch loaf pan with parchment paper, leaving overhang on all sides.

2. In a large bowl, whisk together the flour, baking powder, and baking soda.

3. In a blender, combine the granulated sugar, preserved lemon, yogurt, olive oil, vanilla, and eggs. Blend until smooth.

4. Pour the wet ingredients over the dry ingredients and fold until just incorporated. Pour into the prepared loaf pan, smoothing the top with a rubber or offset spatula.

5. Bake the cake on the center rack for 40 to 45 minutes, until golden and it reaches an internal temperature of 190°F. Let cool in the pan for 15 minutes, then use the parchment overhang to transfer to a wire rack and let cool completely.

6. Make the glaze: In a medium bowl, whisk together the confectioners' sugar and lemon juice until smooth. Drizzle over the cooled cake, then let sit for 10 minutes to set before slicing and serving. Store in an airtight container at room temperature for up to 5 days.

Become the Moses of Loaf Cakes!

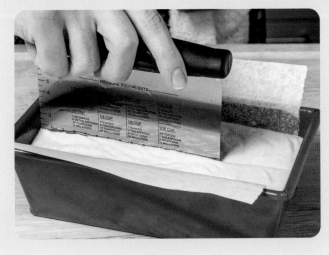

I learned this trick from my friend Edd Kimber, cookbook author and *Great British Bake Off* winner. His secret for loaf cakes that split perfectly is to run a greased knife or bench scraper right down the center of the batter before baking, just barely scoring it. This gives a path of least resistance for the batter to part like the Red Sea as it bakes, making it not only look pretty but cook evenly!

DATE-WALNUT BANANA BREAD

Makes 1 loaf
Prep Time: 20 minutes,
plus cooling time
Cook Time: 1 hour

Nonstick cooking spray, for
  greasing
4 very ripe bananas, peeled
  and coarsely mashed
  (about 1½ cups)
½ cup packed (107g) light
  brown sugar
½ cup olive oil
¼ cup date syrup (silan)
2 large eggs, at room
  temperature
2 cups (270g) all-purpose
  flour
1½ teaspoons kosher salt
1 teaspoon ground
  cinnamon
½ teaspoon baking soda
½ teaspoon baking powder
½ teaspoon freshly ground
  black pepper
½ cup dark chocolate chips
½ cup walnuts, roughly
  chopped
6 Medjool dates, pitted
  and torn
2 teaspoons turbinado
  sugar

I obviously was a sheep and joined the droves of people baking banana bread in 2020. However, my loaf stuck around long after quarantine, becoming the nosh that I always have out on my counter, ready for me to sneak a slice. This recipe takes inspiration from Iraqi charoset, a simple two-ingredient mixture of chopped walnuts and date syrup that just made perfect sense to throw into my banana bread. I doubled down and added chunks of dates for a little chew, and even some chocolate chips, because I felt like it! Scented with cinnamon and a little black pepper (trust me on that), the batter comes together in one bowl, without any dairy (pending you use dark chocolate chips). If you've never had a baked good that's both insanely dense and moist, get ready to go bananas.

1. Preheat the oven to 325°F. Grease a 9 × 5-inch loaf pan with nonstick spray.

2. In a large bowl, whisk the mashed bananas with the brown sugar, olive oil, date syrup, and eggs until well incorporated.

3. Add the flour, salt, cinnamon, baking soda, baking powder, and black pepper, then gently stir together the dry ingredients piled above the wet ingredients a few times before folding together into a smooth batter. Fold in the chocolate chips, walnuts, and dates until incorporated, then scrape the batter into the prepared loaf pan. Smooth the top with a rubber spatula, then sprinkle the turbinado sugar over the top.

4. Bake the banana bread for 1 hour to 1 hour 10 minutes, until golden brown and it reaches an internal temperature of 190°F. Let cool in the pan for 20 minutes, then run an offset spatula or paring knife around the sides of the banana bread and transfer it to a wire rack to cool completely. Slice and serve. Store leftovers in an airtight container at room temperature for up to 5 days.

CHOCOLATE-MARZIPAN MARBLED SNACKING CAKE

Makes 1 (9-inch) square cake

Prep Time: 20 minutes, plus cooling time

Cook Time: 40 minutes

For the Base Batter

8 ounces (2 sticks) unsalted butter, melted and cooled slightly

1 cup (200g) granulated sugar

½ cup packed (107g) light brown sugar

½ cup full-fat sour cream

1 teaspoon almond extract

2 large eggs, at room temperature

2 cups (270g) all-purpose flour

1 teaspoon kosher salt

½ teaspoon baking soda

½ teaspoon baking powder

For the Chocolate Batter

¼ cup (25g) unsweetened cocoa powder

½ cup dark chocolate chips

For the Marzipan Batter

½ cup (56g) finely ground almond flour

1 (7-ounce) tube marzipan, roughly chopped

Nothing was more iconic in my household when I was growing up than my mother's chocolate-marzipan cake, the official dessert of my childhood, and the one requested for every birthday and celebration. She still never fails to bring up that I would help her crack the eggs when she baked it, taking credit for my entrance into the kitchen. What she typically leaves out is that the recipe we were making involved one can of Solo Almond Cake & Pastry Filling mixed into one bowl of prepared Betty Crocker Devil's Food Cake Mix. Nevertheless, bliss was achieved.

I used that core memory to drive the vibe of this fully homemade marbled snacking cake, celebrating the superior combo of chocolate and marzipan! To make your life easier, you make one base batter and then split it up to turn one-half chocolatey and one-half almondy. The two are then swirled together for a fudgy cake packed with both melty chocolate chips and chewy chunks of marzipan. It's hands down my mother's most requested recipe in this book, a sign that our baking roles may have reversed, but I'm still cracking all the eggs.

1. Preheat the oven to 350°F. Line a 9-inch square cake pan with parchment paper, leaving overhang on all sides.

2. Make the base batter: In a medium bowl, whisk together the melted butter, granulated sugar, brown sugar, sour cream, almond extract, and eggs until smooth. Add the flour, kosher salt, baking soda, and baking powder. Gently stir together the dry ingredients piled above the wet ingredients a few times before folding together into a smooth batter. Transfer half of the batter to another medium bowl. (You should have about 1000g of batter total, so 500g per bowl.)

3. Make the chocolate batter: To one of the bowls, fold in the cocoa powder until just incorporated, followed by the chocolate chips.

4. Make the marzipan batter: To the other bowl, fold in the almond flour until just incorporated, followed by the marzipan.

5. In the prepared pan, alternate scoops of each batter until you've used up all the batter and filled the pan. Using the tip of a knife or an offset spatula, gently swirl the two batters together.

6. Bake for 40 to 45 minutes, until golden brown and the cake reaches an internal temperature of 190°F. Let cool completely in the pan, then transfer to a cutting board, slice, and serve. Store the cake in an airtight container at room temperature for up to 5 days.

APPLES & HONEY SNACKING CAKE

Makes 1 (9-inch) square cake
Prep Time: 20 minutes, plus cooling time
Cook Time: 45 minutes

1 cup olive oil
1 cup (200g) granulated sugar
¾ cup unsweetened applesauce
½ cup honey
1 teaspoon vanilla extract
2 large eggs, at room temperature
2¼ cups (304g) all-purpose flour
1 teaspoon ground cinnamon
1 teaspoon ground nutmeg
1 teaspoon kosher salt
½ teaspoon baking soda
½ teaspoon baking powder
2 Honeycrisp apples, cored and chopped
Confectioners' sugar, for dusting

Like every schmuck in the Northeast, I go apple picking in the fall with my family. And while it's mainly for the photo ops, we do always end up leaving with a bushel of apples that I have to bake my way through. This is the cake I revisit every fall on repeat, doubling as the perfect dessert to serve for Rosh Hashanah. The batter itself blends olive oil and applesauce to create the best crumb, while remaining moist for days, making it a great bake-ahead option. Kissed with honey and packed with chunks of apples, it's just as delightful for a sweet breakfast as it is for a late-night snack eaten hunched over the sink.

1. Preheat the oven to 350°F. Line a 9-inch square cake pan with parchment paper, leaving overhang on all sides.

2. In a large bowl, whisk together the olive oil, granulated sugar, applesauce, honey, vanilla, and eggs until smooth. Add the flour, cinnamon, nutmeg, salt, baking soda, and baking powder. Gently stir together the dry ingredients piled above the wet ingredients a few times before folding together into a smooth batter. Fold in the apples until incorporated, then pour the batter into the prepared cake pan.

3. Bake the cake, rotating the pan halfway through the cooking time, for 45 to 50 minutes, until golden brown and it reaches an internal temperature of 190°F. Let cool completely in the pan, then transfer to a cutting board. Dust with confectioners' sugar, then slice and serve. Store leftovers in an airtight container at room temperature for up to 5 days.

TZIMMES CAKE WITH CREAM CHEESE FROSTING

Makes 1 (9 × 13-inch) sheet cake
Prep Time: 30 minutes, plus cooling time
Cook Time: 40 minutes

For the Carrot Cake
Nonstick cooking spray, for greasing
1 cup olive oil
1 cup (200g) granulated sugar
1 cup packed (213g) light brown sugar
1 teaspoon vanilla extract
4 large eggs
2 cups (270g) all-purpose flour
2 teaspoons ground cinnamon
1½ teaspoons kosher salt
1 teaspoon baking powder
1 teaspoon baking soda
1 pound carrots, coarsely grated
8 ounces (1 medium) sweet potato, coarsely grated
½ cup chopped prunes
1 tablespoon finely grated orange zest

For the Cream Cheese Frosting
8 ounces cream cheese, at room temperature

Carrot cake, but make it Jewish! The classic Ashkenazi spiced side of stewed carrots, sweet potatoes, and prunes always deserved to be turned into a dessert, and it just works so well. Grated carrots and sweet potato provide so much moisture to the cinnamon-and-orange-zest-scented batter, while chopped prunes add a fudgy quality that I'll choose any day over raisins. And, in my very best *Mommie Dearest* voice, "NO NUTS IN MY CAKE." I'm partial to the soft texture being uninterrupted, but I won't be too mad if you feel strongly about throwing in some chopped walnuts. The cake is finished with a swoosh of luscious cream cheese frosting, though the cake itself is dairy-free so you can also take your topping in a pareve direction. The biggest takeaway should be that it stays moist for days in the fridge so you can always prepare it ahead. And if you're looking for a standout host gift, my power move is to bring one of these cakes baked in a new fancy ceramic baking dish to leave behind for an extrasweet memento.

1. Make the carrot cake: Preheat the oven to 350°F. Grease a 9 × 13-inch baking dish with nonstick cooking spray.

2. In a large bowl, whisk together the olive oil, granulated sugar, brown sugar, vanilla, and eggs until smooth. Add the flour, cinnamon, salt, baking powder, and baking soda. Gently stir together the dry ingredients piled above the wet ingredients a few times before folding together into a smooth batter. Fold in the carrots, sweet potato, prunes, and orange zest until incorporated. Pour into the prepared baking dish and spread in an even layer.

3. Bake the cake for 40 to 50 minutes, until golden brown and it reaches an internal temperature of 190°F. (Timing is going to depend on the moisture content of your carrots and sweet potatoes, so while on average it takes me 45 minutes, occasionally the proper internal temperature is reached after 40 minutes, so that is when I start checking.) Let cool completely in the dish.

8 ounces (2 sticks) unsalted
   butter, at room temperature
2½ cups confectioners' sugar
1 teaspoon vanilla extract
½ teaspoon kosher salt

4. Meanwhile, make the frosting: In the bowl of a stand mixer fitted with the whisk attachment, whip together the cream cheese, butter, confectioners' sugar, vanilla, and salt until light and fluffy.

5. Spread the frosting over the cooled cake, then slice and serve. Store the leftovers in an airtight container in the refrigerator for up to 5 days.

FLOURLESS CHOCOLATE-SUMAC CAKE

**Makes 1 (9-inch)
round cake**
Prep Time: 20 minutes,
plus cooling time
Cook Time: 45 minutes

8 ounces dark chocolate (70
   to 80% cacao), roughly
   chopped
4 ounces (1 stick) unsalted
   butter or vegan butter,
   cubed
1 cup (200g) granulated
   sugar
1 tablespoon ground sumac
1 teaspoon vanilla extract
1 teaspoon kosher salt
6 large eggs, whites and
   yolks separated
Raspberries, for garnish
Confectioners' sugar, for
   dusting

I've been pushing a ton of culinary combos in this book, but I am once again asking for you to experience the euphoria of chocolate mixed with sumac. If I haven't bullied you yet into buying a jar, consider this your final warning. Made up of dried and ground berries, sumac adds a bright tartness to everything it touches. And while you may be more familiar with it sprinkled on yogurt or grilled meats, the way it plays with the acidity in dark chocolate needs to be shared with the world! There was no better vessel to express my obsession for this duo than a flourless chocolate cake, creating a super decadent ganache lightened just enough with whipped egg whites. Every time I bake one, it collapses a little differently as it cools, but it always tastes like a match made in heaven.

1. Preheat the oven to 325°F. Line a 9-inch springform pan with parchment paper and place on a sheet pan.

2. Set a medium metal or heatproof glass bowl over a small pot of simmering water. Put the chocolate and butter in the bowl and heat, stirring occasionally, until completely melted and combined.

3. In a medium bowl, whisk together ½ cup of the granulated sugar with the sumac, vanilla, salt, and egg yolks until smooth. Slowly whisk in the melted chocolate mixture until combined.

4. In the bowl of a stand mixer fitted with the whisk attachment, whisk the egg whites on medium speed until frothy, then with the mixer running, slowly add the remaining ½ cup granulated sugar. Whisk, gradually increasing the speed to high, until the egg whites hold stiff peaks. Working in three additions, gently fold the whipped egg whites into the chocolate mixture until just incorporated. Scrape the batter into the prepared springform pan.

5. Bake for 40 minutes, until the risen top is matte and cracked. Let cool in the pan for 15 minutes. Run a paring knife around the edge of the cake and remove the springform ring, then let the cake cool completely. Top with raspberries and dust with confectioners' sugar, then slice and serve. Store leftovers in an airtight container at room temperature for up to 5 days.

NANNY'S APPLE CAKE

Makes 1 (9-inch) cake
Prep Time: 25 minutes,
plus cooling time
Cook Time: 45 minutes

For the Dough

2 cups (270g) all-purpose
  flour
1 cup (200g) granulated
  sugar
1 teaspoon baking powder
1 teaspoon ground
  cinnamon
1/2 teaspoon kosher salt
8 ounces (2 sticks) unsalted
  butter or vegan butter,
  cold and cubed
1 large egg, lightly beaten

For the Filling

2 pounds Honeycrisp
  apples, peeled, cored, and
  cut into 1-inch pieces
1/4 cup chopped walnuts
1/4 cup raisins
1/4 cup (34g) all-purpose
  flour
1/4 cup (53g) packed light
  brown sugar
2 tablespoons freshly
  squeezed lemon juice
2 teaspoons finely grated
  fresh ginger (optional)
1/2 teaspoon kosher salt

Meet the almighty half-cake, half-pie hybrid that started it all. It was the first family recipe I learned how to make. It was the first Jewish recipe I had my byline attached to. It was the first time I felt like I was truly representing myself in the food world. I shared a version of it in my last book, transformed into plum crumb bars, but I've spent so much of the last few years exploring old family recipes that I feel like the original deserves its moment.

After fleeing Europe during the Holocaust, part of my family landed in Cuba, rebuilding their lives before having to leave it all again before the revolution. As my aunt Susi tells it, her mother (my great-grandmother, known in our family as Nanny) got this recipe from one of her friends in the vibrant Jewish community that popped up in Havana after the war. It's made of a cookie-like dough used as both a press-in crust and pinched crumble topping that sandwiches a heap of spiced apples. And for all the Jewish mothers obsessed with freezing everything, my mother loves to individually wrap leftover slices and keep them in the freezer to pull out whenever a craving hits!

1. Preheat the oven to 350°F. Set an oven rack in the center of the oven.

2. Make the dough: In a food processor, add the flour, granulated sugar, baking powder, cinnamon, and salt and pulse to combine. Add the butter and pulse until it forms pea-sized crumbles. Add the egg and pulse until the dough just comes together.

3. Press two-thirds of the dough into a 9-inch pie dish across the bottom and up the sides.

4. Make the filling: In a medium bowl, toss together the apples, walnuts, raisins, flour, brown sugar, lemon juice, ginger, if using, and salt to combine.

5. Pour the filling over the pressed dough, then pinch off small pieces of the remaining one-third dough and scatter them over the top of the filling.

6. Place the pie dish on a sheet pan and bake on the center rack for 45 minutes, until golden brown and bubbling. Let cool completely before slicing and serving.

CARAMELIZED HONEY BUNDT CAKE

**Makes 1 (9-inch)
Bundt cake**
Prep Time: 20 minutes,
plus cooling time
Cook Time: 45 minutes

For the Cake
Nonstick cooking spray, for
  greasing
1 cup honey (see headnote)
1 cup brewed Earl Grey tea,
  warm
3 cups (405g) all-purpose
  flour
2 teaspoons baking powder
1½ teaspoons kosher salt
1 teaspoon ground
  cinnamon
1 teaspoon ground ginger
½ teaspoon freshly grated
  nutmeg
½ teaspoon baking soda
4 large eggs
1 cup olive oil
¾ cup packed (160g) light
  brown sugar
1 teaspoon finely grated
  lemon zest
2 tablespoons freshly
  squeezed lemon juice
1 teaspoon vanilla extract

While we typically see honey cake only around Rosh Hashanah, to sweeten the new year, you'll want this recipe to sugarcoat every season. I want you to take this opportunity to explore the terroir of my favorite sweetener, since the type of honey you use is what's going to drive the flavor of this cake. The main factor is what flowers the honeybees are harvesting from, in addition to the time of year. A lighter honey like wildflower will bring more floral tones, while a darker honey like buckwheat carries deeper notes of caramel. Since so much of Jewish food is symbolic ritual, I find it kind of poetic to use honey that's produced locally to you to add some focused intention toward adding sweetness to your new year (or even just your day). No matter the variety, we're going to make the honey really sing by caramelizing it on the stovetop first.

When it comes to any Bundt, which I always pronounce with a *Big Fat Greek Wedding* impersonation, I have some advice to ensure there is no sticking. Most importantly, grease liberally! For a standard pan, a healthy coating of nonstick spray should do the trick. However, for more intricate designs with all those nooks and crannies, my food stylist Barrett Washburne taught me a great trick: Spray your pan and freeze it for 15 minutes before spraying again and adding your batter. Then, never place your Bundt on a sheet pan in the oven, which will restrict airflow and cause uneven baking. Finally, say a little prayer before you flip. Worse comes to worst, a stuck cake still makes a delicious trifle!

1. Bake the cake: Preheat the oven to 350°F. Grease a 9-inch Bundt pan with nonstick cooking spray.

2. In a medium saucepan, bring the honey to a simmer over medium heat. Cook, stirring constantly, for 3 minutes, then remove from the heat. Pour in the tea and whisk to dissolve the honey. Let cool for 10 minutes.

(cont.)

1½ cups confectioners'
   sugar
¼ cup honey
1 teaspoon vanilla extract
Pinch of kosher salt
1 to 2 tablespoons water
Bee pollen, for garnish
   (optional)

3. Meanwhile, in a medium bowl, whisk together the flour, baking powder, salt, cinnamon, ginger, nutmeg, and baking soda to combine.

4. In a large bowl, whisk together the eggs, olive oil, brown sugar, lemon zest and juice, and vanilla until smooth. Slowly whisk in the honey mixture until smooth. Add the dry ingredients to the wet ingredients and fold in until just incorporated. Pour the batter into the prepared pan, smoothing the top with a rubber or offset spatula.

5. Bake the cake on the center rack (with no sheet pan underneath) for 40 minutes, until the top is golden and a toothpick inserted into the center comes out clean. Let cool for 10 minutes, then place a large plate over the top of the cake and use a kitchen towel or oven mitts to invert together. Gently tap on the top to release the cake and carefully remove the pan, then let cool completely.

6. Glaze the cake: In a medium bowl, whisk together the confectioners' sugar, honey, vanilla, and salt with the water until a smooth, thick glaze forms. Drizzle over the cake, then garnish with bee pollen, if using. Slice and serve. Store leftovers in an airtight container in the refrigerator for up to 5 days.

MANISCHEWITZ FRUIT CAKE

Makes 1 (9-inch) Bundt cake

Prep Time: 25 minutes, plus cooling time

Cook Time: 1 hour 5 minutes

For the Cake

Nonstick cooking spray, for greasing

¾ cup Manischewitz wine

1 teaspoon finely grated orange zest

12 ounces chopped dried fruit, such as raisins, golden raisins, apricots, cranberries, and prunes

4 large eggs

2 cups (400g) granulated sugar

1 cup neutral oil, such as vegetable, avocado, or sunflower

1 teaspoon vanilla extract

3 cups (405g) all-purpose flour

1½ teaspoons baking powder

1 teaspoon kosher salt

1 teaspoon ground cinnamon

1 teaspoon ground ginger

1 teaspoon ground nutmeg

½ teaspoon baking soda

While I might not have a taste for alcohol, I do indeed have a taste for the ethereal concord grape flavor of Manischewitz! Other than for kiddush, I'm going to encourage you to always have a bottle on hand to throw together this Jewish fruit cake. I developed it to help me clean out my pantry, using the odds and ends of the dried fruit and nuts I end up accumulating. Though if you need more encouragement, it's a great choice for your dessert table next Tu BiShvat or Rosh Hashanah. My guess is that your cupboard is already stocked up on most ingredients for this recipe, with 4 eggs being the sole item you'll need from the fridge. Once the dried fruit is reconstituted in the wine (something you can do a day in advance), the rest of the batter comes together in minutes, so you can set it and forget it. Finished with a rosy Manischewitz glaze, this cake is chewy and dense, ready to be enjoyed with a cup of tea or coffee or, well, you know.

¼ teaspoon kosher salt

1. Make the cake: Preheat the oven to 325°F. Grease a 9-inch Bundt pan with nonstick cooking spray.

2. In a medium saucepan, bring the Manischewitz and orange zest to a simmer over medium-high heat. Add the dried fruit and cook, stirring constantly, for 2 minutes, then remove from the heat and let cool completely.

3. In a large bowl, whisk together the eggs, granulated sugar, oil, and vanilla until smooth. Add the flour, baking powder, salt, cinnamon, ginger, nutmeg, and baking soda. Gently stir together the dry ingredients piled above the wet ingredients a few times before folding together into a smooth batter. Fold in the dried fruit with any syrupy wine left in the pan and the chopped nuts

(cont.)

1 cup chopped mixed
   nuts, such as hazelnuts,
   walnuts, pistachios, and
   almonds

For the Glaze
1½ cups confectioners'
   sugar
3 to 4 tablespoons
   Manischewitz wine

until incorporated, then scrape the batter into the prepared Bundt pan.

4. Bake the cake for 1 hour to 1 hour 10 minutes, until golden brown and it reaches an internal temperature of 190°F. Let cool for 10 minutes, then place a large plate over the top of the cake and use a kitchen towel or oven mitts to invert together. Gently tap on the top to release the cake and carefully remove the pan, then let cool completely.

5. Make the glaze: In a medium bowl, whisk together the confectioners' sugar, Manischewitz, and salt until smooth. Drizzle over the cooled cake, then let sit for 10 minutes to set before slicing and serving. Store in an airtight container at room temperature for up to 5 days.

11

LOOK TO THE COOKIE

All your problems will be solved.

HAVDALAH SNICKERDOODLES

Makes about 20 cookies
Prep Time: 20 minutes,
plus 1 hour chilling time
Cook Time: 10 minutes

For the Dough
2½ cups (338g) all-
    purpose flour
1½ teaspoons cream of
    tartar
1 teaspoon baking soda
1 teaspoon kosher salt
8 ounces (2 sticks) unsalted
    butter or vegan butter, at
    room temperature
1 cup (200g) granulated
    sugar
¼ cup (53g) packed light
    brown sugar
2 large eggs, room
    temperature
1 teaspoon finely grated
    orange zest
1 teaspoon vanilla extract
1 teaspoon rose water
    (optional)

For the Rolling Sugar
¼ cup granulated sugar
2 teaspoons ground
    cinnamon
½ teaspoon ground
    cardamom
½ teaspoon ground cloves
Pinch of kosher salt

Havdalah is the closing ritual for Shabbat, meant to welcome in the new week by reawakening your senses. To help you on that journey, it's traditional to pass around a spice box, taking a moment to be enveloped by the sweet aroma of cinnamon, cloves, rosebuds, orange peels, and cardamom. These snickerdoodles are meant to bring you on the same sensory experience, perfuming your home with all the spices of havdalah, which have been infused into the dough. On top of the harmony of flavors, the cookies themselves find that idyllic balance of a golden crisp outer ring with a chewy center as soft as a cloud.

1. Make the dough: Line a quarter sheet pan or plate with parchment paper. In a medium bowl, whisk together the flour, cream of tartar, baking soda, and salt to combine.

2. In the bowl of a stand mixer fitted with the paddle attachment, cream the butter and both sugars on medium speed until light and fluffy, 2 minutes. With the mixer running, add the eggs one at a time and mix until incorporated, stopping to scrape the sides of the bowl as needed. Add the orange zest, vanilla, and rose water, if using, and mix to incorporate.

3. Add the flour mixture and mix on low speed until a smooth dough forms. Remove the mixer bowl and, using a 3-tablespoon cookie scoop, scoop balls of dough onto the prepared sheet pan. You should get about 20 balls. Cover with plastic and refrigerate for 1 hour.

4. Meanwhile, prepare the rolling sugar: In a small bowl, whisk together the granulated sugar, cinnamon, cardamom, cloves, and salt to combine.

5. About 30 minutes before baking, preheat the oven to 400°F. Line two sheet pans with parchment paper.

6. After chilling, roll the balls of cookie dough between your hands until smooth, then toss each in the sugar mixture to coat. Place them on the prepared sheet pans, spacing them 2 inches apart. Bake for 10 to 12 minutes, until the edges are golden brown. Let cool slightly on the pans, then serve warm.

PASSOVER CHOCOLATE CHIP COOKIES #K4PCCC

Makes about 2 dozen cookies
Prep Time: 20 minutes, plus chilling and cooling time
Cook Time: 10 minutes

8 ounces (2 sticks) unsalted butter, at room temperature (or ¾ cup olive oil)

¾ cup packed (160g) light brown sugar

⅔ cup (135g) granulated sugar

2 large eggs

2 teaspoons vanilla extract

2½ cups (280g) finely ground almond flour

1 cup (192g) potato starch

1½ teaspoons kosher salt

2 cups milk or dark chocolate chips

3 ounces dark chocolate (70% cacao), finely chopped

Flaky sea salt, for garnish (optional)

The way people react to a warm tray of chocolate chip cookies never fails to fill my heart with joy. When I started playing around with converting my tried-and-true recipe into a kosher-for-Passover creation, I didn't expect to end up with a gluten-free cookie that has a texture that might be better than the original. I found that the combination of almond flour and potato starch is the key to holding together the dough and creating an ultrachewy texture that's beautifully saturated with butter (or olive oil if you're making these pareve).

Since gluten is not in the mix, you don't have to worry about overmixing, but you do have to worry about undermixing. Make sure you properly incorporate the dry ingredients, or you'll end up with some cookies that barely spread and others that spread out way too much. As for the chocolate, I stand by the combo of chocolate chips for richness and chunks for gooeyness, though I've been known to throw in a few mini M&M's on occasion. Any way you stuff this dough, once it's scooped you can pop your balls in the fridge for up to 5 days or in the freezer for up to 6 months. Just know your batch won't last long, since they're too good to Passover! (I'll see myself out.)

1. In the bowl of a stand mixer fitted with the paddle attachment, cream the butter and both sugars on medium speed until light and fluffy, 2 minutes. With the mixer running, add the eggs one at a time and mix until incorporated, stopping to scrape the sides of the bowl as needed. Add the vanilla and mix to incorporate.

2. In a small bowl, whisk together the almond flour, potato starch, and kosher salt to combine, then add to the mixer bowl. Mix on low speed until a smooth dough forms. Remove the mixer bowl and use a rubber spatula to carefully scrape the bottom and sides of the bowl to ensure the dough is evenly incorporated (this step is VERY important; see headnote). Return the mixer bowl and add the chocolate chips and chopped chocolate. Mix on low speed until well incorporated. Cover and chill for 1 hour.

3. Preheat the oven to 375°F. Line two sheet pans with parchment paper. Using a 3-tablespoon cookie scoop, scoop balls of dough onto the prepared sheet pans, spacing them 2 inches apart, and sprinkle with a pinch of flaky sea salt, if using. Bake, rotating the pans halfway through the cooking time, for 10 to 12 minutes, until the cookies are lightly golden around the edges. Let cool slightly on the pans, then serve warm.

CHAROSET RUGELACH

Makes 32 rugelach
Prep Time: 40 minutes,
plus 1 hour chilling time
Cook Time: 30 minutes

For the Dough
1 (8-ounce) package full-fat
  cream cheese, cold and
  cubed
4 ounces (1 stick) unsalted
  butter, cold and cubed
2⅓ cups (315g) all-purpose
  flour, plus more for
  dusting
¼ cup full-fat sour cream
¼ cup (50g) granulated
  sugar
½ teaspoon kosher salt

**For the Filling and
Assembly**
⅔ cup walnuts
⅔ cup raisins
⅓ cup (66g) granulated
  sugar
1 teaspoon ground
  cinnamon
¼ teaspoon kosher salt
½ cup apple butter
1 large egg white, beaten
Turbinado sugar, for
  garnish

I was pretty happy with my rugelach recipe, until my friend Dave Dreifus brought me a batch of his, which put mine to shame. Dave worked his way through some of the country's top three-Michelin-star restaurants before starting Best Damn Cookies in NYC, where he sells just that while following in the footsteps of his grandfather, who ran a kosher bakery in Brooklyn. He came by and we kibbitzed about Jewish food, discussing its absence from our experiences at CIA (Culinary Institute of America) and working in fine-dining restaurants. We didn't think anything of it then, since growing up in America comes with an ingrained acceptance of Jewish food being valued as lesser. But as we've explored our pride for it professionally, we've been able to finally see our truest selves in our biggest passion, an immensely overwhelming feeling that brought us both to tears just discussing it.

Deep conversations aside, Dave's rugelach truly are the best on the planet. Naturally, he makes his own cream cheese and sour cream for the flakiest dough, which gets filled with a jammy charoset compote. I'm not going to have you culturing your own dairy, but I did revisit my recipe to give you a result almost as good. The dough is made in the food processor with cold butter and cream cheese to create pie dough–like flakiness, then covered with a lazy charoset filling of apple butter topped with chopped walnuts and raisins with cinnamon sugar. They're not Dave's cookies, but they're still some of the best damn rugelach out there!

1. Make the dough: In a food processor, combine the cream cheese, butter, flour, sour cream, granulated sugar, and salt. Pulse for about 1 minute until the butter and cream cheese are incorporated into a crumbly dough. Transfer the crumbles to a clean work surface and press and lightly knead them together to form a ball of dough. Divide the dough into 2 equal disks (each should be about 395g), wrap each in plastic wrap, and refrigerate for 1 hour.

2. Meanwhile, preheat the oven to 375°F. Line a sheet pan with parchment paper.

3. Make the filling: Wipe out the food processor bowl and add the walnuts, raisins, granulated sugar, cinnamon, and salt. Pulse until finely chopped, then transfer to a small bowl.

4. Assemble the rugelach: On a lightly floured work surface, roll out 1 disk of the dough into a 12-inch circle, dusting with flour as needed. Brush off any excess flour, then spread half of the apple butter evenly over the dough, leaving a ½-inch border. Sprinkle half of the walnut mixture evenly over the apple butter. Slice the dough into 16 even wedges. Roll each wedge up tightly from the outside edge in, then place the rugelach on the prepared sheet pan, spacing them ½ inch apart. Repeat with the remaining dough, apple butter, and filling, arranging on the pan in 4 rows of 8 rugelach each. Brush the rugelach with the beaten egg white, then sprinkle turbinado sugar on top.

5. Bake, rotating the pan halfway through the cooking time, for 30 minutes, until the rugelach are golden brown. Let cool slightly, then serve.

ANGOSTURA-LIME COCONUT MACAROONS

Makes about 2 dozen macaroons

Prep Time: 20 minutes, plus cooling and chilling time

Cook Time: 20 minutes

For the Macaroons

3 large egg whites

¾ cup (150g) granulated sugar

½ teaspoon kosher salt

4 cups (12 ounces) unsweetened finely shredded coconut

1 tablespoon Angostura aromatic bitters

1 teaspoon finely grated lime zest

For Decorating

1 cup white chocolate chips (a dairy-free variety to make pareve)

1 teaspoon coconut oil

1 teaspoon Angostura aromatic bitters

Pinch of kosher salt

Finely grated lime zest, for garnish

Flaky sea salt, for garnish

I'm not ashamed to say I love canned macaroons. As a kid, I would pop one after another, blissfully unaware of the nutritional facts on the back of the can. As an adult, I can appreciate the artistry of homemade macaroons, while still dabbling in the store-bought on occasion. This recipe feels like a tropical cocktail on the beach, mixing shredded coconut with lime zest and Angostura bitters. Once baked, the macs are dipped in white chocolate infused with more bitters, creating a texture closer to a thick frosting that hardens into the perfect spiced shell. They're a little taste of vacation, whenever you need it.

Now, here's the twist: This recipe isn't technically kosher for Passover because of the bitters (the alcohol we're flavoring with). During Pesach, you can simply swap the bitters with an equal amount of any K4P liqueur. The rest of the year it doesn't matter, so go nuts!

1. Make the macaroons: Preheat the oven to 350°F. Line a sheet pan with parchment paper.

2. In the bowl of a stand mixer fitted with the whisk attachment, whisk the egg whites, sugar, and salt on medium speed for 1 to 2 minutes until white and glossy, but still runny. Add the coconut, bitters, and lime zest, then use a rubber spatula to fold by hand until well incorporated.

3. Using a 1½-tablespoon cookie scoop, scoop macaroons onto the prepared pan, spacing each 1 inch apart. Bake, rotating the pan halfway through the cooking time, for 13 to 15 minutes, until golden. Let cool completely on the pan.

4. Decorate the macaroons: Set a medium metal or heatproof glass bowl over a small pot of simmering water. Put the white chocolate, coconut oil, bitters, and kosher salt in the bowl and heat, stirring occasionally, until completely melted and combined.

5. Dip the top of each macaroon in the white chocolate mixture then return to the sheet pan. Once all the macaroons are dipped, garnish with lime zest and flaky salt. Refrigerate for 10 to 15 minutes to set the white chocolate, then serve. Store in an airtight container at room temperature for up to 5 days.

SUPER FUDGY DATE BROWNIES

Makes 16 brownies
Prep Time: 15 minutes,
plus cooling time
Cook Time: 45 minutes

8 ounces dark chocolate
   (70% cacao), coarsely
   chopped
4 ounces (1 stick) unsalted
   butter or vegan butter,
   cubed
1½ cups (300g) granulated
   sugar
¼ cup date syrup (silan)
4 large eggs
¼ cup (25g) unsweetened
   cocoa powder
1 tablespoon vanilla extract
1½ teaspoons kosher salt
1 cup (135g) all-purpose flour
½ cup milk chocolate chips
½ cup dark chocolate chips
16 Medjool dates, pitted
Flaky sea salt, for garnish
   (optional)

It all started with a really good date . . . like the dried fruit kind. I was gallivanting through the Shuk in Tel Aviv and picked up a bag of the plumpest Medjool dates to nosh on. My first bite was into the sweetest, fudgiest date I'd ever had, causing an unexpected audible sigh of satisfaction. I was immediately struck with the idea to create a brownie recipe that could mimic that same fudginess, and have each square studded with a date. I started testing versions of it the second I was back in NYC, eventually landing on this batter tinged with date syrup for more of those deep caramel tones, and packed with chocolate chips to add gooeyness and help give the brownies that shiny crinkle top. Not only is this recipe easily turned pareve by using vegan butter and all dark chocolate chips, but it even makes for the perfect Passover dessert when you swap the flour with potato starch. Most importantly, I tend to always keep a finished batch in the freezer to pull out whenever the mood strikes for date night!

1. Preheat the oven to 350°F. Line a 9-inch square baking pan with parchment paper, leaving overhang on all sides.

2. Set a medium metal or heatproof glass bowl over a small pot of simmering water. Add the chopped chocolate and butter and heat, stirring occasionally, until completely melted and combined, then remove from the heat.

3. Meanwhile, in a large bowl, whisk together the sugar, date syrup, and eggs until very smooth. Whisk in the cocoa powder, vanilla, and kosher salt until smooth. Slowly whisk in the melted chocolate mixture until smooth. Fold in the flour until just incorporated, followed by both chocolate chips. Scrape the batter into the prepared pan and spread it into an even layer. Stud the batter with the pitted dates, spacing them out in 4 rows of 4 dates each, so when you slice the finished brownies, each will have its own date. Sprinkle with a pinch of flaky salt, if using, on top.

4. Bake for 40 minutes, until the top is matte and the edges begin to crack, then let cool completely in the pan. (For cleaner slicing and firmer texture, once cool, cover and refrigerate for 4 hours.) Use the overhanging parchment to transfer to a cutting board, then slice into 16 brownies and serve.

HINT-OF-ROSE MANDEL BREAD

Makes about 16 cookies

Prep Time: 15 minutes, plus cooling time

Cook Time: 25 or 40 minutes

½ cup (100g) granulated sugar

½ cup vegetable oil, plus more for greasing

1 tablespoon rose water

1 teaspoon almond extract

½ teaspoon kosher salt

2 large eggs

2 cups (270g) all-purpose flour

½ cup (56g) finely ground almond flour

1 teaspoon baking powder

½ cup slivered almonds

½ cup chopped white chocolate (a dairy-free variety to make pareve)

2 teaspoons turbinado sugar

Use this recipe as an excuse to take a pause, pour a cup of coffee or tea, and dunk in something sweet, whether you're alone or with a fellow yenta. The Ashkenazi cousin of Italian biscotti, mandel bread is an equally crunchy, twice-baked cookie that's ideal for any almond lover. I've been playing around with a base recipe from my great-grandmother's recipe box for a while, taking it in a more delicate direction by infusing just a touch of rose water for an ethereal flavor and adding chunks of white chocolate, which caramelize during the second bake for rich notes of butterscotch. While I give you an option to stop after the first bake for a softer version, I'm going to side with tradition and recommend the double bake so you have the best possible cookie to dip into your hot bev.

1. Preheat the oven to 350°F. Line a sheet pan with parchment paper.

2. In a large bowl, whisk together the granulated sugar, oil, rose water, almond extract, salt, and eggs until smooth. Add the flour, almond flour, and baking powder. Gently stir together the dry ingredients piled above the wet ingredients a few times before folding together into a smooth dough. Fold in the almonds and white chocolate to incorporate. Transfer to the prepared pan and, using greased hands, shape into a 4 × 12-inch log. Sprinkle the top with the turbinado sugar.

3. Bake for 25 minutes, until lightly golden. Let cool completely, then slice into ¾-inch-thick cookies. Enjoy as is for a softer mandel bread, or place the cookies cut sides down back on the pan and return to the oven. Bake for 15 minutes more for a more traditional, crisp mandel bread, then let cool completely and serve.

YOU-CAN-GO-YOUR-OWN-WAY FRANGIPANE HAMANTASCHEN

Makes about 20 hamantaschen
Prep Time: 40 minutes, plus cooling time and 1 hour chilling time
Cook Time: 20 minutes

For the Filling

1¼ cups (140g) almond flour

½ cup (100g) granulated sugar

2 tablespoons unsalted butter or vegan butter, melted and cooled slightly

1 teaspoon almond extract

½ teaspoon kosher salt

1 large egg, lightly beaten

+

¼ cup poppy seeds

2 teaspoons finely grated lemon zest

Confectioners' sugar, for garnish postbake

OR

¼ cup rainbow sprinkles, plus more for garnish prebake

OR

1 teaspoon ground cardamom

20 whole raw almonds, for garnish prebake

OR

¼ cup mini chocolate chips

20 dark chocolate chunks, for garnish prebake

Crack out your groggers because this Purim we're making foolproof hamantaschen. This recipe is the result of so many years of testing and tweaking to create a dough and method that yields picture-perfect buttery triangles every single time, no matter your experience or skill level. Instead of the standard jam or jelly, we're leaning into frangipane, a super moist and chewy almond filling that won't ever cause your hamantaschen to explode in the oven like fruit preserves can. It's a blank slate you can take into any direction, from sprinkles to poppy.

There are two issues that I find lead to the most failures when making any hamantasch recipe. First, everyone is so afraid of overworking their dough that they end up underworking it. If you don't mix the dough enough, the flour won't properly hydrate into the elastic Play-Doh-like texture you need, resulting in a lot of cracking and spilled-out filling. It all comes down to the visual cue of your dough staying together in one ball, so if it's still crumbly, keep mixing! Second, everyone has no chill. Once shaped, you must let the cookies firm up in the fridge for an hour before baking so they keep their shape. Go watch an episode of *Housewives* and don't try to rush it. If you keep opening that damn door and letting out all the cold, it will take longer!

1. Make the filling: In a medium bowl, stir together the almond flour, granulated sugar, melted butter, almond extract, salt, and egg until a smooth paste forms. Fold in the poppy seeds and lemon zest OR the rainbow sprinkles OR the cardamom OR the mini chocolate chips.

2. Make the dough: Line two sheet pans with parchment. In the bowl of a stand mixer fitted with the paddle attachment, cream the butter and granulated sugar on medium speed until light and fluffy, 1 to 2 minutes. With the motor running, add the egg and mix until incorporated, stopping to scrape the sides of the bowl as needed. Add the vanilla and salt and mix to incorporate.

3. Add the flour and mix on low until a smooth dough forms. (It's crucial your dough is mixed enough to make one ball; if it's still crumbly, mix more!)

4. Transfer the dough between two sheets of parchment and roll out to ¼ inch thick. Using a 3¼-inch ring cutter, cut out as many circles of dough as you can. Spoon 1 scant tablespoon of filling into the center of each circle

For the Dough

8 ounces (2 sticks) unsalted butter or vegan butter, at room temperature

1 cup (200g) granulated sugar

1 large egg

1 teaspoon vanilla extract

1 teaspoon kosher salt

3 cups (405g) all-purpose flour

of dough. Fold in the dough from three sides and pinch the edges together to seal, leaving a small opening over the filling. Place the hamantaschen on one of the prepared sheet pans. Reroll the dough scraps and repeat the process to form as many hamantaschen as you can.

5. If you went the rainbow sprinkles route, garnish the tops with more rainbow sprinkles. If you went the cardamom route, stud each hamantasch with 1 raw almond. If you went the chocolate chip route, stud each hamantasch with a chocolate chunk.

6. Chill the hamantaschen for 1 hour. Meanwhile, preheat the oven to 350°F.

7. Divide the chilled hamantaschen between the sheet pan you chilled them on and the other parchment-lined pan, spacing them 2 inches apart. Repinch the corners to ensure they're well sealed.

8. Bake, rotating the pans halfway through the cooking time, for about 20 minutes, until the bottoms and corners of the hamantaschen are golden. Let cool, then serve. (If you went the lemon-poppy route, dust with confectioners' sugar before serving.) Store leftovers in an airtight container at room temperature for up to 5 days.

HANUKKAH MARBLE-GLAZED SHORTBREAD COOKIES

Makes about 2 dozen cookies

Prep Time: 30 minutes, plus chilling and setting time

Cook Time: 15 minutes

For the Dough

8 ounces (2 sticks) unsalted butter, at room temperature

¾ cup (150g) granulated sugar

1 large egg

2 teaspoons vanilla extract

1 teaspoon almond extract

1 teaspoon kosher salt

2½ cups (338g) all-purpose flour

¼ teaspoon baking powder

For the Glaze

2 cups confectioners' sugar

¼ cup half-and-half

1 tablespoon vodka

1 teaspoon almond extract

½ teaspoon kosher salt

Blue food coloring

These are my response to Christmas cookies, since we can't let the *goyim* have all the fun. There's a larger conversation to be had about the holiday industrial complex and our part in hyping up Hanukkah like it's Jewish Christmas, which no matter how delicious these cookies are, it's not. But the story of the Maccabees is very much worth celebrating, allowing conversations about our history in overcoming oppression and in fighting for our right to exist. And as long as we're talking about our past and how it impacts our present and future, we might as well nosh on some shortbreads shaped like Stars of David, menorahs, and dreidels. The wow factor is in the marbled glaze, which uses an easy technique of lightly swirling in food coloring before coating your cookies. They're so good, Santa might even drop by while you light the menorah.

1. For the dough: In the bowl of a stand mixer fitted with the paddle attachment (though this dough can easily be made by hand), cream the butter and granulated sugar on medium speed until light and fluffy, 1 to 2 minutes. With the motor running, add the egg and mix until incorporated, stopping to scrape the sides of the bowl as needed. Add the vanilla and almond extracts with the salt and mix to incorporate.

2. Add the flour and baking powder and mix on low until a smooth dough forms. Transfer the dough between two sheets of parchment paper and roll out to ¼ inch thick. Chill for 1 hour.

3. After 30 minutes of chilling, preheat the oven to 350°F. Line two sheet pans with parchment paper.

4. Remove the top sheet of parchment from the dough and cut out cookies using 2½-inch Hanukkah cookie cutters. Carefully transfer the cookies to the prepared sheet pans, spacing them 1 inch apart from one another. Reroll the scraps between the parchment and repeat, chilling again as needed if the dough becomes too soft.

5. Bake, rotating the pans halfway through the cooking time, for 13 to 15 minutes, until the edges are lightly golden. Let cool completely on the pans.

6. Meanwhile, make the glaze: In a medium bowl, whisk the confectioners' sugar, half-and-half, vodka, almond extract, and salt until smooth. Drip a few drops of food coloring on top of the glaze, then swirl with the tip of a paring knife for a marbled effect. (For more distinct marbling for all the cookies, divide the glaze between two bowls before swirling in the food coloring.)

7. Dip the cooled cookies into the glaze, letting any excess drip off, then place on a wire rack to set for 15 minutes before serving (the vodka will evaporate, leaving a matte finish and no booze!). Store leftovers in an airtight container at room temperature for up to 5 days.

Look to the Cookie • 273

CRISPY PERSIAN RICE TREATS

Makes 16 bars
Prep Time: 15 minutes,
plus cooling time
Cook Time: 5 minutes

Nonstick cooking spray, for
 greasing
4 tablespoons (2 ounces)
 unsalted butter or vegan
 butter
1 (10-ounce) bag
 marshmallows (I prefer
 mini but regular size
 work, too)
¼ teaspoon saffron
 threads, finely ground
 with a mortar and pestle
6 cups Kellogg's Rice
 Krispies cereal
½ cup dried barberries
 (zereshk)
½ cup chopped pistachios
½ teaspoon kosher salt

If you love a highbrow-lowbrow mash-up and/or tahdig, this recipe is for you. Like many of my favorite noshes, it was born out of the need for a very last-minute dessert. I was cooking a Persian-themed Shabbat with my friends Benny Blanco and Jess Damuck, so I threw these squares together just to have something sweet and on theme. It's the same combo of butter, marshmallows, and Rice Krispies you know and love, but with a luxurious kiss of saffron, chopped pistachios, and dried barberries. You get that sweet taste of nostalgia but reimagined with powerful Persian flavors that add some extra texture and tang. I knew these treats couldn't be bad, but I wasn't prepared for them to be such a huge hit. It's now the recipe I jump to whenever I want to drum up the biggest reaction for the least amount of work, which is pretty often!

1. Grease a 9-inch square baking pan with nonstick cooking spray and line with parchment paper, leaving overhang on all sides.

2. In a large pot or dutch oven, melt the butter over medium heat. Add the marshmallows and ground saffron and cook, stirring constantly, until the marshmallows are almost melted. Remove from the heat and stir in the cereal, barberries, pistachios, and salt until well incorporated. Scrape into the prepared pan and, using an offset spatula or measuring cup greased with nonstick cooking spray, press into an even layer. Let cool completely.

3. Transfer to a cutting board and slice into 16 bars, then serve. Store leftovers in an airtight container at room temperature for up to 5 days.

HONEY-NUT BAKLAWA

Serves 8 to 10
Prep Time: 30 minutes,
plus cooling time and
4 hours soaking time
Cook Time: 40 minutes

1½ cups raw pistachios

1½ cups raw walnuts

1 pound (about 20 sheets)
frozen phyllo (13 × 18-
inch sheets), thawed

8 ounces (2 sticks) unsalted
butter or vegan butter,
melted

1¼ cups (250g) granulated
sugar

1 cup water

½ cup honey

½ teaspoon ground
cardamom

½ teaspoon kosher salt

1 tablespoon rose water

1 teaspoon finely grated
lemon zest

Baby got bak! I adore any syrup-soaked dessert with a viscous sweetness that oozes out as you chew. This saturated beauty is brought to you by my husband's aunt Diana who, unlike most of Alex's family, has her recipes written down! As one of my culinary guides through the world of Iraqi and Persian dishes, all our cooking lessons would end with me rummaging through her recipe book, picking out what I'd want us to make together next. Her baklawa (the Arabic spelling/pronunciation) is perfumed with rose water, cardamom, and lemon, making for the sweetest pastry diamonds, which are also surprisingly easy to throw together and perfect to prepare in advance.

Past store-bought phyllo dough, this whole recipe comes down to three customizable components. First, the nuts are negotiable! You just need 3 cups total, so use a blend that fits your palate and pantry (Diana typically uses walnuts and almonds). Second, choose your fat. I use butter, but Diana's original recipe uses oil (or vegan butter) to keep it pareve. Third, pour on the syrup. The way the flavors of lemon, rose, and cardamom seep into every corner of this dish is what I adore so much, though you can swap or omit depending on your floral sensitivities. And while many swear by only pouring cold syrup onto hot baklawa or vice versa, my preference is to make the syrup right when the tray goes into the oven so it's still warm when you pour it on top. And just like us, you must make time for your tray to have a good, long soak!

1. Preheat the oven to 375°F.

2. In a food processor, combine the pistachios and walnuts together and pulse until fine crumbs form.

3. Open the stack of phyllo sheets on a cutting board and slice crosswise to create two equal stacks, each 9 × 13 inches. In a 9 × 13-inch baking dish (I prefer metal), place one stack of the phyllo sheets. Sprinkle the crushed pistachios and walnuts over the phyllo in an even layer, then top with the other stack of phyllo sheets.

4. With your sharpest knife, cut the phyllo into 6 rows lengthwise, and then into 8 columns crosswise on an angle to form diamonds, making sure you cut all the way to the bottom of the dish. Drizzle all of the melted butter on top, making sure to evenly coat all the phyllo.

5. Bake, rotating the pan halfway through the cooking time, for 40 to 45 minutes, until golden brown and crisp.

6. Meanwhile, in a medium saucepan, combine the sugar, water, honey, cardamom, and salt over medium-high heat. Bring to a simmer and cook, stirring often and reducing the heat as needed to maintain a simmer, for 10 minutes. Remove from the heat and stir in the rose water and lemon zest, then set aside.

7. As soon as the baklawa is baked, gently pour the syrup over it. Let cool completely, then cover and let rest at room temperature for at least 4 hours before serving. Store leftovers in an airtight container at room temperature or in the refrigerator for up to 5 days.

MATZO CRUNCH

Serves 8 to 10

Prep Time: 15 minutes,
plus 30 minutes chilling time

Cook Time: 20 minutes

4 sheets matzo

8 ounces (2 sticks) unsalted
    butter or vegan butter

1 cup packed (213g) light
    brown sugar

1 teaspoon vanilla extract

1 teaspoon kosher salt

1½ cups dark, milk, or
    white chocolate chips

Toppings for Dark

Chopped apricots

Chopped pistachios

Chopped dates

Flaky sea salt

Toppings for Milk

Rainbow sprinkles

Mini M&M's

Crushed potato chips

Toppings for White

Crushed Aleppo pepper

Flaky sea salt

Even the bread of affliction can be transformed into one of the most wildly compelling sweets when soaked in butterscotch and covered in chocolate! Popularized by cookbook author Marcy Goldman in 1985, matzo crunch (one of the many names it has taken on) has become a staple K4P dessert in Jewish households everywhere, including my own. It's wildly simple, addictively brittle, and infinitely customizable, making it another Passover staple we shouldn't turn our backs on during the rest of the year. I've included some of my most frequented topping combinations for dark, milk, and white chocolate that illustrate the range of this sugary canvas, from an elevated nosh to a magical munchie!

1. Preheat the oven to 350°F.

2. Line a sheet pan with parchment paper and arrange the matzo on top, breaking the sheets to fit.

3. In a small saucepan, combine the butter and brown sugar over medium-high heat. Cook until the sugar has dissolved and the mixture is violently bubbling, 5 to 6 minutes. Remove from the heat and stir in the vanilla and kosher salt. Pour over the matzo, using an offset spatula to spread evenly.

4. Bake for 12 to 15 minutes, until caramelized and the bubbling begins to dissipate. Remove from the oven and immediately scatter the chocolate chips over the top. Let sit for 5 minutes, then using an offset spatula, spread evenly over the matzo.

5. Scatter on your desired toppings, then refrigerate until set, about 30 minutes. Break into pieces and serve. Store leftovers in an airtight container at room temperature or in the refrigerator for up to 5 days.

Holidays of Our Lives

While this book is set up to bring Jewish flair to your everyday kitchen, these recipes will, of course, also help you step up your holiday entertaining game!

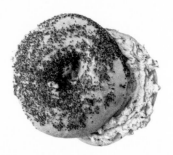

Universal Conversion Chart

OVEN TEMPERATURE EQUIVALENTS

250°F = 120°C

275°F = 135°C

300°F = 150°C

325°F = 160°C

350°F = 180°C

375°F = 190°C

400°F = 200°C

425°F = 220°C

450°F = 230°C

475°F = 250°C

500°F = 260°C

MEASUREMENT EQUIVALENTS

Measurements should always be level unless directed otherwise.

⅛ teaspoon = 0.5 mL

¼ teaspoon = 1 mL

½ teaspoon = 2 mL

1 teaspoon = 5 mL

1 tablespoon = 3 teaspoons = ½ fluid ounce = 15 mL

2 tablespoons = ⅛ cup = 1 fluid ounce = 30 mL

4 tablespoons = ¼ cup = 2 fluid ounces = 60 mL

5⅓ tablespoons = ⅓ cup = 3 fluid ounces = 80 mL

8 tablespoons = ½ cup = 4 fluid ounces = 120 mL

10 ⅔ tablespoons = ⅔ cup = 5 fluid ounces = 160 mL

12 tablespoons = ¾ cup = 6 fluid ounces = 180 mL

16 tablespoons = 1 cup = 8 fluid ounces = 240 mL

Acknowledgments

As always, thank you to my husband, Alex. You are my muse, my better half, and my extra-crispy chicken nugget.

This book is really a love letter to the women in my life who I've been lucky enough to learn from in the kitchen. Thank you to my mother, Dr. Elizabette Cohen (she was mad I didn't mention her name in my last book since obviously she's Mom), for being my biggest cheerleader, letting me tweak and twist your recipes, and telling everyone in your Barre classes to follow me on Instagram. Thank you to my grandma Annie for spending countless hours on the phone with me, telling me stories of your childhood and step-by-steps of all of your recipes. The way you built your home around the kitchen was a huge inspiration for this book. Thank you to my aunt Susi for being a constant source of knowledge on our family's history and letting me borrow your mother's recipe box (I promise I'll give it back!). Thank you to my mother-in-law, Robina Shapiro, for showering me with love and tahdig, while always sharing countless stories and recipes from your upbringing to help me continue to preserve tradition. Thank you to Alex's aunt Diana Phillips for your endless hospitality and cooking classes.

Past the women who inspired these recipes, I'm lucky to have such an incredible family behind me. Thank you to my father, Mike, for always being a beacon of support throughout all my endeavors and buying a book to send to everyone you know. Thank you, Jamie, for being the best sister I could ever ask for, even if you think my Havdalah Snickerdoodles are the worst thing you've ever tasted in your life. Thank you to my late grandma Marilyn. Not a day goes by in which I don't pass somewhere in the city that reminds me of you. Thank you to my brother-in-law Avi Savar and sister-in-law Leigh Savar for your never-ending support and your focus on creating the most wonderful spaces to gather and blend our families. Thank you to my sisters-in-law Tanya Shapiro and Kristen Stilwell for your friendship and love of challah and brisket, respectively. Thank you, Manu, for always being there to help Alex and me eat all the leftovers as I powered through every version of every recipe in this book.

I'm beyond blessed to have a team behind me to help make my dreams come true.

Thank you to the best literary agent / neck snapper in the world, Sarah Passick. I'm so lucky to have your guidance and friendship. It was truly beshert that we would meet in the Holy Land and become family with Daniel Geneen and Allison Milam. Thank you to my editor, Sarah Pelz, for helping shape this book into what it is and giving me the freedom to be my eccentric self on every page. Thank you to my managers, Megan Brown and Noah Swimmer at Underscore, who've helped me navigate these wild and wonderful past few years and been there every step of the way. Thank you to my photographer, Matt Taylor-Gross, for making every photo more stunning than the next and humoring my wild headshot ideas. Your talent is matched by your kindness. Thank you to my food stylist, Barrett Washburne, for making every dish look beyond perfect. I've always been such a huge fan of your work and I continue to be honored that my books get to be a part of that. Thank you to my prop stylist, Marie Sullivan, for taking the most obscure descriptions of how I want the photos to look and so expertly translating them on set in a way I couldn't verbalize. Thank you to the rest of the team that made this shoot happen: Lauren Radel, Dinah Bess Rotter, Lori Reilly, and Matt Christian Jackson. Thank you to my book designer, Bonni Leon-Berman, for building the book of my dreams.

Thank you to Dana Golub for being such an incredible recipe tester and friend! You cranked through these recipes and gave such magnificent feedback! Thank you to all my other recipe testers who helped make this book perfect: Jessica Cohen, Sam Goldberg, Dr. Pam, Austin Friedman, Max Hoffman, Rabbi James Feder, Jon Lindefjeld, and H. Alan Scott.

Special thanks to some of my favorite Jews: Richie Jackson, Jordan Roth, Mike Solomonov, Adeena Sussman, Katie Couric (ish!), Judy Gold, Modi Rosenfeld, Alex Edelman, Benj Pasek, and Shoshana Bean. You all inspire me endlessly, and your love and support these past years will never be forgotten.

Thank you to OneTable for letting me serve on your board and contribute to your incredible mission of helping young Jews find passion in Shabbat and Jewish ritual.

Thank you to my haters; if you're reading this, it means you need to get a hobby!

Thank you to everyone who's sat at my table and allowed me to test these recipes in action.

And, of course, thank YOU! If you bought this book, it means you're supporting my dreams and I will forever be grateful.

Index

About the Author

Jake Cohen is a *New York Times* bestselling cookbook author and nice Jewish boy from New York City. After working in some of the city's best restaurants and test kitchens, he wrote his first book, *Jew-ish*, about his love of modern Jewish cooking and baking. Jake and his recipes have been featured on *Good Morning America*, *Rachael Ray*, *Live with Kelly and Ryan*, *The Drew Barrymore Show*, and the Food Network, and in the *New York Times*, *Food & Wine*, *The Wall Street Journal*, *Bon Appétit*, *Food52*, and *Forbes*, among others. When he's not posting challah-braiding videos and recipes on his Instagram and TikTok (@jakecohen), he's watching *Seinfeld* reruns with his husband, Alex, to gain inspiration for his author photos.

HarperCollins books may be purchased for educational, business,
or sales promotional use. For information, please email the Special
Markets Department at
SPsales@harpercollins.com.

FIRST EDITION

Designed by Bonni Leon-Berman

Photography by Matt Taylor-Gross

Library of Congress Cataloging-in-Publication Data

Names: Cohen, Jake, 1993– author.
Title: I could nosh : classic Jew-ish recipes revamped for every day
/ Jake Cohen.
Description: New York : Harvest, an imprint of William Morrow,
[2023] | Includes index.
Identifiers: LCCN 2023010135 (print) | LCCN 2023010136 (ebook)
| ISBN 9780063239708 (hardcover) | ISBN 9780063239715
(ebook)
Subjects: LCSH: Jewish cooking. | LCGFT: Cookbooks.
Classification: LCC TX724 .C5377 2023 (print) | LCC TX724
(ebook) | DDC 641.5/676–dc23/eng/20230310
LC record available at https://lccn.loc.gov/2023010135

LC ebook record available at https://lccn.loc.gov/2023010136

ISBN 978-0-06-323970-8

23 24 25 26 27 TC 10 9 8 7 6 5 4 3 2 1